TANK ACTION

FROM THE GREAT WAR TO THE GULF

The Shermans which took part in the Korean War were M4A3E8s, mounting the 76 mm gun, the first being A Company, 8072 Medium Tank Bn, a provisional organization which had been hastily activated in Japan. Not all had a 'Tiger in their tank'! (Simon Dunstan)

TANK ACTION

FROM THE GREAT WAR TO THE GULF

GEORGE FORTY

BCA

LONDON   NEW YORK   SYDNEY   TORONTO

This edition published 1995 by BCA by arrangement with
Alan Sutton Publishing Limited
Phoenix Mill · Far Thrupp · Stroud · Gloucestershire

CN 1295

British Library Cataloguing in Publication Data

A catalogue record for this book is available from the British Library.

ISBN 0–7509–0479–8

Library of Congress Cataloging in Publication Data applied for

Endpapers: front: FT 174, near Juvigny, 28 August 1918; back: M1 Abrams.

Typeset in 10/13 Sabon.
Typesetting and origination by
Alan Sutton Publishing Limited.
Printed in Great Britain by
Butler & Tanner, Frome, Somerset.

CONTENTS

PART THREE: POSTWAR CONFLICTS

LIST OF ILLUSTRATIONS

LIST OF DRAWINGS

LIST OF MAPS

INTRODUCTION

Some years ago I wrote a book about great tank commanders in which I endeavoured to deal with the most successful armoured battlefield commanders since the inception of the tank, who, like knights of old, have led their armoured troops into battle from the 'sharp end' – men like Generals Elles, Patton, Rommel, Guderian and Tal. I also included in that same book reference to some of the men who have rightly been described as 'tank aces', namely those whose prowess as individual tank commanders deserved special recognition. However, in the Introduction to that book I was careful to explain that a tank commander is only as good as the rest of the crew, and that a tank crew was a team, all members of which played their own vital part. No tank commander will be able to engage and destroy the enemy unless his driver, gunner and loader/radio operator all do their jobs efficiently and effectively. For a long time I wrestled with my conscience over the selection of these 'ace' tank commanders because I know from personal experience just how much a tank commander depends upon his crew, especially when he is learning his trade.

Having talked to tank commanders of other nations, I am well aware that the term 'tank ace' does not find universal favour for a variety of reasons, the strongest one being that it is invidious to single out from such a great company of armoured soldiers just a few who have 'hit the headlines'. Others will argue that in the same way as the award of gallantry medals is to some extent a lottery, many heroic acts passing unnoticed in the

heat of battle, then so too is the selection of the best of any bunch of tank commanders and the subsequent classification of them as 'aces'.

By the same token, surely one cannot select as an 'ace' the commander of a team in preference to his driver, who through his individual skill and ability gets the tank to its correct place on the battlefield and then, just as importantly, gets it out again to live and fight another day, or the gunner, who physically aims at and engages the target. Nevertheless, it is the tank commander who leads his tank crew and who therefore normally receives both the brickbats and the bouquets. The 'buck stops with him', so he is the inevitable best choice.

I thought it might be interesting to examine this special breed of men, to explain what they did and how they did it. However, such a book would be in danger of becoming a litany of names and actions, which, despite the heroism of the individuals, could become both boring and repetitive. I have decided instead, therefore, to examine a series of good tank actions, hence the title of this book, spread throughout the history of tank warfare, looking at each in as much detail as possible; I have included descriptions of the armoured fighting vehicles involved, the types of terrain over which the action was fought and, where possible, the ranges of engagements, the types of ammunition used, etc. – in other words, some of the more technical aspects of tank battles. I believe in this way one can get a far better idea of what tank commanding is all about, rather than just describing the life story of the chosen tank ace.

The book follows the development of armoured warfare from the first tank engagement of the First World War up to the recent Gulf War conflict, much as my *Tank Commanders* did. I have deliberately chosen as many different types of tanks, terrains and targets as possible, so that Sgt Waterhouse's remarkable effort in getting an M3 Lee tank up a seemingly impossible jungle hillside onto the District Commissioner's tennis court in order to deal with dug-in Japanese infantry at Kohima is covered, along with Obersturmführer Michael Wittmann's more well known, but equally remarkable battle with the 7th Armoured Division's advance guard at Villers-Bocage and Lt Frank Mitchell's first tank-versus-tank engagement at Villers Bretonneux. The time-scale, range of choice and so on is vast, so I am bound to be brought to book by some readers for not mentioning their favourite commander.

The book starts with a chapter on what goes into the making of a good tank commander and how this training has changed over the years. From this survey I believe it is clear that, although the technology gets more and more complicated, the basic skills of the tank commander – efficiency, bravery, quick-wittedness and the ability to act on his own initiative – are still of paramount importance. I have also dealt here with the question of how tank aces are selected, highlighting some of the views which can be brought both for and against the various methods employed.

As always I have many people to thank for their invaluable help with the provision of the battle accounts, photographs, sketch maps,

etc. Their names appear in the particular chapter. However, I am particularly grateful to the following:

Maj Gen Israel Tal, Brig C.J.A. Hammerbeck, Col James H. Leach, Lt Col Haynes Dugan, Lt Col Richard East, Lt Col David Eshel, Lt Col Robert Kendell, Maj Hugh Fane-Harvey, Maj G.A.S. Hancock, Maj Peter R. Mansoor, Maj Norman Plough, Capt H.R. McMaster, 1st Lt Richard M. Bohannon, Mr Simon Dunstan, Mr A.W. Green, Mr Michael J.R. Green, Ms Ann Hassinger, Mr Kevin R. Ingraham, Mr Stephen L. Sewell, Mr John J. Slonaker, Mrs Katie Talbot, Mr Gordon Williamson, Mr Steven J. Zaloga.

My thanks to all those who have generously allowed me to quote from their books and magazines, or have provided material and/or photographs, in particular RTR Publications Ltd (*Tank* magazine), US Naval Institute (*Proceedings* magazine), and the *US Armor* magazine, Panzermuseum Munster Oertze, US Army Center of Military History, US Army Military History Institute, MOD Library, the Tank Museum, Central Armed Forces Museum Moscow, Patton Museum of Cavalry and Armor, and HQ USMC.

Finally I must thank my wife, who has drawn all the sketch maps, the Tank Museum staff (Librarian David Fletcher, Assistant Librarian Graham Holmes and photographer Roland Groom) for supplying the bulk of the AFV drawings and a great number of the photographs.

George Forty
Bryantspuddle
1995

THE TANK COMMANDER

ESSENTIAL QUALITIES

Tank commanders of today possess certain qualities which are as necessary when commanding a modern main battle tank as they were when tanks first appeared on the battlefield during the First World War. If they are to get the best out of their crew, their armoured fighting vehicle (AFV) and all its weapons and equipment, then tank commanders must not only understand the tank's basic characteristics, but they must also have the ability to exploit its full potential, whenever and wherever it is needed. This calls for certain special qualities, such as a sense of awareness and speed of reaction, as well as the more obvious skills of leadership and knowledge which all successful commanders at any level must possess. In the late 1980s the RAC saw the following as the essential qualities of an armoured commander:

a. **Sense of Awareness.** The armoured commander must be tactically aware. He will look outwards at what the enemy and other friendly forces are doing. If he becomes obsessed with the detailed actions of his crew or sub-unit, he will miss opportunities for destroying enemy and fail in his task.

b. **Grip and Leadership.** Every leader has his own style, and this is right and proper. However, an armoured commander must lead from the front, must be clear and concise in his actions and orders, and must not accept second best from those under him.

c. **Speed of Reaction and Anticipation.** A commander without a flexible attitude of mind and a sense of urgency will get left behind in armoured warfare. Quick reaction, initiative and the ability to anticipate are vital.

d. **Knowledge.** A commander must know his enemy, his men and his equipment. Modern warfare is complex and he must also understand the procedures and capabilities of the other arms with whom he may be grouped if he is to cooperate effectively with them.

e. **Commonsense.** Commonsense tempers the more volatile qualities and prevents mistakes.

Examples of these qualities will no doubt shine out from the pages of this book. However, it is as well to list them at the beginning and, by way of introduction, to briefly examine the training of tank commanders since the creation of the post during the First World War. This will help to set the scene and explain some of the difficulties which tank commanders face, both on and off the battlefield.

EARLY DAYS: CHOOSING THE COMMANDER

'Volunteers are required for an exceedingly dangerous and hazardous duty of a secret nature. Officers who have been awarded decorations for bravery, and are experienced in the handling of men, and with an engineering background, should have their names submitted to this office . . .', so read the 'strictly secret and confidential' order from the War Office, which asked for volunteers to command the first ever tanks. There was no shortage of volunteers of the right calibre, but there were other problems.

The armbadge tank, designed by Swinton as the unifying symbol for the new arm and worn by all ranks of the Tank Corps. (Tank Museum)

A SHORTAGE OF TANKS

The first essential for the thorough training of the tank commander and his crew is naturally to have the necessary AFVs, weapons and equipment with which to train. This was a major problem for the first volunteers to the 'Tank Detachment', as the infant British Tank Corps was called in 1916, because the men arrived before the delivery of the initial batch of Heavy Mk I tanks. Not only were there no AFVs at the volunteers' camp at Bisley, but also only three naval 6-pounder guns

The Heavy Section wore the Machine Gun Corps badge from 16 February 1916, but officers seconded to the new arm continued to wear their old regimental capbadges. (Tank Museum)

(selected as the tank's main armament) could be found for instructional purposes and no range was available on which to fire the guns – the War Office having quickly put a stop to the firing of unfilled shells on a Bisley rifle range. Fortunately the Royal Navy came to the rescue, allowing gunnery training to take place at Whale Island, Portsmouth. Driver training for the 'secret weapons' was also impossible at Bisley, so there was a further delay until a suitable, secure location could be found, namely on Lord Iveagh's estate at Elveden, near Thetford, in a remote corner of Norfolk. The area was turned into an imitation of the trench-front in France, 1½ miles wide, designed by Capt G. le Q. Martel, Royal Engineers. In addition, there was the need to formulate a tactical system for use as a guide to training for battle, but at least on that score they were ahead of the game.

'OLE-LUK-OIE'S TIPS

Fortunately for the 'Heavy Section, Machine Gun Corps', as it was now called, their founder, Col Ernest Swinton, was well prepared, and in February 1916 he completed his 'Notes on the Employment of Tanks', which he had drafted in early October 1915. The notes are aptly illustrated by his often-quoted 'Tank Tips', which provides a set of rules for tank commanding, many of which still apply on the modern battlefield. Col Swinton wrote in his autobiography, *Eyewitness*:

'At Elveden training continued at full blast in driving, negotiating the obstacles of a battlefield, and maintenance. There was no time for practising the Tanks in accordance with any elaborate tactical scheme. All that could be taught was the art of manoeuvring together with the straightforward object of searching out and destroying machine guns emplaced in every kind of artfully concealed

TANK TIPS

Remember your orders

Shoot quick

Shoot low. A miss which throws dust in the enemy's eyes is better than one which whistles in his ear.

Shoot cunning

Shoot the enemy while they are rubbing their eyes. Economise ammunition and don't kill a man three times.

Remember that trenches are curly and dugouts deep – look round the corners

Watch the progress of the fight and your neighbouring Tanks

Watch your infantry whom you are helping

Remember the position of your own line

Shell out the enemy's machine guns and other small guns and kill them first with your 6pdrs

You will not see them for they will be cunningly hidden

You must ferret out where they are, judging by the following signs: Sound, Dust, Smoke

A shadow in a parapet

A hole in a wall, haystack, rubbish heap, wood-stack, pile of bricks

They will be usually placed to fire slantways across the front and to shoot along the wire

One 6pdr shell that hits the loophole of a MG emplacement will do it in

Use the 6pdr with care; shoot to hit and not to make a noise

Never have any gun, even when unloaded, pointing at your own infantry, or a 6pdr gun pointed at another tank

It is the unloaded gun that kills the fool's friends

Never mind the heat

Never mind the noise

Never mind the dust

Think of your pals in the infantry

Thank God you are bullet proof and can help the infantry, who are not

Have your mask always handy

Tank Tips

position. Had there been time the next step would have been combined operations with infantry. Of the various instructions prepared and issued the following child's guide to knowledge is reproduced as an example of dignified official language.'[1]

Maj (later Maj Gen) J.F.C. 'Boney' Fuller was the first GSO2 of the Tank Corps and architect of most of its tactical thinking. This photograph shows him as a Staff Colonel. (Tank Museum)

FULLER'S 'INSTRUCTIONS ON TRAINING'

If it was Swinton who began it all, then it was Maj (later Maj Gen) J.F.C. Fuller of the Oxfordshire and Buckinghamshire Light Infantry, when appointed to Elles' staff in France in December 1916 as his chief general staff officer, who devised the tactics that were ultimately to make the tank so successful. He had issued his first 'Instructions on Training' by the end of December and in January and February of 1917 organized and ran a large indoor exercise for all Heavy Branch officers. It was a great shame that Swinton's 'Notes on the Employment of Tanks' was unknown to Elles' HQ, as it would have saved Fuller much effort. However, with the glaring stupidity that coloured so much British staff work in the First World War, it had been totally ignored by GHQ and was never issued.

AMERICAN PROBLEMS

Patton had similar problems when he began training the American Tank Corps, as he wrote in January 1918, 'Unless I get some Tanks soon I will go crazy for I have done nothing of any use since November and it is getting on my nerves'. However, in his own inimitable way, Patton overcame all training difficulties. His training ideas were innovative and thorough, making use of what he called 'machine foot drills' to make up for the lack of vehicles. These drills were designed to conform with the Infantry Drill Regulations, yet accustom the crews to a variety of methods of signalling and battle drills which they would use to manoeuvre their tanks in

Col (later Gen) George S. Patton Jr, c. 1918. Patton was the prime mover in armoured warfare in the AEF in France and commanded 304 Tank Bde in the first US tank action on 12 September 1918. He also wrote the initial tactical handling manuals for American armour. (The Patton Museum)

combat. It is interesting to note that some tank units in the US Army still employ similar techniques today, to make up for modern financial constraints.

CANVAS AND WOOD 'TANKS'

When the Germans began their initial preparations for war in the late 1920s/early 1930s, Gen (then Col) Heinz Guderian, architect of the build-up of the Panzerwaffe, quickly saw the value of using ad hoc machines for basic tactical training. Push-along dummy tanks, followed by slightly more sophisticated motorized dummies, based on NSU, 'Dixi' and Adler cars, caused great amusement among the Allied generals when the Germans first used them on their summer military exercises in 1929. However, the last laugh was definitely at the expense of the Allies when they realized, all too late, how well trained the Panzer crews were when war began in earnest. In *Achtung – Panzer!* Guderian, after explaining how tank crews should be trained individually, goes on to say that 'crew training culminates in the process of unit training, which builds up to large-scale exercises and manoeuvres'.[2] He stresses the importance of training in order to build up what he calls 'small unit cohesion', with all sharing the same testing conditions of combat and all playing their full part. The Germans were also quick to use any opportunity to gain combat experience, for example, sending Panzer officers and men to join the so-called 'volunteer' Condor Legion in Spain, to fight for Franco in the Spanish Civil War (July 1935–March 1939). Four German tank battalions and thirty anti-tank companies were among the ground element of the Legion and it was here that the Germans perfected their new 'Blitzkrieg' tactics which would prove so successful against the Allies in Poland and France.

The modern-day use of driving and gunnery simulators, training tanks, computerized

Architect of the German Blitzkrieg, Col (later Gen) Heinz Guderian grins happily as he strides through conquered French fields. (Imperial War Museum)

tactical trainers and other such equipment has its place in the training of tank commanders and their crews, and helps to save wear and tear upon the most expensive of all the equipment, namely the tanks themselves. However, the use of this equipment cannot entirely replace proper tank training and one is inclined to wonder sometimes whether it is used not to promote better training necessarily, but because of financial and terrain restrictions. In the end nothing can truly replicate the 'real thing' and tank crews must always be allowed to learn how to live and fight on their own tanks, before they have to do so in earnest.

Dixi, NSU and Adler cars (the latter shown here) were transformed into AFVs by using wooden armour. They proved ideal training vehicles for the burgeoning Panzer crews of the early 1930s. (Tank Museum)

Great interest was shown by Germany in the British Army mechanized exercises held on Salisbury Plain between the wars and they based many of their blitzkrieg tactics on what they had gleaned from watching such training. (Tank Museum)

CREW TRAINING

Experiences from the First World War showed that casualties among crews varied greatly from tank to tank and that on some occasions tanks had been employed with as few as just one crewman, who had alternately driven the tank and fired the gun. Also, during lengthy battles, it was often necessary to redistribute surviving crews to surviving tanks. It was therefore essential that crewmen should be skilled in each other's tasks. Ideally, every crewman should be able to drive, work the radio, shoot the main and secondary armament and know how to maintain the vehicle; only then can he work as a fully fledged member of a cohesive team. This principle was opposed from the outset by the Finance Branch of the War Office, who controlled mileage, ammunition and tradesmen's rates of pay. However, it remains just as important today as it did in 1916, although Treasury opposition remains just as strong. From personal experience, when manning my Centurion Mk III in Korea in 1953, I know how essential it is that all the crew are able to do each other's jobs. When coupled with the requirement to ensure 24-hour-a-day availability, all night 'operational stags' could only be maintained over a sustained period if the commander, gunner and loader/operator could drive the tank in an emergency and if all the crew were capable of loading, aiming and firing the guns, working the radios and answering calls, and so on.

The emphasis placed on sensible crew training is obvious, but 'practice makes perfect', as is evidenced by the story of the 'War of the Waters' fought by the Israelis in 1964–5 (see Part Three). As Gen Patton said, 'A pint of sweat will save a gallon of blood'. He also went on to say that soldiers must be trained to such an extent that what they do becomes second nature to them and that they must know their equipment and train with it,

until they can do their jobs 'in their sleep'. He felt so strongly about training and discipline as to aver that a soldier must be so well trained that, '. . . nothing short of death will stop him from fulfilling his mission. If brevity is the soul of wit, then, for the soldier, repetition is the heart of instruction.'

TRAINING OF COMMANDERS

No one can disagree that tank commanders should be selected from the best available tank crewmen, and, at NCO level, this happens in every armoured corps worldwide. It is only in the training and selection of AFV troop/platoon commanders that major differences occur, that is to say in young officer training. If one wants the best tank troop leaders then logic demands that one selects them from among the best tank commanders. However, using this method does not necessarily mean that one gets the best all-round officers. It is strange that although this is the method invariably adopted in wartime, in so-called 'peacetime' we send our potential officers to separate academies to learn how to become officers, then give them a short 'special to arm course' when they learn about armoured fighting vehicles, but which lasts only a few months, and is their only real tank training before they join their units. This means that they do not learn how to command tanks until they reach their regiments. This system has worked fairly satisfactorily in the past, when any build-up to war has been fairly lengthy, thus allowing the young officer time to gain tank commanding experience in his unit. There is also normally a leavening of experienced senior NCO-led tank troops to be found in most squadrons, who would undoubtedly receive battlefield commissions in wartime. However, how many ex-troop leaders would admit that they had to be 'led by the hand' (or should it be by the nose?) by their troop sergeant for many months before

The workings of the internal combustion engine must be understood by all. (Tank Museum)

Gunnery training normally begins in the classroom, with the inevitable detailed lessons on the weapons and ammunition, before going on to the vehicle itself. (Tank Museum)

Wireless instruction in progress at the Tank Corps Centre prewar. (Tank Museum)

they became sufficiently competent and confident enough to lead their troop in combat without getting them all killed in the first battle?

Whether this still holds true is a matter for conjecture, but I suspect that it might. This inevitably means that we are in danger of putting our most sophisticated and expensive tank ever in service, under the command of the most inexperienced members of the regiment. Not all nations do this of course. Some lengthen the syllabus for their young potential officers to include far more 'special to arm training', while others, such as the most battle-experienced armoured nation in the world today, namely Israel, still use the wartime method, which means that all its armoured officers have become experienced tank commanders before their selection to become officers. My personal preference is for this method, but there are many valid arguments for and against it and this is not really the place to air them.

TANK ACES

This book is not essentially about tank commander training, but rather about its end result, namely looking at low-level tank battles to see how they were fought and who did well enough to be classified as a tank ace. This in itself is not as easy a process as one might imagine. Some years ago the Americans tried to do it at Fort Knox, instituting an award programme to honour the very best of their past tankers. They immediately found that it was not a simple business to lay down the criteria to be used in making such a selection. The US Air Force, for example, awards the title of 'ace' to a pilot after five confirmed combat kills, but US Armor does not have a similar award which recognizes tank aces, nor does any other army. When looking for tank aces in the context of the Second World War, then inevitably German tank commanders such as Wittmann and Barkmann immediately spring to mind. One is therefore led to ask the question, were they

Driving instruction must always include practical work. A Vickers Medium crosses the River Wylie, *c.* 1935. (Tank Museum)

really so much better than their Allied opposite numbers? I am quite certain that the correct answer to that question is 'No, but perhaps they lived longer!' or, alternatively, that the German system of honouring their top tank commanders and the general high level of prestige which was given to their armoured troops, especially after their initial successes in Poland, France, Russia and North Africa, made it easier to spot the tank ace.

In the confusion of a large tank battle, where it is not just one tank up against another single tank, then it is never easy to say who actually knocked out the enemy. The example I have given of the assault on the Pacific island of Peleliu is a classic case, but I could have cited many others. A well-

respected ex-tank gunner friend of mine gave me two different examples from engagements in the Western Desert. In the first, a much depleted 5th Royal Tank Regiment (5 RTR) managed to manoeuvre into hull-down positions overlooking the Ariete Division during the Crusader battles of November 1941. The Italian tanks were moving broadside on, across its front, at a range of some 500 yd. At this range they were perfect targets for the 37 mm guns of the Fifth's Honey tanks and about twenty were quickly knocked out before the Italians beat a hasty retreat. Later inspection of the knocked-out enemy tanks showed that all of them had been hit several times and were probably claimed as 'kills' by many different tank commanders and gunners. On another

In the same way, live firing on the ranges, even with practice rather than full charge ammunition, is vital. (Tank Museum)

occasion, during the early battles around El Alamein in July 1942, a German battlegroup, led by a tank flying a large flag, attacked the sector held by a composite regiment made up of some thirty tanks – all that was left of 3 and 5 RTR. The attack had hardly begun when the order went out to all stations on the radio net: 'Get that bastard with the flag!' And they did so, all thirty of them. Who could positively say that theirs was the tank which had knocked out the enemy, despite the fact that it was such an obvious target? The answer of course is that no one could be certain, nor did they really care; what counted at the time was merely to knock out the enemy as quickly as possible.

THE TANK
Certainly the general excellence of German AFVs had a great deal to do with the life-expectancy of would-be tank aces in the Second World War. For example, would SS

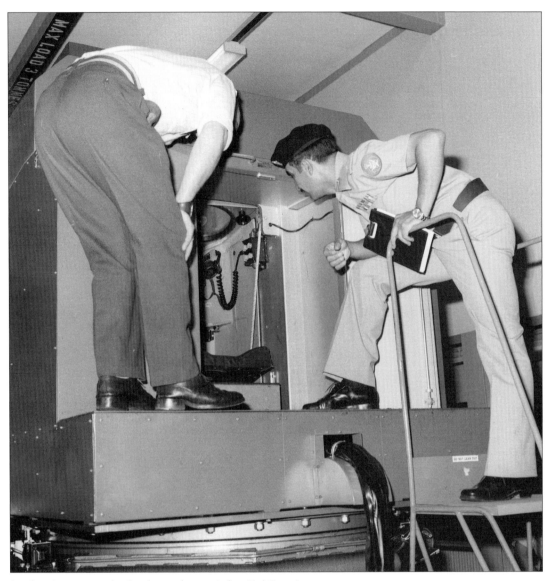

Some basic driver training can be achieved using a classroom simulator. (Tank Museum)

Hauptsturmführer Michael Wittmann have lasted as long as he did, or gained so much adulation, if he had been commanding a 30 ton Sherman or a 28 ton Cromwell, each with its 75 mm gun, instead of his dreaded '88 mm toting', 56 ton Tiger? The chances are that he would have finished up, like so many brave Allied tank commanders, being burned to death in the infamous 'Tommy Cooker' as the Germans nicknamed the Sherman. Yet there were, as we shall see, many Sherman and Cromwell tank commanders who achieved remarkable feats of bravery and knocked out Tigers and other better armoured and better armed German tanks. And of course, the courageous Wittmann suffered the same fate in the end. However, the fire-power, protection and

TEWTs (Tactical Exercises Without Troops) form the basis of tactical training. (Tank Museum)

The Battlegroup Tactical Trainer is a computerized indoor tactical trainer for practising battlegroup level exercises. (Tank Museum)

mobility attributes of a would-be tank ace's AFV clearly have a distinct bearing on the subject, as the recent Gulf conflict has shown once again, both the Abrams and Challenger proving far superior in every respect to the vast mass of Soviet-built, Iraqi-crewed AFVs.

THE CREW

The tank ace can never really be separated from his crew. His driver must get the tank into position (and out again in a hurry sometimes); the loader must do his job quickly and efficiently, while it is, or has been, the gunner's finger on the trigger and eye on the gunsight/telescope which has meant life or death to both the enemy tank and their own AFV. Their roles in ensuring that first round 'kill' before the enemy can react cannot be overemphasized. So it follows that the tank ace cannot become one, without an ace driver, ace loader and ace gunner. Even in three- or two-man tanks, or in those where the commander can lay and fire the gun himself, he still does not perform single-handed, so cannot be separated from his crew. Only when we get one-man tanks (perish the thought!), like single-seater fighter aircraft, will it really be possible to say that any one individual is truly a tank ace.

A FINAL BRIEFING

To close this short introductory chapter I would like to quote from the final briefing given by Maj Gen Israel Tal, then Director of the Israeli Armoured Corps, to his commanders on 5 June 1967, just before their surprise assault on the Egyptian Army at the start of the Six-Day War. Maj Gen Tal is a remarkable man, having begun his military career as a sergeant in the British Army during the Second World War. After arriving in Israel, he became a member of the 'Hagana' underground during Israel's war of independence and then entered the IDF as commander of machine-gun officer courses

Maj Gen Israel Tal, one of Israel's greatest soldiers. (Israel Defence Forces)

with the rank of major. His senior armoured corps appointments have included commanding an armoured brigade and an armoured division, while he is of course equally well known for his work on designing and producing the Merkava main battle tank. His words contain many of the essentials required by any good armoured commander, so they encapsulate much of what the following chapters will cover:

'Now that the plan is clear to us all, and, with it, all the moves nicely drawn on our maps, I want to say this to you: once the battle starts nothing that happens in the field will accord with what we have marked on these sketches of ours. The lines and axes of the actual battles will be quite different. But none need be worried by this, for combat

The Royal Tank Corps capbadge adopted in 1923, which incorporated the Corps motto: 'Fear Naught'. Note that the tank faces the opposite way to the one on the Tank Corps badge because of the change from peaked cap to beret. (Tank Museum)

Original capbadge of the RAC, which was formed on 4 April 1939, bringing together into one Corps the regiments of the now mechanized Cavalry of the Line and the battalions of the Royal Tank Corps. (Tank Museum)

never develops quite in accordance with the arrows on the map. However, one thing must be executed exactly as planned: the principle and concept lying behind these map markings. All will charge forward to the assault and all will penetrate as deeply as possible without paying concern to flanks and the rear. Whoever loses contact with our forces must continue to battle forward, knowing that the rest of his comrades – in all our formations – are doing the same.

'This opening battle will be the test battle for all the land engagements of the campaign. We face an enemy whose morale is high, who is confident in himself and his weapons. Our immediate objective is thus not only a physical one involving terrain and troops, but primarily a psychological one – an objective of morale. The one who wins this first battle will harbour the offensive spirit, the one who loses will feel retreat in his soul. The implication therefore is clear: the success of the campaign hinges on our immediate battle. Thus the fate of the State is bound up with what we do now, how we act and how we fare.

'I must now add this very grave injunction: this battle must be fought, if necessary, to the death. There is no other course. Each man will charge forward to the very end, irrespective of the cost in casualties. There will be no halt and no retreat. There will be only the assault and the advance.'

In this address Tal was echoing the words of other great Panzer leaders. Guderian, for example, talked about only having room in the Panzerwaffe for 'lively, open-minded spirits' and about having to overcome the inertia of the individual, just like the immovability of the broad mass. 'Only when the Panzer forces are full of verve,' he wrote, 'only when they are fanatically committed to progress, will they win through and achieve their great aim, which is to restore the offensive power of the army.'[3] This was, and still is, the prime task of the tank commander.

NOTES TO THE TANK COMMANDER
1. *Eyewitness*, Maj Gen Sir Ernest D. Swinton.
2. *Achtung – Panzer!*, Maj Gen Heinz Guderian.
3. Ibid.

PART ONE

THE FIRST
WORLD WAR

FLERS: THE FIRST ACTION

TO BREAK THE STALEMATE

Although this book deals primarily with armoured battles, especially tank-versus-tank engagements, it would be unthinkable to leave out the early operations of the First World War, during which the first tanks were used for the purpose for which they had been designed, namely to counter the impasse of static trench warfare. Together with all the other elements of static trench warfare – wire, mines, gas, pillboxes, strong points and, above all, miles and miles of trenches themselves – the machine-gun bullet and the artillery shell had caused mobile warfare on the Western Front effectively to grind to a halt. The tank was invented to break this

The capbadge of the Tank Corps from 28 July 1917 until it became the Royal Tank Corps on 18 October 1923. (Tank Museum)

stalemate and bring back the vital element of mobility onto the battlefield. The first occasion on which they were able to prove some of their capabilities was on the Somme, at Flers, on Friday 15 September 1916. Although this action was far too precipitate and the tanks spread far too thinly and on too wide a front to enable them to achieve very much success, their initial impact on the enemy was little short of amazing. 'The devil is coming!' is how someone in the trenches reported their appearance, and his words were passed along the line like wildfire.

The great Somme offensive, which had opened on 1 July 1916, was not going well. The Allied attack was not successful, the enemy defences were just too strong, and the horrific number of casualties rose – the British alone lost nearly 60,000 men on the very first day, of whom over one-third were killed without any appreciable gain being made. Gen Sir Douglas Haig, C in C British Expeditionary Force, was desperately seeking a solution to the mounting criticism over this blood-bath and seized upon the tank as his salvation, despite the fact that the number of tanks available was very small and, moreover, they were completely untried in battle.

Of the burgeoning Tank Corps there were just forty-nine tanks available for this attack and Haig decided quite arbitrarily and without any advice from, or reference to, Swinton,[1] to spread them in twos and threes across an entire three corps front: seventeen tanks each were allocated to XIV and XV Corps on the right and centre right, eight to III Corps in the centre, while the remaining seven were to be kept with the Reserve Army. The tanks' main tasks would be to deal with the enemy strong points and provide fire support for the infantry. The six companies (lettered A to F) which at the time made up the 'Heavy Section, Machine Gun Corps' (as the embryo Tank Corps was then called) were not all in France, and those that had arrived

were not all available. The forty-nine tanks that were ready came from just two companies – C and D. We shall be following the fortunes of one of these tanks, namely D 17, *Dinnaken* as it was called, commanded by Lt Stuart Henderson Hastie. Hastie was 2nd Lt (Temporary Lt) of the Highland Light Infantry, who had volunteered to join the newly forming Corps which would man these strange new weapons. He and his tank were destined to win worldwide fame when they were reported as 'walking up the High Street of Flers, with the British Army cheering behind'.

THE TANK

D 17 was a Heavy Mk I, male tank, weighing 28 tons, armed with two 6-pounder guns in its side half-turrets (known as sponsons) and four machine-guns in separate ball mountings (one front, one rear and one in each sponson). It had a crew of eight men, armour 6–12 mm thick, a top speed of about 4 m.p.h. and a radius of action of just under 24 miles. Its 'partner', the Heavy Mk I, female tank, was identical except for its armament – four Vickers .303 machine-guns replacing the two 6-pounders (two MGs in each sponson). [In the extract from C Company orders which appears later, the female tank is called either a 'Vickers car' or 'Tank MG'.] The initial build was for 100 Mk I tanks (fifty male and fifty female).

The Mk I is immediately recognizable from other marks of British Heavy Tanks because of the length of its gun barrels. (The 6-pounders were the original Admiralty pattern 8 cwt 40 calibre, but were replaced in the Mk IV onwards with the short 6 cwt 23 calibre gun whose barrel was less liable to be damaged by trees or houses, or get stuck in the mud during steep descents.) The Mk I was also fitted with a pair of tail wheels, which would assist the driver in steering the tank. Designed to be used on good going, the

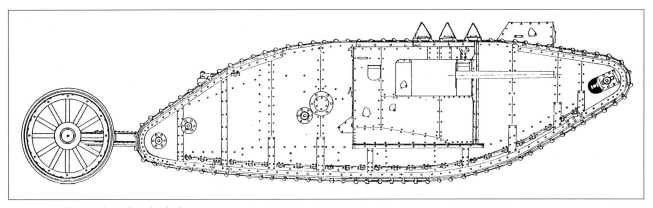

The Heavy Mk I (Male) tank, side elevation.

wheels were operated by means of a steering wheel, which was fixed to the glacis plate in front of the driver, and were supposed to be able to turn the tank in a circle of about 60 yd in radius. In action they proved to be a complete failure, due to the bad going and the cloying mud of the Somme, where they sank up to the axle, fell into shellholes and so on. As they did not help the tank's climbing

ability either, they were quickly dispensed with, all tail-wheel assemblies being removed by November 1916.

The original long-barrelled 6-pounders were obviously designed for long-range shooting in the Royal Navy, so the potential gun range was far in excess of any necessary tank engagements. The gun could traverse 100° from dead ahead. Between 324 and 332

A Heavy Mk I on its way up to take part in the first tank battle at Flers, 15 September 1916. (Tank Museum)

rounds of main gun ammunition could be stowed in the tank (estimates vary), comprising High Explosive (HE), Armour Piercing (AP) and case shot (anti-personnel for use against infantry in the open). It had a muzzle velocity of 554 m per second (m/sec) as opposed to only 441 m/sec for the 23 calibre gun.

THE SETTING

The morning of 15 September 1916 was typically autumnal for that part of France – fine, but with a thin ground mist. A couple of days earlier the tanks had been moved by

train up to their concentration area at a railhead known as 'The Loop', near Bray-sur-Somme. Then on the night of the 13th they had moved forward to their respective assembly areas, D Company going to 'Green Dump' behind Delville Wood (see map). They motored forward on their tracks, following the tapes which had been laid along their respective routes.

From Green Dump, which was only some 3 miles behind the front trenches, the tanks advanced to their 'jump-off' positions. It still took them a full 9 hours to reach these starting locations, due to the bad going and

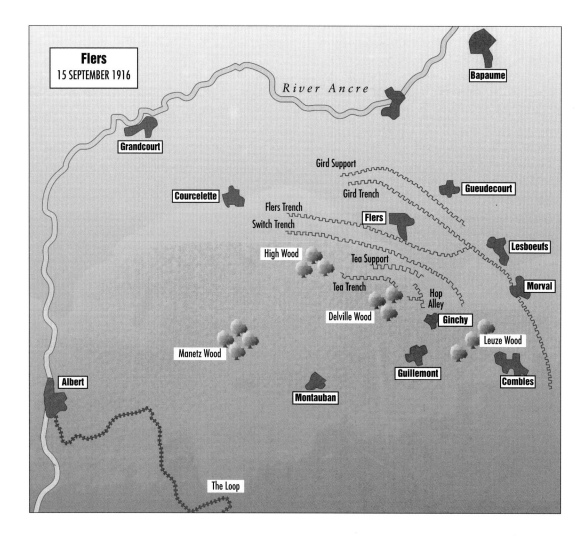

the darkness. The drivers had to use bottom gear most of the way and at times one of the crew had to dismount to look for routes round some very bad patches of ground. One can imagine the strain this placed upon the crews, even before the battle had begun. One commander (Lt Arnold of D 16) was so worried about the length of time it was taking him that he contemplated sending off his carrier pigeon, but decided against it and fortunately managed to get to his starting position just as the infantry were leaving their trenches.

D 17 was grouped together with D 9 and D 14, their outline orders being as follows:

'To proceed from starting line at 5.45AM, ahead of the infantry to TEA SUPPORT, then to 1st objective SWITCH TRENCH. Thence to FLERS AVENUE on to FLERS VILLAGE and on from there to GIRD TRENCH, GIRD SUPPORT to GUEUDECOURT.'[2]

The orders which Hastie actually copied down are well worth repeating here, despite the fact that some of his references are difficult to follow:

'COMPANY ORDERS FOR 'D' GROUP OF TANKS FOR 15 SEPT 1916
HASTIE (D 17) COURT (D 14) HUFFAM (D 9)

'You will leave your starting line at Zero minus 35 (Zero Hour being 0620am). Distance – 480 yards out is taken at 600 as you are in column ie: at 10 yards per minute – 60 minutes.

'You must arrive at plus 25 as you are W of Flers Road 60 minus 25 equals 35. Throughout the advance you will follow the route laid down on map and adhere to times given you. The following points in your advance are to be noted. The first Vickers car of the Group that arrives at TEA TRENCH will stop there – where he will deal with the German machine-guns and advance posts until the arrival of the Infantry when he will advance in line with them, overtaking the Group at SWITCH TRENCH. All Tanks of Group on arrival at SWITCH TRENCH wait until arrival of Infantry when the Group will advance 150 yards and thence conform to time-table.

'The objectives, routes and responsibility for dealing with strong points encountered by Group of Tanks D will be as follows. TEA SUPPORT TRENCH (where one Tank MG will be dropped until arrival of Infantry). SWITCH TRENCH – FLERS TRENCH sunken road at TIA35 thence to follow sunken-ditch at NW Corner of FLERS VILLAGE N31A82 HOG HEAD strong point. During the advance to the second objective from SWITCH to FLERS TRENCH along the routes chosen.

'You will make every effort to deal with sunken-roads and machine-gun emplacements as far as FLERS TRENCH. Should any strong point succeed in holding up the Infantry the Tanks will immediately proceed to deal with it.'

Hastie made the following observation below this last sentence:

'PS: While writing out these Company Orders I have realized that Huffam and Court were in our Group and when they both got stuck in a sunken road on the morning of the attack it put all the burden of the attack on to us – no wonder Maj Summers sent them in on their own once they got unditched – the following day. Looking back I think we should have done remarkably well as a Group – had we remained intact.'

THE BATTLE
The best description of D 17's part in the battle is taken from an account written by Gunner A.H.R. Reiffer, MM, who was the No. 2 Gunner of the starboard side 6-pounder, with Percy Boult as No 1. In 1957 he wrote:

'It was only half-light on this misty September morning when the barrage from hundreds of our guns signalled our start. Four of the crew – including myself – swung the starting handle and the 105 hp Daimler engine of D 17 roared into life and we were off. And that is how it seemed to be throughout the action. There was hell outside all right, but there was such a hell of a noise inside and we were such a tight-packed crew, that we didn't concern ourselves with what was happening outside. Our main preoccupation was doing our job – keeping our feet and keeping a wary eye out for the rock and roll of the tank. I was No. 2 gunner to Percy Boult on the starboard 6-pounder gun and our day started when Boult excitedly told me he was going to fire at a German observation balloon (spotting for the artillery). Several rounds were fired and Boult claimed a direct hit. The balloon disappeared and this may have had some bearing on the partial success of the tanks attacking Flers.

'As we approached our first objective we were stopped by an infantry runner who carried a message from his Brigadier asking for our help to clear up a strong point near Flers. Lt Hastie refused, saying his orders were to attack Flers. As we came into the village, which was a heap of rubble with (in places) a few skeletons of houses still standing – Boult (of the eagle eye) spotted a couple of German machine-gunners – at first floor level – who were firing at us. Four rounds of 6-pounder aimed at their only means of support, at almost point blank range, was enough to put them "hors-de-combat".

'A few yards further on Lt Hastie stopped the tank and told us to strip to the waist on the starboard 6-pounder as we were approaching a crossroads in the centre of the village and 100 yd to our right there was a German field gun battery. As we crossed this road we were to engage the enemy guns. We stripped to the waist and then the tank lumbered on up the main street of Flers. We were within 50 yd of the crossroads when we were stopped again by a runner who told us that we were in our own barrage and we had orders to retire. The infantry had apparently run into stiff opposition and the second objective had been abandoned. Lt Hastie turned us about and I think all of us (with perhaps the exception of Boult) heaved a sigh of relief. We retraced our tracks and turned back for Delville Wood and a ridge about [¾] mile away (on the Flers side). Lt Hastie stopped D 17 – stopped the engine and told Cpl Shelson that he was going to see the tank lying under the ridge (Lt Head's I believe). For the first time since the action started our engine was silent and we then realised there was indeed hell to pop outside. We were sitting, rather helpless, in the middle of one of the fiercest German barrages of the whole war. Within 5 minutes we had received a direct hit on a track and were ordered to abandon tank by Cpl Shelson. We all made for Lt Head's tank and fortunately no one was wounded running the gauntlet of this barrage.'

The crew stayed in the comparative safety of Lt Head's damaged tank under the sheltering ridge and, when night came and the barrage eased, they were able to get back to base.[3]

In 1963 Hastie received an interesting letter from a retired officer – Lt Wilfrid Staddon of the East Surrey Regiment – who explained that he and Hastie had met in Flers on the morning of the battle, when Hastie had shouted to him '. . . from the port side of the now famous tank, for verification of the direction of the fourth objective'. In his reply Hastie confirmed that it was his tank and goes on:

'Owing to having to force the engine due to steering being carried out by using brakes

Rear view of Heavy Mk I tank, C 5 *Creme de Menthe*, which had its tailwheels damaged by artillery fire during the battle, on Poziers Ridge. It was Capt Inglis's tank. (Tank Museum)

alternately on the tracks (the steering wheels in rear were hit early and out of action), the bearings were "run" . . . and the old Daimler was in a sorry state. Eventually I withdrew to Flers Trench on our end of Flers main street and distinctly remember discussing the situation with an infantry officer . . . so you must have been that officer.

'Owing to the mechanical condition of the tank (I expected the engine to pack up any time) I eventually withdrew and struggled very slowly back up the Flers–Delville Wood road for a short distance, when I swung left-handed and had just reached the edge of a hillock about 200 yd from the road when our engine packed up for good. That was 15 Sept for us!'

Hastie's letter thus clarifies the real reason why D 17 stopped in such an exposed position, but does not give any more clues on targets engaged and destroyed. However, Liddell Hart in his history *The Tanks* does say that D 6, D 16 and D 17 (the only three tanks left of the ten allotted to the 41st Division in the centre of XV Corps sector):

'. . . pushed into or along the eastern edge of Flers, smashing machine-gun nests, breaking into fortified houses, and spreading panic among the defenders – most of whom fled towards Gueudecourt. *Dinnaken* D 17 drove right through the village.'

A MILITARY CROSS FOR HASTIE

Lt Stuart Hastie was awarded an immediate Military Cross for his bravery at Flers, the citation in the Tank Corps Book of Honour reading: 'For conspicuous gallantry in action. He fought his tank with great gallantry,

Drawing by Sam Goddard Crowder of the first tank attack at Flers, giving details of some of the tanks and crews around the edge. (Tank Museum)

reaching the third objective. Later he rendered valuable service in salving a tank lying out under very heavy fire.'

THE AFTERMATH

All the individual tanks had performed bravely and in some cases very successfully, although many had been disabled, bogged or broken down, so it cannot be said that the new weapons had either fully proved themselves or had a great influence on the battle. Many senior officers viewed their performance with scorn and talked only about the obvious faults, making no allowances whatsoever for the crews' inexperience or the fact that they had been rushed into action on bad going and spread far too thinly across a very wide front. The press, on the other hand, had a field-day, claiming that the new weapon was invincible and inventing names for it such as 'Land Dreadnought', 'Jabberwock with eyes of Flame', 'Metal Monster' and 'Touring Fort'. When an air observer reported that he had seen a tank in the main street of Flers, with large numbers of troops following it, the press coined the now-famous headline 'A tank is walking up the High Street of Flers, with the British Army cheering behind!' – which Liddell Hart aptly notes as being 'a rendering which, though not precise, was prophetic'.

Fortunately Haig was pleased with the Heavy Section's performance and told Swinton that although the tanks had not achieved all that had been hoped for, they had saved many lives and fully justified themselves. Haig is reliably reported as saying, 'Wherever the tanks advanced we took our objectives and where they did not advance we did not take our objectives'. Perhaps the biggest bonus was the fact that he also said that now he wanted as many tanks built as possible, this being translated into a firm order for 1,000 bigger and better tanks, plus a further 100 Mk Is just to keep the factories going while the new design was

being finalized. That alone made worthwhile all the efforts of the gallant little band of C and D Companies, Heavy Section, Machine Gun Corps, that had fought at Flers. The newly emerging Tank Corps would have to wait until Cambrai before the tank would be able to show its true worth.

COMMENT

Lt Hastie was a brave and valiant commander. However, he could not by any stretch of the imagination be classified as a tank ace. The obvious difficulties of intercommunication between crew members meant that gunners had largely to use their own initiative – which Percy Boult clearly demonstrated, on both long-range (the observation balloon) and close-range (the MG nests) targets. Lt Hastie took charge when a major target was about to present itself (the enemy battery in Flers), preparing his gun crews for action, but would presumably then have let them correct their own fire in any subsequent engagement.

Mk Vs move forward during the final stages of the First World War, October 1918. Note that they are fitted with 'Cribs' which replaced the brushwood fascines for trench crossing.

BERRY AU BAC:
THE FRENCH BEGINNING

16 APRIL 1917

UN CUIRASSE TERRESTRE

Great Britain's main ally, France, was also experimenting with armoured tracked vehicles and their first 'land battleship' was little more than a turretless armoured box, containing a 75 mm short calibre gun on its starboard side, sitting on top of an American Holt caterpillar tractor, the brainchild of Col Jean Baptiste Estienne. Built by the Schneider works at Le Creusot, initial production was slow, so Estienne was 'pipped at the post' by the British at Flers. Eventually, however, by 1 April 1917, over two hundred had been delivered, although they were minus their self-starters and over thirty were immobilized through lack of spare parts.

Nevertheless, rather like Haig, the French C in C on the Western Front, Gen Robert Nivelle, decided to use the new weapons as part of a massive attack designed to break the stalemate on the Somme Front, before they had a proper chance to sort out their teething problems. The area chosen was Berry au Bac on the River Aisne, the date 16 April 1917, some seven months after Flers. The plan involved 132 Schneiders, organized into eight companies and divided into two groups, debouching from west of Berry au Bac, north-west towards the plain between the Aisne at Neufchâtel and Soissons.

The two groups were led by Capt Chaubes in the west and Chef d'Escadrons Bossut in the centre (this was the main group, consisting of eighty-one tanks). The mission of the latter group was to penetrate 9 km, from the village of Cholera to the village of Prouvais, across four successive lines of defences supported by heavy artillery. Bossut is the subject of this study, his Schneider bearing the name *Trompe-la-Mort* (Cheat Death) and flying his personal pennant, which bore the motto 'À fond et jusqu'au bout' ('All the Way').

THE TANK

Bossut's Schneider was a 13½ ton tank (nearer 15 tons when combat loaded), armed with a 75 mm pack howitzer and two 8 mm Hotchkiss model 1914 machine-guns. It had a crew of six, was powered by a four-cylinder Schneider petrol engine producing 55 b.h.p. Its armour was 6–11½ mm thick, it had a top speed of 4.6 m.p.h. and a range of about 30 miles. Just over 400 were built (including the CA2 which mounted a 47 mm gun). It was vulnerable to being easily 'brewed up', due to its badly protected fuel tanks located high up on each side of the AFV. A machine-gun bullet penetrating the side usually led to the tank catching fire almost immediately.

Part of Groupement Chaubes at Berry au Bac, 16 April 1917. They were operating to the north of Bossut's Groupement. (Musée de Berry au Bac)

Commandant Bossut (on left) stands in front of his Schneider tank *Trompe-la-Mort* (Cheat Death) before the battle. (Musée de Berry au Bac)

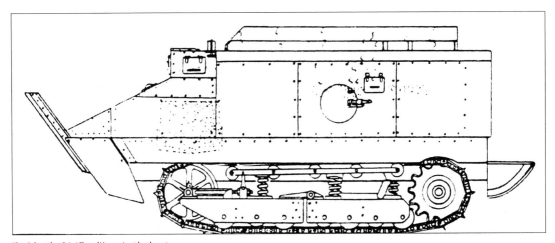

The Schneider C A (Char d'Assaut), side elevation.

The 75 mm gun was mounted in a sponson on the right-hand side of the tank, with limited traverse. The MGs were in ball mountings – one on each side. It carried ninety-six rounds of ammunition for the main gun.

THE SETTING
Reconnaissance before the attack showed that the Germans had widened their trenches and concentrated more artillery – possibly as a result of experience gained at Flers and subsequent British tank actions. The ground was very flat, which meant that it was easy for the enemy to observe the assault; there was consequently little chance of the French achieving any surprise.

Just as at Flers, the tanks had to make a long approach march before getting to their 'jumping-off' positions. However, unlike Flers, this was not all done during the night and much of this approach march had to be made in broad daylight. The tanks were soon spotted by German recce aircraft, the result being that heavy artillery fire was directed onto them. In addition, part of the approach route was in full view of the enemy artillery ground observation posts (OPs). Added to

these difficulties was the tendency for the Schneider to 'brew up' easily when the AFV was struck with shell splinters, all of which led to heavy tank casualties even before the actual attack began.

Bossut had considerable misgivings about the attack and had made them known to higher command, but they had not been heeded. 'We are attacking under very bad conditions', he had confided to his brother (a warrant officer in his unit) on the night before the battle. 'Few of us will come back tomorrow, but our sacrifice will not be in vain.'

THE BATTLE
Chef d'Escadrons Louis-Marie-Ildefonse Bossut had insisted that he be allowed to lead the attack and at 06.30 hrs on the 16th, his group moved out of the assembly area in a 2 km long column along the Pontavert–Gouignicourt road, towards Cholera Farm and the bridge over the Miette. They crossed the Start Line at 08.00 hrs and made good progress initially, although it took 45 minutes to cross the first German line. During this advance Bossut had spent much time on foot, going

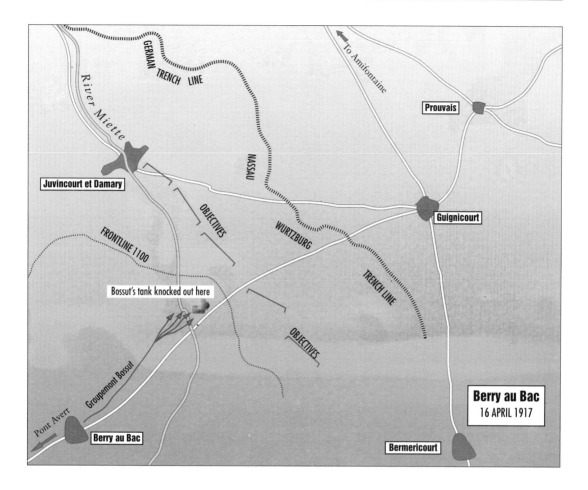

Berry au Bac
16 APRIL 1917

from tank to tank, checking on their progress and encouraging his men.

As they approached the second line at about 11.00 hrs, Bossut remounted his Schneider and almost immediately his tank was struck by an artillery shell which came down from a high angle, passed through the roof and exploded inside. All six members of the crew were killed, Bossut being blown out of the tank. It was the eve of his 44th birthday. That night his brother recovered the body, just before being wounded himself.

The attack continued past the trench lines of Nassau and Wurtzburg, and the fortified position of Hindenburg, and on towards the objective at Prouvais. However, the terrain and artillery bombardment made it impossible for the infantry to follow (as had happened at Flers). Many of the tanks were destroyed – in Bossut's group 44 out of the 81 which began the attack were lost, and there were some 180 casualties among the crews. The overall offensive did not achieve its aim, even though the armoured thrust had been partially successful. Gen Nivelle was replaced two weeks later.

FRANCE'S FIRST TANK HERO
Maj Bossut was the holder of the Légion d'Honneur, the Croix de Guerre (with seven citations) and the Croix de Sainte-Anne. He

Commandant Bossut (marked with a cross) guiding his tank towards the start line at Berry au Bac. (Musée de Berry au Bac)

Chef d'Escadrons Louis-Marie-Ildefonse Bossut, France's first tank hero. (Tank Museum)

was undoubtedly one of France's first tank heroes, despite the fact that he was killed in this his first tank action, without apparently firing a single round at the enemy. His heroism is obvious. He, like so many armoured commanders since those early days, led his troops from the 'sharp end', imposing his will on the battle by his physical presence. However, on the evidence of Berry au Bac, he cannot truly be classified as a tank ace.

AMERICAN OPERATIONS IN THE ST MIHIEL SALIENT

THE YANKS ARE COMING!

The third major Allied partner was of course the USA, whose armour was first used in the St Mihiel Salient on 12 September 1918 when the 304th Tank Brigade (304 Tank Bde), under Lt Col George Smith Patton Jr,[4] supported an attack by the 1st and 42nd Divisions (1 and 42 Div) of the US IV Corps. The action which I have chosen, however, took place two days later, when 2nd Lt Edwin A. McClure of A Company, 344th Tank Battalion (344 Tank Bn), led his platoon of little Renault light tanks in a mad dash through a barrage of German artillery fire some 2 km into the enemy rear, shooting up the enemy artillery and destroying eight machine-gun nests. This action ended in him successfully towing home two broken-down tanks and resulted in him being awarded the Distinguished Service Cross.

THE TANK

The tank battalions of the American Expeditionary Force (AEF) were equipped with either British heavy tanks or French light tanks. McClure had the latter – the Renault FT 17 of which some 3,500 were built in France. The US Army received 514 Renault FT 17s during war, and, although plans were laid to produce them in quantity in the USA

as the 6 ton special tractor, this did not happen until after the war was over. There were various models of the FT 17, the simplest being armed with an 8 mm machine-gun. However, McClure's was one of the later versions which mounted a 37 mm Puteaux light gun. It was a two-man tank, the first in the world to have a fully traversing turret. Armour was thin, it weighed only 6.9 tons, had a top speed of 4.7 m.p.h. and a range of 22 miles.

The 37 mm gun could fire AP or HE shells, 240 rounds being carried. Muzzle velocities were 388 m/sec (AP) and 367 m/sec (HE). Because of its one-man turret it was really only suitable for close infantry work, the commander also having to act as gunner and loader.

THE SETTING

Fifteen tanks of 344 Tank Bn (including McClure's), together with twenty-two tanks of the 14th and 17th French Groupements (Schneider tanks), had arrived just south of St Benoit (see map overleaf) at noon on 13 September 1918. They remained in position for the remainder of that day and were joined during the afternoon by a further fifteen tanks of 345th Tank Battalion (345 Tank Bn). Having replenished with fuel, which did not arrive until late evening, the tanks moved off

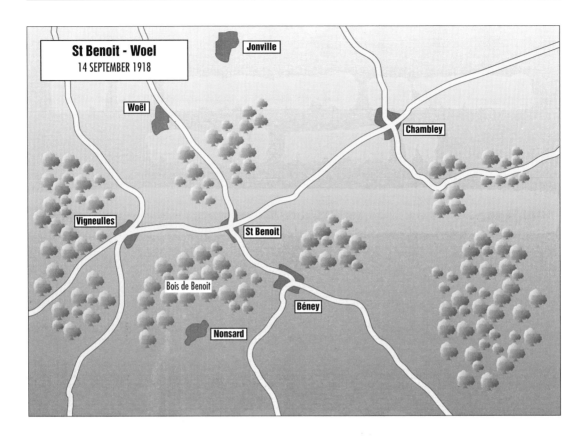

through Nonsard to Vignouelles, arriving there at midnight.

As they were out of touch with the 1st Infantry Division (1 Inf Div), whom they were supporting, it was decided to move on to Woel in the hope of linking up with the division somewhere en route. At 09.00 hrs on the 14th the leading tanks were some 2 km west of Woel, when they were told that the Germans had been driven out of the town and that it was now in French hands. However, contact with the division had still not been established, so a patrol was sent into the woods to the south to try to regain contact. At the same time the resupply column arrived and the tanks were replenished and the men fed. During this operation the trucks were attacked by enemy aeroplanes and one man was wounded. Then at 12.00 hrs it was decided to send a patrol of

three tanks (McClure's platoon), with five dismounted men, to Woel and thence 2 km south-east down the road towards St Benoit.

At 13.30 hrs the patrol commander (McClure) reported that Woel was clear of enemy and that he was returning. However, just half an hour later, he was attacked south of Woel by an enemy infantry battalion, supported by a battery of artillery and at least eight machine-guns. He sent a runner back to Battalion HQ, saying that he was attacking and five more tanks (under 2nd Lt Gordon M. Grant) were sent to his assistance. The eight tanks then attacked, succeeded in driving the enemy eastwards as far as Jonville, destroying at least a dozen machine-guns and capturing four 77 mm artillery guns. During this action they were shelled and both McClure and Grant, as well as four of their soldiers, were wounded as they attempted to

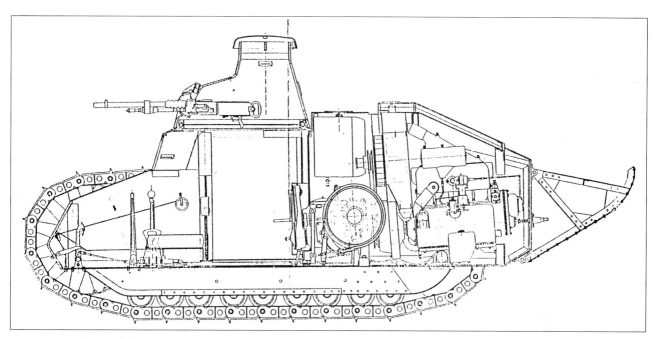

Renault FT 17, side elevation.

French-built Renault FT 17s in American Army service. The tiny two-man vehicles were armed either with a machine-gun in the one-man turret, or a 37 mm Puteaux gun (as seen here), which was the same type as commanded by Lt McClure. (US Army)

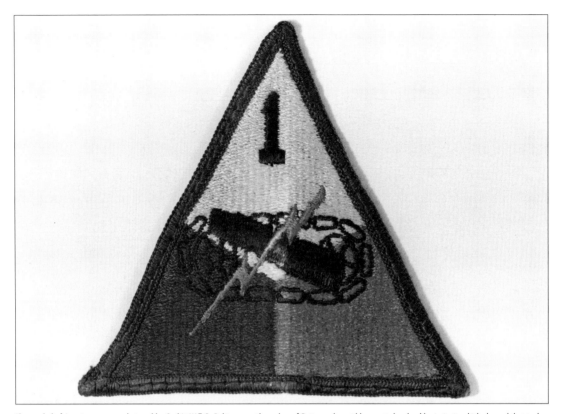

The symbol of American armour, designed by 2nd Lt Will G. Robinson on the orders of Patton, who said he wanted a shoulder insignia which showed that tanks had '. . . the fire-power of artillery, the mobility of cavalry and the ability to hold ground like the infantry, so it must have red, yellow and blue in it'. The resulting 'pyramid of power' was later embellished with an endless track, a cannon and a lightning bolt and divisional numbers were added as appropriate – the one shown is the patch for 1 Armd Div. (Tank Museum)

attach the field guns to the backs of their tanks. McClure then ordered the breech blocks of the artillery guns to be removed to make the guns useless and subsequently abandoned them. Two of the Renaults were mechanically disabled during the action, so he towed them back to Battalion HQ, then 2 km west of Woel. The patrol got out of the area just in time as the enemy laid down an intensive barrage with its heavy 150 mm guns.

2nd Lt Edwin McClure received a Distinguished Service Cross for this action and a few weeks later won a similar award in the Exermont area for another mad dash against the enemy. On that occasion he cleared out a number of machine-gun nests while climbing the high ground north-west of Exermont. He was wounded again, as was his driver, and his gun and its sights put out of action. McClure immediately dismounted, ran to another tank, dodging machine-gun bullets on the way, and changed places with the tank commander. He continued to lead his platoon and his new tank was hit and penetrated by an anti-tank bullet which 'wounded driver, and struck two 37 mm cartridge cases causing the powder to burst into flames in my face, and setting fire to four maps; fighting our blazing paper with our hands before it could explode'.[5] While this was going on the driver stalled the tank and they took more fire from the anti-tank rifle

American Doughboys, supported by FT 17s, advancing during one of the final campaigns of 1918 in which tanks played a major role. (US Army)

American FT 17s undergoing maintenance and repairs before the drive northwards. (The Patton Museum)

until McClure was able to locate it and deal with it using his 37 mm. He then knocked out an enemy 55 mm gun and drove off an infantry platoon with his trusty 37 mm.

An impassable stream prevented him from following up the enemy and, while halted, he was engaged by several 77 mm guns, over open sights. He managed to zigzag his way out of trouble, then tried to collect more tanks and resume the attack, but was prevented by more heavy artillery fire, which included gas shells. Only then did McClure set off back to his HQ, to report and to get his wounds dressed, but he passed out while walking down the road to Baulny. He was picked up by a passing lorry, taken to hospital, but managed to 'escape' and locate a Tank Corps LO at 1 Div HQ, to whom he made his report. He then allowed himself to

be evacuated. After seven weeks in hospital, the gallant McClure was promoted to 1st lieutenant and given command of A Company.

COMMENT

McClure was undoubtedly an early tank ace. He possessed all the attributes of a fine tank commander, including bravery and panache. In addition, he had to load, aim and fire his 37 mm gun, as well as locating and acquiring his targets, guiding his driver, map reading, leading the other tanks in his platoon, and so forth, all without the aid of radio and the other modern devices on which a modern tank commander now depends so heavily. He was thus commander, loader and gunner all rolled into one – quite an undertaking, which make his exploits all the more remarkable.[6]

VILLERS BRETONNEUX: THE FIRST TANK-VERSUS-TANK ENGAGEMENT

24 APRIL 1918

Although the Germans were very slow to build tanks in the First World War, and then only built a handful compared with the thousands produced by the British and French, it was inevitable that there would eventually be a tank-versus-tank engagement and that a tank commander would be able to claim to be the first to have knocked out an enemy tank. Quite fortuitously, this honour fell to a tank commander in No. 1 Section, A Company, 1st Tank Battalion (1 Tank Bn), of the British Tank Corps, although later in the same action a German tank commander would knock out three British tanks.

The British tank commander, 2nd Lt Francis (known as Frank) Mitchell, fortunately wrote a detailed account of the battle and there are also detailed accounts from the German side, so it is possible to piece together a reasonably accurate account of the action. Mitchell was later to describe the action as being 'very much the German Cambrai', which perhaps rather over-embellishes what was a far more localized engagement, despite the fact that it was the first time German tanks had been used in any numbers.

BACKGROUND

By April 1918 the Germans had advanced within 7 miles of Amiens, an important rail centre and junction point of the British and French armies. If they could capture Villers Bretonneux and the high ground between there and Cachy (see map overleaf), it would be possible to dominate Amiens with accurate artillery fire and perhaps capture it, with serious consequences for the Allies. To prevent this from happening the French brought up crack troops, including units of the Foreign Legion, some of whom were positioned in the Bois de Blangy about 4 miles west of Villers Bretonneux, together with British tanks of A Company, 1 Tank Bn. These tanks were engaged in what were known as 'Savage Rabbit' tactics – this required the tanks to be used in the counter-attack role, waiting in concealed ambush positions and then 'emerging like savage rabbits from their holes', as Gen Hugh Elles put it, 'to fall upon the flanks of any German advance'.[7]

THE TANKS

A Company, which had recently suffered a number of casualties, was equipped with hastily renovated old Heavy Mk IV tanks. No. 1 Section, under Capt J.C. Brown, MC, comprised three tanks – two female and one male (No. 4066), the male tank commanded by 2nd Lt Frank Mitchell. Apart from having the short-barrelled 6-pounders and no tail

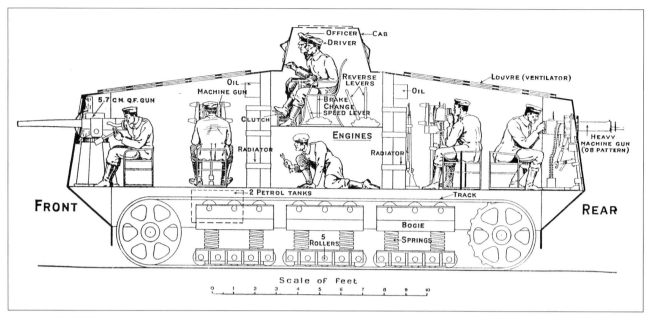

The A7V Sturmpanzerwagen.

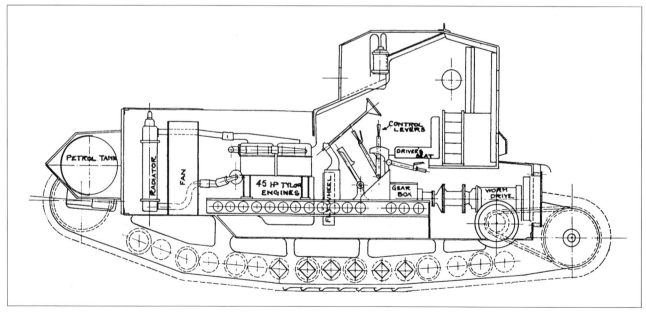

The Medium 'A' Whippet.

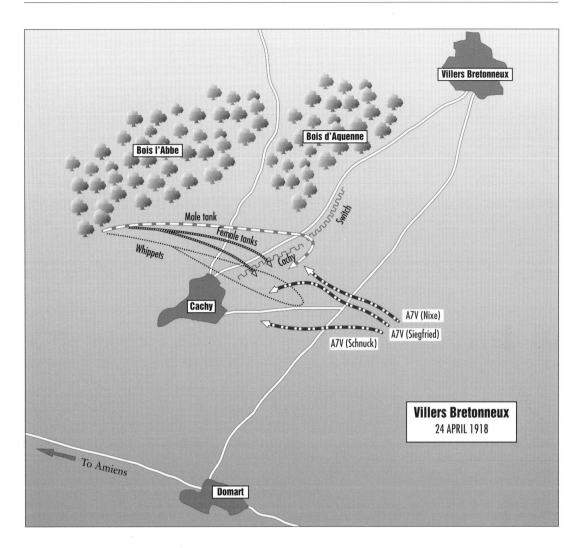

wheels, it was little different to the Mk I which I have already described, so let us look instead at the German heavy tank, the A7V Sturmpanzerwagen. Weighing 33 tons combat-loaded, with a crew of eighteen (commander, driver, gunner, loader, two engineers and six two-man machine-gun teams), it had armour 15–30 mm thick, was armed with a single 57 mm Russian Sokol gun, mounted in the centre of the front of the tank, plus six Spandau or Maxim machine-guns spread all over the vehicle (see drawing). It had a top speed cross-country of about 4 m.p.h. and a radius of action of 20 miles. It was in essence a heavily protected mobile gun platform, basically there to support the infantry. However, it was badly balanced, under-powered and had a poor cross-country performance. Only twenty A7Vs were ever built.

The third type of tank involved in the battle was the British Medium A Whippet, seven in all, belonging to C Battalion, Tank Corps and commanded by Capt T.R. Price. The Whippet weighed 14 tons, was armed only with four machine-guns, had a crew of three, thin armour, but could manage a top speed of over 8 m.p.h., with a good cross-country performance.

Two German A7Vs shelter in a farmyard. Some of the tank's enormous eighteen-man crew can be seen on the nearest tank. (Tank Museum)

THE SETTING

The Germans decided to attack in order to capture the dominating ground between Villers Bretonneux and Cachy. They might then move on to take Amiens if the situation allowed them to do so. This somewhat hesitant approach was because they were short of troops for the attack, and lacked artillery ammunition to support it properly. However, on the plus side, fourteen A7Vs were available. British tanks had been seen in the area of the woods north of Cachy, so they had been shelled continuously, with both HE and mustard gas. Mitchell comments that on the night of 23/4 April the shelling became unbearable. An enemy aircraft had flown low, dropping flares, and discovered them, so there was nothing for it but to move (at 01.00 hrs) to the western edge of the Bois

l'Abbe. However, towards dawn they were once again completely overwhelmed with gas shells. Two of Mitchell's crew collapsed and had to be evacuated. Nearby a battery of 18-pounders was firing, their crews all in masks. Wounded infantry then appeared and told Brown and Mitchell that Villers Bretonneux had been captured and the enemy had broken through. The battery had lost its FOO,[8] so was firing blind. It was agreed that if the Germans advanced, the tanks would move out to attack them, while the guns fired over open sights.

About 08.00 hrs the GOC of 23rd Brigade (23 Bde) arrived and went forward with Capt Brown to discover the true situation. They found that the line was still holding between Cachy and Villers Bretonneux. However, they did not discover that there were enemy tanks in the area. Brown's section was given orders to move up to the Cachy switch line and hold it at all costs.

Mitchell recalls:

'As the wood was still thick with gas we wore our masks, while cranking up a third member of my crew collapsed and I had to leave him behind propped up against a tree trunk. A man was loaned to me by one of the females, bringing the crew, including myself, up to six instead of the normal eight. Both my first and second drivers had become casualties, so the tank was driven by the third driver, whose only experience of driving was a fortnight's course at Le Treport (the base camp). Capt Brown rode in my tank. I was the only tank commander familiar with the lie of the land.'

They set off at 08.45 hrs, making for the Cachy switch line, with Mitchell's tank on the left, nearest the wood, and the two females to his right. Soon they were able to remove their gas masks, as they zigzagged undamaged through a heavy enemy barrage. As they approached the switch line at about 09.30 hrs, an infantryman jumped out of a trench, waving his rifle and shouted to Mitchell, 'Look out there's Jerry tanks about!' This was the first indication that the enemy were using tanks, and looking ahead Mitchell saw, 'three weirdly shaped objects moving towards the eastern edge of Cachy, one only some 400 yd away, the other two being further away to the south. Behind the tanks I could see lines of advancing infantry.'

Capt Brown immediately left Mitchell's tank to run across to warn the two females, while Mitchell turned right and, travelling parallel to the nearest German tank, threaded his way in between the small isolated trenches that formed the Cachy switch line, in the direction of Cachy. The left-hand 6-pounder gunner began to range on the German tank, but there was no reply from the A7V.

Although there was mist overhead, at ground level it was clear and Mitchell was able to use his forward Lewis machine-gun against the German infantry.

'Half-way to Cachy I turned round as the two females were patrolling the other part of the switch line. My attention was now fully fixed on the German tank nearest me which was moving slowly. The right-hand gunner, Sgt J.R. McKenzie, was firing steadily at it, but as I kept zigzagging and there were many shellholes, accurate shooting was difficult.'

Mitchell's tank then came under fire from the German tank:

'Suddenly there was a noise like a storm of hail beating against our right wall and the tank became alive with splinters. It was a broadside of armour-piercing bullets. . . . The crew lay flat on the floor. I ordered the driver to go straight ahead and we gradually drew clear, but not before our faces were splintered. Steel helmets protected our heads.'[9]

Turning to the German account of the action, the fourteen A7Vs supporting the German advance had been divided into three groups – group 1 (three tanks) made directly for Villers Bretonneux; group 2 (seven tanks) were on the right flank making for Bois d'Aquenne; group 3 (four tanks) drove towards Cachy. It was this latter group which Mitchell had seen and was engaging. The fog had caused the German tanks to lose their way and one of the four (Elfriede) went too far north, then fell into a quarry and, although the crew continued to fight bravely as infantry, the tank itself took no further part in the battle. The remaining three A7Vs of group 3 were the ones Mitchell had seen and the tank which he had started to engage (Nixe) was under the command of 2nd Lt Wilhelm Biltz.

Artist's impression of the first tank-versus-tank engagement, which took place on 24 April 1918. (Tank Museum)

As soon as he saw the enemy tanks Biltz put his tank into reverse and, at the same time, ordered his gunners to engage them.

Clearly if Mitchell was going to give his gunner a decent chance to hit the enemy, then he had to halt, thus providing a static, stable gun platform. And this he did. Biltz, however, seeing Mitchell halt, thought that he had knocked him out, so turned his attention onto the two female tanks, managing to hit them both, so that they were forced to retire and took no further part in the action. Mitchell again takes up the story:

'I continued carefully on my route in front of the switch line. The left-hand gunner (named Carter, as far as I can remember) was now shooting well. His shells were bursting very near to the German tank. I opened a loophole at the top side of the cab for better observation and when opposite our opponent, we stopped. The gunner ranged steadily nearer and then I saw a shell burst high up on the forward part of the German tank. It was a direct hit. He obtained a second hit almost immediately lower down on the side facing us and then a third in the same region. It was splendid shooting for a man whose eyes were swollen by gas and who was working his gun single-handed, owing to shortage of crew.

'The German tank stopped abruptly and tilted slightly. Men ran out of a door at the side and I fired at them with my Lewis gun. The German infantry following behind stopped also. It was about 10.20 a.m.'

Inside *Nixe* there was chaos. The first strike had killed the front gunner, mortally wounded two more crewmen and slightly injured a further three. Biltz was afraid that a large box of armed hand grenades, carried in the forward fighting compartment, was going to explode and ordered his crew to bail out. The tank was hit twice more, but damage was apparently insignificant. After some time had passed, the driver noticed that the tank engines were still running, so Biltz, after

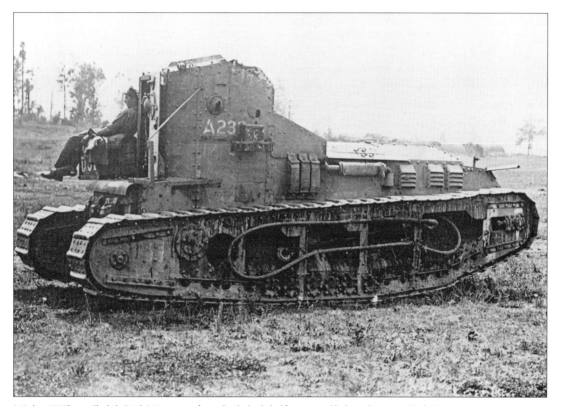

A Medium 'A' Whippet. The little British 14 tonner was fast and agile, but lacked fire-power and had very thin armour. (Tank Museum)

making very sure that his tank would not blow up, ordered his crew to remount. They were then able to drive the damaged A7V back about 2 km before the engines ran out of oil and seized. This damage had been caused by the hits on the side, so Mitchell could rightly claim to have knocked out the first enemy tank.

After dealing with *Nixe*, Mitchell then began to engage the other two A7Vs, which seemed to be coming in his direction. However, after a while, they withdrew slowly southwards and Mitchell clearly thought he had seen them off.

The rest of the battle was not so good from the British point of view. Mitchell had a grandstand view but took no part, as he was still patrolling the switch line and firing case shot at the attacking German infantry. About 11.00 hrs he saw seven Whippets appear from the northern edge of Cachy, then drive out at top speed past the wire and on over the ground in front of the Cachy switch line. They initially played havoc with the German infantry, scattering them right and left, as they drove among them firing their machine-guns. Then suddenly, one stopped and Mitchell saw great clouds of smoke coming from it. Then a second burst into flames. The remaining five withdrew towards Cachy, but one stopped about 100 yd from the village and Mitchell saw a crewman get out and run over to another Whippet, which picked him up. A fourth Whippet broke down near an orchard, close to Cachy, so only three actually made it home undamaged.

Capt T.R. Price, who had been commanding the seven Whippets, had been told that he was going out to attack unsupported infantry, hence his rather reckless, but highly effective, 'charge' directly at the enemy. He did not know about the other two A7Vs of group 3 (*Siegfried* commanded by 2nd Lt Friedrich-Wilhelm Bitter and *Schnuck* commanded by 2nd Lt Albert Mueller). Bitter saw the Whippets come charging in among the infantry, immediately moved his tank forward and opened fire, as did the supporting artillery. It is impossible to tell which of these actually knocked out the Whippets, but clearly the A7Vs played an important part in forcing them to withdraw.

Then it was Mitchell's turn to get hit. (He had actually already been bombed by a friendly aircraft which had mistaken him for the enemy.) Having engaged another German tank at a range of some 1,000 yd in the direction of Villers Bretonneux (presumably one of group 1), Mitchell's tank was then hit by a light mortar belonging to the German Guards Grenadier Regiment 5, which broke one of its tracks. 'We had been hit at last. We got out and made for the nearest trench some 50 yd back. It was about 12.45 p.m.'

A MILITARY CROSS FOR MITCHELL

For his gallant action 2nd Lt Francis Mitchell was awarded the Military Cross and Sgt J.R. McKenzie the Military Medal. Mitchell's citation reads:

'For most conspicuous gallantry and devotion to duty in action against enemy tanks at Cachy on April 24, 1918. This officer was in command of a male tank in action east of Cachy Switch Line, when hostile tanks came in action. He fought his tank with great gallantry and manoeuvred it with much skill in order to bring the most effective fire on the enemy one, but to avoid offering a greater target than possible. As a result of his skilful handling of his tank and his control of fire,

he was able to register five direct hits on the enemy tank and put it out of action. Throughout he showed the greatest coolness and initiative.'

COMMENT

Undoubtedly both Mitchell and Bitter deserve their place in this book. Both manoeuvred skilfully, despite their cumbersome machines. Their gunners equally deserve high praise. Anyone who has tried firing a tank gun with a gas mask on knows how difficult it is, but I doubt very much if there are many gunners alive today who have had to aim and fire their tank guns with their eyes swollen by mustard gas.

NOTES TO ON THE WESTERN FRONT

1. Maj Gen Sir Ernest Swinton, 'Father of the Tank Corps' and one of the prime movers in tank development, had come over to France at Haig's behest and wrote later of this encounter with Haig: 'On 19 August I paid a hurried visit for one day to Advanced GHQ at Beauquesne. Sir Douglas saw me and pointed out on the map the sector where he proposed to throw in the tanks. He did not enter into any discussion of his reasons for using them at the time.'

2. Taken from the War Diary (Army Form C 2118), held by the Tank Museum Library.

3. That evening Gunner Reiffer and Gunner Smith of D 1 went out to tank D 9, which had been disabled during the battle and lay about 30 yd in front of the German lines, to discover whether or not it had been turned into a strong point by the Germans. After a hair-raising night recce, they confirmed that the tank was not being used by the Germans and brought back one of its Hotchkiss machine-guns. Both Reiffer and Smith were awarded with the Military Medal for their bravery.

4. George Smith Patton Jr would have a spectacular and at times controversial career

in two world wars, reaching the rank of four star general in command of the US Third Army in the Second World War. Love him or hate him, he was undoubtedly one of the finest armoured commanders the world has ever known.

5. Taken from a Personal Experience Report written by 1st Lt Edwin A. McClure, Co A, 329 Bn Tank Corps, held by the Patton Museum Library.

6. Sadly tank designers did not learn and continued to build two-man tanks right up to the start of the Second World War, principally because they were cheap and easy to manufacture.

7. This tactic had been forced upon the Tank Corps due to shortages of serviceable tanks in France and especially a grave shortage of the new light Whippet tanks.

8. FOO = Forward Observation Officer, who spotted for the guns and sent back target information to the battery gun position.

9. Mitchell credits the A7Vs with this fire but other historians, who have analysed Biltz's battle reports carefully, consider that it was more probably an infantry machine-gunner.

PART TWO

THE SECOND WORLD WAR

BLITZKRIEG!

FRANCE 1940

On 10 May 1940 the 'Phoney War' was well and truly ended, with the savage German blitzkrieg onslaught on the West. The main German thrust was through the Ardennes and Luxembourg by strong armoured and mechanized forces, designed to seize bridgeheads across the Meuse between Namur and Sedan, then to overrun France as quickly as possible. The other operations – the airborne assaults on Holland and Belgium, both swiftly followed up by land assaults – were merely cleverly planned diversions to draw the Allied armies away from the main German attack. However, in the event, both went so well that the Germans were able to advance on all fronts. The plan, codenamed *Fall Gelb* (Case Yellow)

Oberstleutnant von Jaworski was one of very few tank commanders (perhaps unique?) to be credited with the sinking of an enemy destroyer off the French coast in 1940. (Tank Museum)

was breathtakingly simple – and it worked. One essential ingredient was the blitzkrieg tactics of the Panzers, who spearheaded all the German thrusts. One such formation was 6th Panzer Division (6 Pz Div), which was part of Reinhardt's XLI Panzer Corps, the centre Corps of the enormous mass of armour comprising some seven Panzer divisions, which was to force the crossing over the Meuse and provide the main *Schwerpunkt* that would seal the fate of the Allied armies.

6 Pz Div was somewhat different to the majority of the other Panzer divisions in that it had started life as the 1st Light Division, one of four *leichte* divisions which became 6th, 7th, 8th and 9th Panzer Divisions after the Polish campaign. Its main equipment was also different, because in mid-April 1939, while the division was stationed at Paderborn, it had been issued with some

hundred plus Czechoslovakian tanks – the Skoda LT vz 35,[1] which had been developed from the British Vickers 6 ton tank. It was a three-man tank (commander, driver and gunner), although CO 11th Panzer Regiment (Pz Regt 11) sensibly ordered that it should be manned by four men, adding a loader in the turret. German radios were also fitted. With a total of 235 tanks in the division (65 x PzKpfw II, 128 x PzKpfw 35(t) [including 10 x command] and 42 x PzKpfw IV), it had a powerful tank content.

Under Generalmajor Werner Kempf, 6 Pz Div had moved its leading elements forward of the Rhine, into the Mayen area on 9 May, ready for the assault on the West the following day. Crossing the Meuse at Montherme, at dawn on the 13th, they burst through the weak Maginot line defences that evening and were soon west of the Meuse, pressing on deep into the enemy rear. By

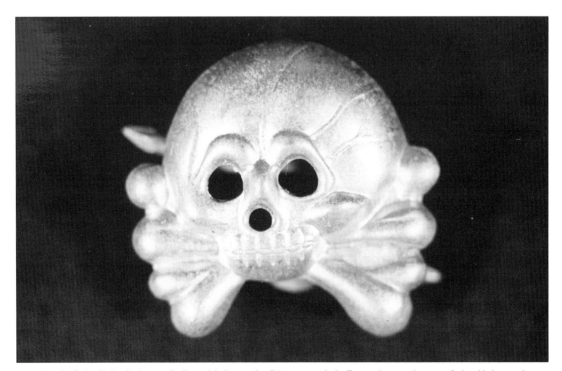

Panzer 'Totenkopf' (Death's Head) white metal collar patch badge worn by all Panzertruppe, both officers and men, in the centre of a long black rectangle piped around the outside in pink. (Tank Museum)

20.00 hrs on the evening of the 15th, having been given orders to pursue the retreating enemy, their advanced guard had reached Montcornet, some 40 miles west of the river. By the following evening, they had reached the River Oise at Guise, which is where this account begins.

The subject of this study is Dr Franz Bake, a tank ace, seen here at the beginning of his Panzer career in the Second World War. Born in 1898, he had served during the First World War, being awarded both the Iron Cross First and Second Class for bravery while serving with the 53rd Infantry Regiment. He left the army at the end of the war, but had rejoined the Wehrmacht in December 1937 as a leutenant and had volunteered for the newly emerging, élite Panzer arm. During the Polish

campaign he was a battalion adjutant, but now, for the assault on France, he was commanding 1 Kompanie of Panzer Battalion 65, Pz Regt 11, and was eager to show his true worth.

THE TANKS

Developed by Skoda in 1934–5, the LT vz 35 light tank weighed 10½ tons, mounted a 3.7 cm KwK 34(t) (Skoda A-3) anti-tank gun, which had an armoured cowl fitted over its recoil cylinder because it stuck out of the front of the fully traversing turret. The gun was an adapted field gun, with a muzzle velocity of 675 m/sec. Alongside it was a ball-mounted coaxial 7.92 mm machine-gun, which could be disconnected so that it and the 37 mm could be fired independently when

Tank crews belonging to Oberleutnant Dr Franz Bake's No. 1 Kompanie of Pz Bn 65, Pz Regt 11, are seen here with their PzKpfw 35(t)s. (Bake is the one in the forage cap.) (Panzermuseum)

The Char B1 bis was a formidable tank, with a 47 mm gun in the turret (replacing the 37 mm of the B1) as well the 75 mm howitzer in its hull. (Tank Museum)

necessary. A second MG was fitted in a ball socket in front of the driver. Its armour was 8–35 mm thick, it had a top speed of 25 m.p.h. and a range of 125 miles. In German service it had a crew of four. Although it was never considered to be as good as the other Czech tank 'seized' by the Germans when they invaded Czechoslovakia – the PzKpfw 38(t) – it was still a good tank, being described by a member of 6 Pz Div as 'that fine and reliable offspring of the Vickers six-ton tank'.[2]

Opposing the Germans were various French AFVs, including one of the most formidable heavy tanks of the period – the Char B1 bis. This was the ultimate development of the 15 ton 75 mm gun tanks which had been advocated as long ago as 1918 by Gen Estienne and was produced in the early thirties. Weighing 32 tons, with a crew of four, armour 14–60 mm thick and mounting a 47 mm gun in its turret, plus a 75 mm howitzer in the hull and two machine-guns, it was a formidable tank. It had a top speed of 17½ m.p.h. and a range of 87 miles. The major drawback to the hull-mounted howitzer was that it had only 5° of traverse.

THE SETTING

Since crossing the River Meuse, 1 Kompanie, the battlegroup's breakthrough force, had gone hell for leather for Guise, intent on capturing a crossing place over the River Oise, bypassing columns of fleeing French troops, dealing swiftly with any opposition. Bake was at the head of his eighteen tanks (four of his company's full complement of twenty-two had been left behind east of the

Bake stops to talk with Oberst von Esebeck, his Battlegroup commander, on the way to capture a crossing over the River Oise, 1940. (Panzermuseum)

Meuse with mechanical problems). As darkness fell, the column closed up and orders were given to use minimum lighting. As they approached Flavigny, a village close to Guise, the leading motorcyclists of the vanguard came under machine-gun and cannon fire from the village. The battlegroup commander, Oberst Freiherr von Esebeck, ordered up some of the 3.7 cm anti-tank guns of the 41st Anti-Tank Battalion, but as soon as they began to fire they were engaged by a number of French heavy tanks – the Char B1 bis – which quickly knocked out the leading anti-tank guns. The 3.7 cm anti-tank guns could not penetrate the frontal armour of the French heavy tanks – hardly surprising as it was 60 mm thick.

The French tanks belonged to 2ème Division Cuirassée (2 DCR), which had originally contained two demi-brigades of

tanks, each with a battalion of Char B and B1 bis (thirty-four tanks) and a battalion of forty-five Hotchkiss light tanks. Unfortunately, in line with current French armoured policy, these tanks had been scattered along the front in 'penny packets', and in many cases ordered to defend bridges and other vital points, without any proper infantry support.

THE BATTLE

Dr Bake, faced with this situation, sent patrols forward to scout the enemy position, at the same time bringing his tanks up to a suitable 'jumping off' point, from where they would be able to outflank the enemy and press on past Guise. He personally went forward to look for a good route for his Panzers, first in his tank and then on foot, accompanied by his adjutant. They walked

PzKpfw 35(t)s in action in France, 1940. (Tank Museum)

The Tank Battle badge was awarded in silver to tank crews and bronze to support troops. There were also two further classes – one for 25–50 battles and one for 75–100 battles. (Tank Museum)

right up to a French outpost and captured the surprised occupants. Bake sent them to the rear, guarded by two slightly wounded anti-tank gunners.

Following his recce, Bake conferred with Oberst von Esebeck and it was decided that the attack on Guise should begin at first light on the following day (17 May). The Panzers moved forward and the enemy tanks began to engage them. Bake sent some of his armour round to the flank where he reckoned that their 37 mm guns would have a better chance of penetrating the sides of the enemy heavies. The attack had begun. The motorcycle troops dismounted and were working their way forward, supported by fire from the anti-tank guns and Bake's tanks. Bake spotted an enemy tank, which had started to fire at the tanks he had sent around the flank. He ordered his driver to advance and guided him into a good fire position. His gunner had already laid onto the French Char B1 bis, so as soon as Bake ordered his driver to halt, he

Dr Bake, now an Oberst, talks with two of his officers in Russia. He wears his Knight's Cross (Ritterkreuz) and three tank destruction badges; the latter can be seen on his right arm. (Panzermuseum)

Adolf Hitler presents Oberst d.Res. Dr Bake, commander of Pz Regt 11, with Oakleaves (Eichenlaub) to his Knight's Cross, 14 November 1943.

engaged the enemy, but his first shot struck the frontal armour of the heavy tank and bounced off.

Bake ordered his driver to advance again, moving at maximum speed into another firing position just to the left of the enemy tank. The French gunner had fired as they moved off and a shell had whistled past fortunately missing Bake's tank. They halted again some 70 m further on, slewed round to face the enemy and began another engagement. The loader had already rammed the next round into the chamber, the gunner corrected his aim slightly and fired. A hit! The 37 mm AP round struck the gap between the enemy tank's turret and hull, jamming the turret, so that it could not be traversed. Bake rapidly fired two more rounds, both hits, and the enemy tank blew up before the crew could escape.

The tanks which Bake had sent around to the flank now opened fire, moving forward to deal with the anti-tank gun positions, while the dismounted motorcycle troops fought their way into Guise and then began to clear the houses systematically one by one. It required several hours of hard fighting before Guise surrendered. In total, Dr Bake's company had knocked out three Char B1 bis heavy tanks, four anti-tank guns and a large number of enemy trucks.

The German advance had been so swift that when the newly appointed commander of the 9ème Armée, Gen Henri Giraud,[3] endeavoured to withdraw his command post from Wassigny to Le Catelet, he found every crossroads held by German armoured cars.

His party was forced to abandon their vehicles and make for the town on foot. On 19 May, after hitching a ride on a gun-carrier, which was part of a small French column, his party was attacked by Panzers and had to take refuge in a nearby farm. They were then surrounded by tanks from Pz Regt 11, who took prisoner Gen Giraud, his chief of staff and fifty officers – quite a prize.

A GALLANT AND DISTINGUISHED CAREER

Guise was Bake's first successful Panzer action, which he followed with more spectacular blitzkrieg battles all the way through France, for which he was awarded the Iron Cross First Class. From then on he held various appointments within Pz Regt 11 in Russia, rising to command the regiment in 1943–4. At Kursk he won the coveted Tank Destruction Badge no fewer than three times – quite a feat because it was only awarded for the *single-handed* destruction of an enemy AFV with a hand-held weapon. He next commanded 'Heavy Panzer Regiment Bake', whose Tigers and Panthers achieved 'extraordinary results in a number of engagements' (Oberst Helmut Ritgen's words). In 1945 he reached the pinnacle of his career as the commanding general of 13th Panzer Division. He was awarded the Knight's Cross of the Iron Cross on 1 January 1943, then his Oakleaves and finally his Sword. Generalmajor Dr Franz Bake died in December 1978, as a result of a traffic accident; undoubtedly a tank ace, he fully merits his place in this book.

THE BATTLE IN FRONT OF THE GEMBLOUX GAP

13 MAY 1940

THE ASSAULT ON BELGIUM

North of the main thrust through the Ardennes and south of the assault on Holland, the air and land attacks on Belgium were deliberately designed to draw the Allied armies forward into their Dyle Line positions[4] and away from the main German assault. Nevertheless, following the highly successful paratroop operations against the Belgian fortress of Eben Emael,[5] the German Sixth Army launched a major ground assault in the Maastricht–Liège area. Although this was exactly the attack the Allies had expected, they were slow to react, muddled in their thinking and hopelessly outclassed by the German blitzkrieg tactics. The French High Command had always assumed that the Belgian defence of its frontier, bolstered up by a British and French cavalry screen, would be sufficient to delay the Germans from reaching the Dyle Line before the Allies had completed their move forward. This did not happen. Thanks to the spectacular seizure of the Eben Emael fortress and, more importantly, the capture of the Albert Canal bridges, the Germans were rapidly able to establish their forces on the western side of the canal. The Belgians then reacted far too hastily, giving orders to withdraw to the Dyle Line positions on the evening of 11 May, after only token resistance.

The following two days (12–13 May), in the area between Hannut and Gembloux, the Panzers of Gen Erich Hoepner's XVI Panzer Corps, consisting of 3rd and 4th Panzer Divisions (3 and 4 Pz Div), fought what was probably the largest tank battle of the campaign against Gen René Prioux's 1er Corps de Cavalerie, consisting of 2ème and 3ème Divisions Légères Mécaniques (2 and 3 DLM). Both sides suffered considerable losses – in excess of a hundred AFVs each – and both claimed victory. However, as the French then withdrew westwards into the First Army's prepared defensive positions, while the Germans moved forward and thus retained possession of the battlefield, the Panzer recovery teams were able to recover and repair many of their disabled vehicles. Undoubtedly, the battle also did much to keep Allied eyes fixed firmly on the Belgian front and thus away from the major German major assault in the Ardennes.

THE TANKS

As this was such an important tank battle, I have decided to describe a tank from each side and also to look in more detail at the organization and method of operation of each tank force. To start with the French 1er Corps de Cavalerie, its two DLMs were equipped as follows:

The Somua S35 was one of the best medium tanks in service in any army at the start of the Second World War. It was the first in the world to be constructed with both a cast turret and hull. Weighing 20 tons, its main armament was a 47 mm gun. (Tank Museum)

2 DLM

3ème (Brigade Légères Mécaniques) BLM
    13ème Dragons – 40 x Somua S35 and 40 x Hotchkiss H35
    29ème Dragons – 40 x Somua S35 and 40 x Hotchkiss H35

4ème BLM
    8ème Cuirassiers – 40 x Panhard P178 (armoured cars)
    1er Dragons Portes – 60 x AMR Renault light tanks

3 DLM

5ème BLM
    1er Cuirassiers – 40 x Somua S35 and 40 x Hotchkiss H39

2ème Cuirassiers – 40 x Somua S35 and 40 x Hotchkiss H39

6ème BLM
    12ème Cuirassiers – 40 x Panhard P178
    11ème Dragons Portes – 60 x Hotchkiss H35

TOTALS – 160 Somua, 220 Hotchkiss H35/39, 60 AMR and 80 Panhard P178 (440 tanks and 80 armoured cars)

(Based on information given in *Blitzkrieg in the West, Then and Now* by Jean Paul Pallud.)

Tank Details

Type of tank and year built	Weight (tons)	Armament	Crew	Top speed (mph)	Armour (mm)
Somua S35 (1936)	20	1x47 mm & 1xMG	3	25	20–55
Hotchkiss H35 (1935)	11.4	1x37 mm & 1xMG	2	17.5	12–34
Hotchkiss H39 (1939)	12	ditto	2	22.5	12–45
Renault AMR VM (1933)	6	1xMG	2	31	5–13
Renault AMR ZT (1938)	6	1x25 mm & 1xMG	2	ditto	ditto

Unfortunately, French tactics were based upon subordinating the tank to the infantry. Although the DLM was, on paper, a well-balanced force, it lacked artillery and recce potential, while its infantry travelled in unarmoured vehicles and it really needed some heavier tanks. In addition, French armoured commanders had had little opportunity to train for modern armoured warfare, generally lacked initiative and allowed the enemy to take charge of the battle far too often.

Opposing them was Hoepner's XVI Panzer

French Hotchkiss H39, photographed in a bombed town in France, 25 May 1940. (Tank Museum)

Corps, comprising 3 and 4 Pz Div, made up of, respectively, Panzer Regiments 5 and 6 (Pz Regt 5 and 6), and Panzer Regiments 35 and 36 (Pz Regt 35 and 36).

Each division had an establishment of 76 PzKpfw III/IV and 181 PzKpfw I/II, plus 50 armoured cars. There was of course some variation between divisions, due to breakdowns and so on. However, the most important aspect was that each Panzer division was a balanced force of all-arms, with its own lorried infantry brigade, recce battalion, motorized artillery regiment, anti-tank battalion, pioneer battalion and, most importantly, on-call Junkers 88 dive-bombers to provide close air support. All had trained and fought together and were now moulded into a superb fighting machine.

Tank Details

Type of tank and year built	Weight (tons)	Armament	Crew	Top Speed (mph)	Armour (mm)
PzKpfw I (Ausf A 1934, Ausf B 1935)	6	2xMG	2	22	6–13
PzKpfw II (Ausf A, B & C) (1937)	9	1x2 cm & 1xMG	3	30–5	5–16
PzKpfw III (Ausf A to G) (1937–40 dependent upon Mark)	15½–20	1x3.7 cm & 2xMG	5	20	5–30
PzKpfw IV (up to Ausf D) (1937–40 dependent upon Mark)	18½–20	1x7.5 cm & 2/3xMG	5	20	5–30

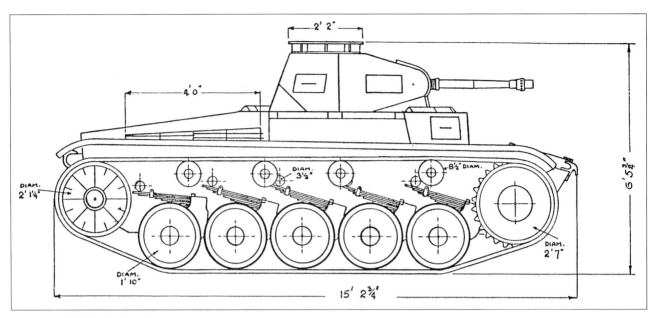

PzKpfw II Ausf c, A B and C.

It was the training, discipline, communications, crew efficiency, and above all the dash and *élan* of the German tank crews which made them so dangerous. By the time they came to attack the West, these skills had been honed to perfection in training and put into practice against the brave Poles. Nevertheless, above everything they needed leaders who would lead from the front, impose their personality upon the battle and make things happen.

THE BATTLE

After an enforced delay on the River Meuse due to the destruction of the bridges at Maastricht, which had necessitated it crossing on pontoons until bridges could be built, Hoepner's XVI Panzer Corps had made good progress across Belgium, with its leading elements reaching Grandville (on the road between Liège and St Trond) on 11 May. The Belgian 7th Infantry Division had all but ceased to exist, over 7,000 of its soldiers being captured by 4 Pz Div. Having followed 4 Pz Div across the river, 3 Pz Div was now on the right flank of the Corps as the whirlwind advance continued. They were aiming for the Gembloux Gap, north-west of Namur, an obvious approach route and one which the planners of the Dyle Plan had anticipated.

By the afternoon of Sunday 12 May, Gen Prioux's Corps de Cavalerie were on a line Tirlemont–Huy with '3 DLM between Tirlemont and Hannut, and 2 DLM between Hannut and Huy. Here across a broadly undulating landscape, with only scattered woods and villages well apart, armour was in its element.'[6] Until that moment the only action that had taken place between the two Corps since the previous day had been minor skirmishes, when recce units of both sides had clashed. However, things would soon change, as the Stuka dive-bombers began to systematically soften up the French positions, and the leading elements of 4 Pz Div began to probe in earnest.

One interested spectator (soon to be a player) was Lt Robert Le Bel, who was commanding a platoon of Hotchkiss H39s in

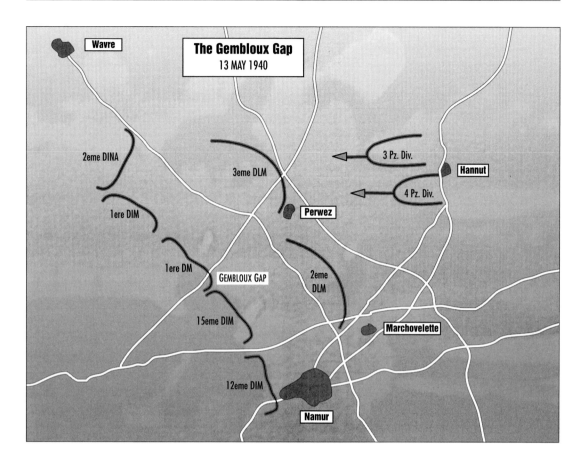

The Gembloux Gap
13 MAY 1940

Wavre

2eme DINA

3eme DLM

3 Pz. Div.

Hannut

4 Pz. Div.

1ere DIM

Perwez

1ere DM

GEMBLOUX GAP

2eme DLM

15eme DIM

Marchovelette

12eme DIM

Namur

3 DLM. He was standing in his turret on the outskirts of Jandrain and recalled seeing the enemy division getting ready for battle some 3 km away: 'The massive gathering of this armoured armada was an unforgettable sight . . . it appeared even more terrifying through the field glasses. How many were there? It was not possible to tell from so far away, but they were numerous and their guns seemed to be potent.'[7] As Lt Le Bel's later recollections reveal, being at the receiving end of a blitzkrieg attack was a most unnerving experience. Contact was soon made and all that afternoon the battle raged, with tanks being knocked out on both sides. The French gave as good as they got and no doubt the 47 mm gun on the Somua accounted for a fair share of German casualties. However, under the continued pressure from the two Panzer divisions, supported by air and artillery, the French armour was forced to give ground and also to avoid the outflanking manoeuvres of the blitzkrieg tactics. By the end of the day Hannut had been taken (see map).

After a tense but quiet night and early morning, the Stukas resumed their attacks about 11.30 hrs, timed to coincide with yet another artillery barrage. An hour later the Panzers advanced, closely followed by motorized infantry. A German observer, Hauptmann Ernst von Jugenfeld, who was commanding 2nd Battalion of Pz Regt 35, after extolling the prowess of the Stukas who, he said, rarely missed their targets, went on to say that the Panzers '. . . had to work hard to get the better of the French tanks'. He described the battlefield as being like a 'witch's cauldron' that seethed all day. By

A PzKpfw II held up by a partially demolished bridge in Belgium, May 1940. (Tank Museum)

evening the leading elements of 4 Pz Div had entered Ramillies, some 10 km west of Hannut, although they had had to fight every inch of the way, the French by no means completely overwhelmed. On the right flank, 3 Pz Div had taken Jauche after fierce house-to-house fighting.

Gen Prioux then ordered his two DLMs to withdraw to new positions, roughly parallel to and screening the line Namur–Gembloux–Wavre, which was where the next major defensive position was to be established. This disengagement was completed with some difficulty during the

night of the 13th, but by dawn on the 14th the two divisions were in their new positions – 2 DLM on the right, between Marchovelette (just in front of Namur) and Perwez, while in the north, 3 DLM was spread from Perwez up to Beauvechain. At 05.00 hrs on the 14th the Germans resumed their artillery bombardment, followed irresistibly by the Panzers, who finally breached the DLMs screen and were soon some 5 km beyond it, making contact with the main French positions.

3 DLM counter-attacked, but as it was now down to about half strength this was not

Two PzKpfw IIs negotiate a small ditch in France, May 1940. (Tank Museum)

entirely successful and it was pulled back behind the infantry line to reorganize. 2 DLM also pulled back, with the Germans literally snapping at its heels. Indeed, some German Panzers, following close behind 2 DLM, managed to get right inside the main infantry positions before they were destroyed at close range by anti-tank gunfire. French artillery then restored the situation with a heavy barrage, halting the German advance at about 17.00 hrs.

That was the end of the tank battle. The two DLMs had lost many of their tanks, but they had held the enemy, and the line Namur–Gembloux–Wavre was still intact. This is of course exactly what the German High Command wanted, as it undoubtedly kept the Allies convinced that they had been right all along and that the threat through

Belgium was definitely the main thrust, thus diverting their attention (and their armour) away from the real major attack unfolding in the Ardennes, until it was far too late to stop it.

TANK ACES?

I have yet to discover if any tank aces emerged from this battle, although Oberleutnant Bruno Nolde, who was commanding 8 Kompanie of Pz Regt 6, 3 Pz Div, was singled out for praise in the Army Report of 20 May, which spoke of his 'extraordinary coolness during the tank battles of recent days'.[8]

However, it was clearly a battle which restored some pride to French armour. Later, between the 14th and 17th, Gen Charles de Gaulle would restore a little more in an attack with 4 DCR in the Laon–Montcarnet area. But it was all 'too little, too late' to really worry the rampant Panzers, who swept on, virtually unhindered.

The only real armoured set-back they received in France was a British counter-attack in the Arras area, in which the 4th and the 7th Royal Tank Regiment (4 and 7 RTR) fought a stubborn action that caused great anxiety to Rommel and others (Hitler included), and held up the Germans long enough to allow the British Expeditionary Force time to reach its escape port of Dunkirk. As Sir Basil Liddell Hart says in his history of the RTR:

'It may well be asked whether two battalions have ever had such a tremendous effect on history as the 4th and 7th RTR achieved at Arras. Their effect in saving the British Army from being cut off from its escape port provides ample justification for the view that if two well-equipped armoured divisions had been available the Battle of France might also have been saved.'[9]

THE ATTACK ON NIBEIWA FORT

OPERATION 'COMPASS'

The scene now changes to the Western Desert, where the Italian Tenth Army, after much huffing and puffing, had advanced into Egypt on 13 September 1940, occupying Sidi Barrani on the 16th, and had started to build a series of eight forts, starting at Maktila and Sidi Barrani on the coast and working down to Sofafi about 40 miles to the south-west. The other five posts were: Tummar West, Tummar East and Point 90 to the south of Sidi Barrani; Nibeiwa, south of the Tummars; and Rabia, south-west of Nibeiwa. They were all well-constructed camps, Nibeiwa being rectangular in shape – 2,400 yd by 1,800 yd – and garrisoned by Gen Pietro Maletti's group. This comprised four Libyan Infantry battalions, three Saharan auto companies, plus Italian field, AA and anti-tank artillery units and Italian engineers, in total some 2,500 men. Tank support was supposed to contain both a medium and a light tank company. The former was equipped with either the Carro Armato M11/39 or M13/40 medium tanks, armed with 37 mm and 47 mm guns respectively, while the latter were tiny 3 ton tankettes – Carro Veloce 3/33 and 33/11 – capable only of carrying light machine-guns. The latest air reconnaissance, however, had seen only some 250 MT vehicles, no tanks had been positively identified. The report concluded:

'Although ground troops have reported medium tanks, it is impossible from the available photos to identify any tanks among the MT. APW states that the tanks taking part in the Hileiquat engagement were brought forward specially for the recce, and it is not accordingly thought that tanks are permanently stationed at Nibeiwa.'[10]

Total Axis forces manning these forward positions was some 60,000 Italian and Libyan troops; the Germans of course had not yet arrived.

There the Italians stayed. Marshal Rodolfo Graziani, commander of the Italian forces in North Africa, had much to say about future Italian advances to capture the Suez Canal, but the inept and cowardly 'Butcher of the Desert' had no real intentions of making any further forward moves. Wavell's reply to this ponderous advance was to plan Operation 'Compass', initially proposed as just a 'five-day raid' to deal with the Italian incursion. The 'raid' began on 9 December, under the brilliant leadership of Lt-Gen Sir Richard O'Connor. His Western Desert Force basically comprised just two divisions – the 7th Armoured Division (7 Armd Div) and the 4th Infantry Division (4 Inf Div) – which together with Corps troops amounted to some 32,000 men in total. However, their 'ace in the hand' was 7 RTR, equipped with Matilda Mk II heavy infantry tanks, soon to earn the nickname 'Queen of the Desert'.

THE TANK

The Infantry tank Mk II, Matilda II (A 12) was a 26½ ton tank with a crew of four, a

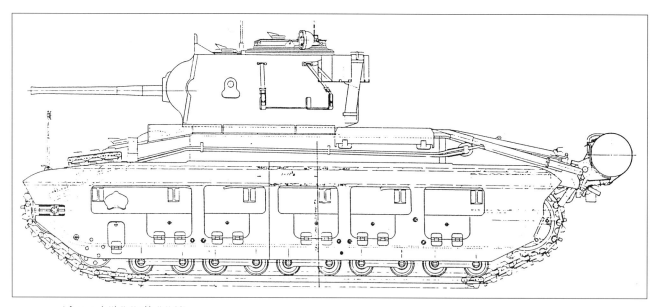

Infantry tank Mk II, Matilda II (A 12)

cross-country speed of about 8 m.p.h. (up to 15 on good going) and a road radius of 160 miles (only 80 cross-country). Armed with a 2-pounder Ordnance Quick Firing (OQF) gun (ninety-three rounds carried) and a coaxially-mounted Besa machine-gun, it had performed well in France, the Arras counter-attack by 4 and 7 RTR in May 1940 being the only serious set-back the German Panzerwaffe had suffered. Most importantly, it had armour 13–78 mm thick, which made it virtually invulnerable to the Italian tanks and anti-armour weapons of the period, at anything other than point-blank range. During the battle for Bardia in January 1941, one commander told me that his tank received no fewer than forty-six direct hits without a single penetration. All this changed, of course, when the dreaded German 88 mm arrived on the scene. Its main drawback was that its turret ring was not wide enough to allow a larger gun to be fitted, so it was soon to be outgunned by the PzKpfw IIIs and IVs of the Deutsches Afrika Korps. However, for the time being, it was

able to deal with anything the Italians could muster.

The OQF 2-pounder gun, firing AP solid shot, had a muzzle velocity of 853 m/sec, which would defeat 40 mm of armour angled at 30°, at 1,000 m, whereas the Italian 47 mm (47/32Mod37) on the M13/40 would only penetrate 29 mm at the same range, and 55 mm at 100 m. Much of the Matilda's armour was therefore invulnerable even at such short ranges.

Weighing 11 tons, with a crew of three and armour only 6–30 mm thick, the M11 was almost obsolescent by the time it went into action in North Africa. Nevertheless, it mounted a respectable 37 mm gun plus two machine-guns. The tank was of riveted construction.

THE BATTLE

In view of the complexity and strength of the Italian defences, O'Connor decided to hold a full-scale dress rehearsal. Known as 'Training Exercise No. 1', it took place on 26 November, with 'Training Exercise No. 2'

'Queen of the Desert'. Matilda Mk IIs of 7 RTR advancing in the Western Desert. (Tank Museum)

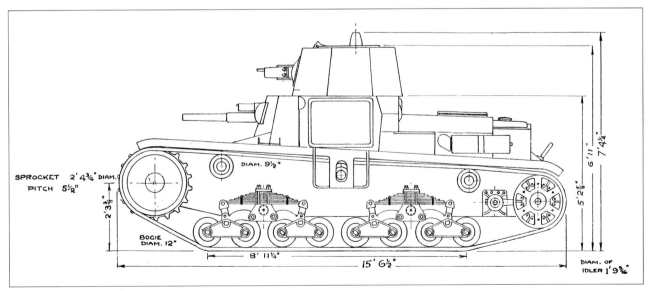

Carro Armato MII/39.

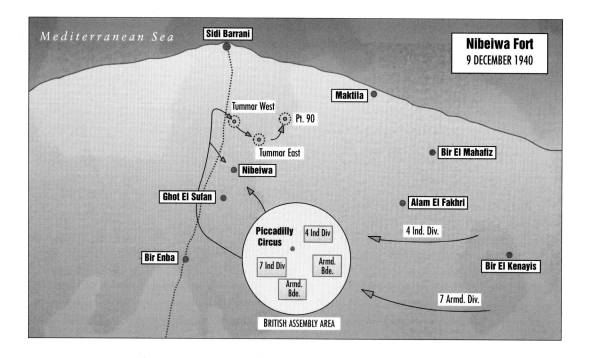

scheduled for the second week in December. This would actually be the 'real thing', but nobody guessed. The rehearsal took place against an accurate replica of the Italian forts built by the Royal Engineers. It had been decided that, for the attack on Nibeiwa, the Matildas would carry out a surprise assault without any preliminary artillery bombardment, relying instead on their shock action. Meanwhile, the infantry, the 4th Battalion, 7th Rajput Regiment, would create a diversion to the east of the camp and then follow up the armour, rather than leading the advance as was the normal accepted practice of the day.

The attacking infantry had moved forward in their lorries to within 3 miles of the fort, and had then worked their way forwards until they bumped the Italian listening posts, opening fire all along the east side of the camp with

'Tracer, star shells, flaming footballs, flares and the flashes from the guns and bursting

shells lighting the place up beautifully. . . . The enemy had been kept busy, had used up a quantity of ammunition and most important of all, it had drowned the sound of our tanks and vehicles getting round to the west face of the camp.'[11]

At the opposite side of the camp, A Squadron 7 RTR, under the command of Maj Henry Rew (the Army and England rugby forward), and B Squadron, under Maj Ted Hawthorn MC, were moving into position for their surprise attack. They knew that there were anti-tank mines laid around the camp, two minefields covering both the south-east and south-west faces of the fort having been definitely located by patrols. In addition, they knew about an anti-tank obstacle which comprised a ditch and bank in the same area, patrols having seen part it being dug. They also knew that there were at least three field artillery batteries in the fort (one specifically in the anti-tank role), plus twenty-six light AA/anti-tank gun positions, a battery of

Panorama of the battlefield outside Nibeiwa Fort, showing some of the knocked-out Italian tanks. (Imperial War Museum)

heavy AA guns and at least 120 to 150 machine-gun emplacements. What they did not know was that twenty-three Italian M11/39 medium tanks had moved into the gap between the minefields exactly where they were intending to make their final approach. However, at least that meant the area was not mined and Italian tanks were easier to deal with than anti-tank mines.

The two squadrons attacked at dawn, aiming at different entrances on the west side of the camp. B Squadron 7 RTR attacked the fort through the more northerly entrance, which was not fully mined, while A Squadron's entrance was mined and casualties resulted, one being Henry Rew, the squadron commander, who was shot by a sniper in the armpit as he got out to inspect mine damage to his tank. Sadly he died in the ambulance on the way back to hospital.

Leading the Matildas of B Squadron into Nibeiwa was No. 6 Troop, under the command of 2nd Lt Hugh Fane-Hervey who told me:

'From the start line to the north-west of the camp we started our advance two up, until we hit the broad desert track leading right into the camp. It was during this movement we saw and knocked out two M11s and then saw the stone walling, set at various angles, inside the camp. The troop more or less stayed together driving here and there within the camp, dealing with gun positions, and where identified, machine-gun nests and infantry. We kept this up until the white flags started to appear, extreme caution was still taken because we knew that the Itis had some very nasty hand grenades, which from time to time were thrown out from hide-outs in the stone walls.

'My tank, *Gitana*, took some direct hits from the artillery and a hell of a lot of machine-gun and small arms fire. The shell hits simply left 'sploshes' but we did have fuses blowing and we spent quite a lot of energy running over guns with our tracks. The Iti gunners were quite brave and stood their ground.

'We encountered the M11s on the way into Nibeiwa and I remember engaging them with two pounder and having the satisfaction of seeing direct hits and the crews bailing out before they were fully engaged. . . . Many of the camp incumbents were caught in their pyjamas, we actually saw them jumping in and out of their dugouts in panic. There were a lot of stone walls to contend with and their wretched soldiers were jumping on either side trying to take cover from our fire. We knew that an awful lot of Libyan soldiers took their boots off and escaped into the night when the bombardment started.'

One of the enemy caught by surprise was the garrison commander, Gen Maletti, who was killed by a burst of machine-gun fire from a Matilda as he came out of his tent, machine-gun in hand. A brave but foolish commander, Maletti had been completely misled by the daring British plan. By 10.00 hrs the camp had been captured, together with large quantities of guns, ammunition, lorries and between 2,000 and 3,000 prisoners. Casualties were minimal for 7 RTR and they had knocked out every single Italian tank. A British medical officer entering the camp on the morning it fell recalled seeing the perimeter trench full of dead and dying Tunisians. He went on:

'The roofs of the tents were riddled with bullet holes. The Italians had lived in deep dugouts and many of their officers had been killed still in pyjamas where they slept. . . . I had to help the Italian MOs sort out their wounded and take some of our surgical team to treat them. . . . Two things stood out. Their SMO did not know where he was on the map and they had no drill for treating the wounded.'[12]

Hugh Fane-Hervey went on to lead the attacks on Sidi Barrani and then Bardia:

'My poor old Matilda took a hell of a hammering in Phase 1 (some forty direct hits) so when I came out of that, Roy Jerram[13] then said: "Hugh, here's my tank, you are in Phase 2, off you go!" Well, Bardia fell on 5 Jan with the 9th Australian Division mostly drunk on the wine they had found in the Bardia encampment.'

The Aussies had a great regard for the Matildas, the Australian commander stating that each Matilda tank was worth a whole infantry battalion to him.

A MILITARY CROSS FOR 2ND LT FANE-HERVEY
The citation for Hugh Fane-Hervey's Military Cross reads:

'This officer directed his troop with great gallantry during the attack on an enemy camp. He led his troop into the camp and engaged anti-tank and field guns at point-blank range receiving many direct hits, putting a number of guns out of action, he then rallied the remainder of his troop, his third tank having been put out of action in the camp.

'Later in the morning he again led his two tanks into another position and attacked guns and put them out of action fighting and directing his troop with coolness and deliberation. He withdrew his troop from the rally, the second tank was hit in one of its radiators and put out of action but managed to return to the rally on one engine. The next

2 Lt Hugh Fane-Hervey gives his report to Maj E. Hawthorn after the capture of the fort. (Maj H. Fane-Hervey)

day he was again in action and fought his tank regardless of danger until put out of action by a direct hit. He then set his tank on fire before being taken prisoner.

'He then persuaded the enemy they were surrounded and marched a number of prisoners to our lines and handed them over. During two days of action this officer showed a coolness and devotion to duty regardless of personal danger.'

Fane-Hervey went on to win a Bar to his Military Cross and to be wounded during the battle for Tobruk in June 1942. Taken to a South African hospital at El Adem, which was subsequently overrun by the Germans, he escaped but was eventually recaptured and sent to a POW camp in Italy. He managed to escape again while being transferred to a

camp in Germany and eventually reached the United Kingdom in August 1944. Rejoining the 2nd Royal Tank Regiment (2 RTR) in Italy, he was badly wounded in April 1945, but recovered to continue his army career until retiring in April 1959.

TANK ACES

Following the highly successful start at Nibeiwa, Operation 'Compass' went on to clear the entire Italian Army out of Cyrenaica, as we shall see in the next battle description. 7 RTR played a major part in the success of 'Compass' and, as a result, many decorations were awarded to the tank commanders and crewmen. It would be invidious to pick out one individual from this fine regiment and to label him a tank ace when success was secured by the combined

Matilda Mk IIs of 7 RTR carrying out maintenance in the Tummar area after the battle for Nibeiwa Fort. (Tank Museum)

effort of the whole regiment, brilliantly led by Roy Jerram. At troop leader/tank commander/ tank crewman level, the recommendations for immediate awards covering just Nibeiwa, the Tummars and Sidi-Barrani, numbered 5 Military Crosses, 3 Distinguished Conduct Medals and 10 Military Medals, the last of these including Military Medal recommendations for both Cpl Reginald Reader, the driver of Hugh Fane-Hervey's tank *Gitana*, and for his gunner, Tpr Walter Coombs. Sadly not all these recommendations resulted in the award of medals, although 7 RTR's 'medal tally' for this period was considerable.

'FOX KILLED IN THE OPEN': THE BATTLE OF BEDA FOMM

8 FEBRUARY 1941

'TELL DICK HE CAN GO ON'

Instead of O'Connor stopping after he had successfully completed the aims of Operation 'Compass', the Western Desert Force went on to capture Bardia on 5 January 1941, Tobruk two weeks later, then Mechili on the 27th. On 29 January O'Connor held a conference at his HQ, then at Bomba, which was attended by Maj Gen Dickie Creagh, GOC 7 Armd Div, Brig John Harding, O'Connor's BGS, and Brig 'Chink' Dorman-Smith, Wavell's BG OPs, who had been sent forward as his personal representative. Information had been received that several large Italian motorized columns had been seen leaving Benghazi and heading for the frontier. O'Connor rightly deduced that Graziani had decided to retreat back all the way to Tripoli – 'rather than expose my person needlessly at the front' was the way the heroic Italian C in C had put it. O'Connor had decided on a bold plan, which involved sending part of 7 Armd Div across unchartered desert to cut off the Italians. Speed was essential, he could not afford to wait for reinforcements, but further petrol supplies had to be ferried forward before the armour could move.

Having heard the plan from Dorman-Smith, Wavell said, 'Tell Dick he can go on and wish him luck from me. He has done well.'[14] Dorman-Smith was back at O'Connor's HQ (now at Mechili) on 2 February and two days later, 7 Armd Div began its desert crossing, while the 6th Australian Division (6 Aust Div) pressed on along the coast road, via Barce and Benghazi, keeping the Italians on the move and thinking that this was still the main thrust. The 'Desert Rats' moved swiftly, reaching Msus on 4 February, then Antelat, where they turned towards the coast making for the Sidi Saleh/Beda Fomm area, where the ambush position would be established. The advanced guard consisted of three squadrons of armoured cars: A and C from the 11th Hussars, plus B from the King's Dragoon Guards (KDG), who had just arrived and were anxious to get some practical experience from the old hands. Behind them was the main body, with two days' supplies of food and water, plus just enough petrol to enable the ninety-five Light Mk VIs and fifty A9, A10 and A13 Cruiser tanks to complete their journey. In addition, they carried as much ammunition as they could squeeze into remaining spaces.

When the main body stopped to replenish with fuel, it was passed by a 'flying column' of the 2nd Battalion of the Rifle Brigade (2RB), C Battery of the 4th Royal Horse Artillery (C Bty 4 RHA) and some anti-tank guns of the 106th Regiment of the Royal

Artillery (106 Regt, RA), all mounted in wheeled vehicles. The tanks leading the main body comprised the three armoured regiments of the 4th Armoured Brigade (4 Armd Bde): 3rd Hussars, 7th Hussars and 2 RTR, all equipped with Cruisers.

While the advanced guard dealt with the Italian garrisons at Msus and Antelat, the 'flying column' pressed on to the ambush position at Sidi Saleh, which it reached at noon the following day. First contact with the enemy was made at 14.30 hrs that afternoon, when the head of a large convoy appeared on the road from Ghemines. It was estimated to contain 20,000 men – ten times the strength of the 'flying column'. The Italians, however, never really knew what hit them. They thought the British were some 150 miles away behind them, but now their way of escape was blocked. So, instead of putting in a properly co-ordinated attack or trying to outflank and encircle the road-block, they

made a number of half-hearted attempts to break through directly down the road, all of which failed. Nevertheless, sheer weight of numbers was having its effect and things were just becoming a little difficult for the gallant 'flying column' when over the horizon came the leading tanks of 4 Armd Bde – 7th Hussars, shortly followed by the other two regiments, who took up positions to the north between Sidi Saleh and Beda Fomm, from whence they proceeded to wreak havoc on the unfortunate retreating Italian Tenth Army. It was now early evening.

We shall take up the battle here, looking at it through the eyes of Maj Norman Plough, then a troop leader in A Sqn, 2 RTR, and his A13 Mk II tank crew.

THE TANKS
A Sqn was equipped with the fast A13 and A13 Mk II Cruiser tanks and had left the main column on the last section of the march

Lt Norman Plough (reading) and some of his crew before the battle at Beda Fomm. (Maj N. Plough)

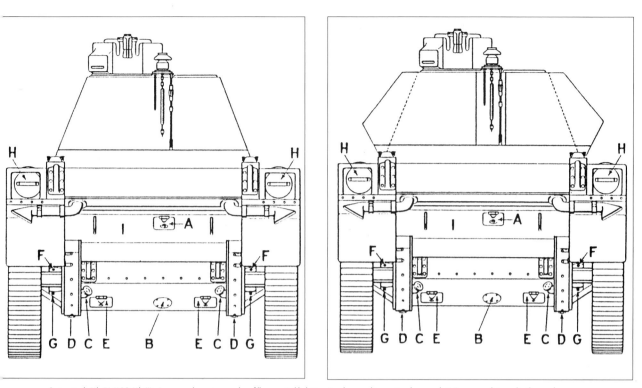

Cruiser tank Mk IV (A13 Mk II). A: access door over gearbox filler cap, tail-light junction box, and inspection lamp socket; B: access plate under the gearbox drain plug; C: final drive filler caps; D: final drive drain plugs; E: access doors under brakes; F: greasers for rear axle arm pivot bearing; G: greasers for rear shock absorber bottom eyes; H: air cleaner handles; I: rear sloping plate over transmission compartment.

to block the road at Beda Fomm. The A13, Cruiser tank Mk III, was the first of the cruiser line to be fitted with the Christie suspension,[15] which gave it a remarkably high cross-country speed of 24 m.p.h. (approx), although even this could be improved on as Norman Plough explains. 'Earlier in the campaign we had removed the governors on our Napier engines and with the help of our excellent fitters, our tank engines were very carefully maintained and tuned to achieve 35–40 m.p.h.' The A13 was a 14 ton tank, built in 1939 and powered by a Nuffield Liberty V12 engine developing 340 b.h.p. It had a road radius of 90 miles and a good performance. However, its armour was very thin – only 6–14 mm thick. It was armed with a 2-pounder (eighty-seven rounds carried) and a coaxially mounted Vickers .303 MG. Thus it was both under-gunned and under-armoured and had to rely upon its speed for protection (compare its armour thickness with the 78 mm of the Matilda II).

The A13 Mk II, Cruiser tank Mk IV was essentially an up-armoured version of the A13, with armour up to 30 mm thick, which put the weight up by 3 to 4 tons, thus reducing its performance slightly. The Vickers MG was changed for a 7.92 mm BESA, while a Bren gun was also occasionally carried for AA defence. A Close Support version was also built which mounted a 3 in howitzer instead of the 2-pounder.

The main Italian tank in the Italian Tenth Army was the Italian medium Carro Armato M13/40. Designed to spearhead the Italian armoured forces, this 14 ton tank, with armour 9–30 mm thick, was a most

Italian M13/40 medium tanks in the desert. (Author's collection)

respectable performer, with a good 47 mm high-velocity gun. Its problem, however, was its crew, who invariably showed no desire to fight, so many were knocked out by the lighter armed and armoured A13s.

THE BATTLE
Norman Plough writes;

'On the last section of the march from Msus all fit A13s were sent ahead to cut the Benghazi-Agedabia road . . . we dropped 3 or 4 tanks on this last run to Beda Fomm (only chosen from a map reference with a windmill water tower – a recognizable feature), mostly loss of tracks. This was a serious design fault

with the A13 tank. The track plates were connected together with steel pins and held in position with lead dowels. The rough volcanic debris and sand caused the lead dowels to vibrate and fall out, then the pins. A13 tank commanders spent a lot of time during a move checking for loose pins, often stopping to hammer back track pins and replace lead dowels. I always carried a pocketful of lead dowels – it was the tank commander's responsibility to control the problem, as he was the only man in the crew who could get out quickly and do the job.

'An hour before dusk we picked up the landmark of the steel-framed wind-powered waterhole at Beda Fomm. It was surrounded

The windpump at Beda Fomm. (Maj N. Plough)

was some talking, then complete silence and, as the Italians did not send anyone to discover what was behind the road-block, Plough decided to investigate himself and moved his tank forward until he was closer to the road-block and could see the enemy convoy. At its head were two M13 tanks, closed down, now about 20 yd away. He told his operator, 'Taff' Hughes, to go forward and tap on the lid of the first tank with his revolver to see if there was a crew inside. Hughes did so while two tanks of the troop moved forward behind to cover him. Hughes captured both tank crews and was later awarded the Distinguished Conduct Medal for his bravery. Hughes explained:

'I marched the Eyties back towards our tanks, on the road was this big naval gun, which had been mounted on wheels. I was marching them past and there was an Eytie officer in a beautiful powder-blue uniform with gold braid everywhere. I said to him "fall in" and there were some objections from him, but I made him march back with his hands on his head as well!'

Norman Plough again:

'The sketch [overleaf] shows the position of our A13s before dawn. We were hull down behind the low ridge across Beda Fomm mound around the road. I remember very well the early part of the engagement with tanks of the Italian 1st Ariete Armoured Division, recently arrived at Benghazi – just three weeks before so I was told later by an Italian prisoner.

'Two groups of M13 tanks attacked our position. The first group in two waves was destroyed without loss to us. The second group about 40 minutes later advanced down our right flank and three of our A13s moved across to the Arab grave cairns and tombs. About the same time a few M13s advanced

by Arab graves and tombs. Adjacent to this tower was the main road, cutting through a mound about 30 ft high, with a small ridge on its west side. We moved into position around this small feature.

'A short time after our arrival two single-decker coaches appeared on the road coming from Benghazi. A small burst of machine-gun fire stopped them near the cutting through the mound. The two coaches were full of Italian civilians and women, who were unloaded and sent to safety in the direction of the sand dunes on the coast. We moved the coaches to form a road block about 50 yd from the cutting, where there was soft sand on both sides of the road. Light faded and it was soon pitch dark.'

About 2 hours later the ambushers heard tanks and transport moving down the road and stopping at the coach road-block. There

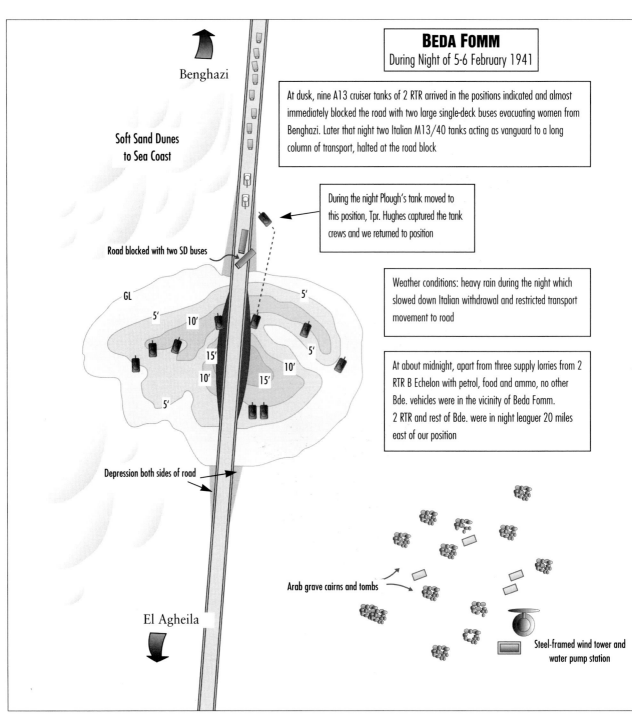

BEDA FOMM
During Night of 5-6 February 1941

Benghazi

Soft Sand Dunes
to Sea Coast

At dusk, nine A13 cruiser tanks of 2 RTR arrived in the positions indicated and almost immediately blocked the road with two large single-deck buses evacuating women from Benghazi. Later that night two Italian M13/40 tanks acting as vanguard to a long column of transport, halted at the road block

During the night Plough's tank moved to this position, Tpr. Hughes captured the tank crews and we returned to position

Road blocked with two SD buses

Weather conditions: heavy rain during the night which slowed down Italian withdrawal and restricted transport movement to road

GL

5'

5'

5'

10'

5'

15'

10'

At about midnight, apart from three supply lorries from 2 RTR B Echelon with petrol, food and ammo, no other Bde. vehicles were in the vicinity of Beda Fomm. 2 RTR and rest of Bde. were in night leaguer 20 miles east of our position

10'

15'

5'

Depression both sides of road

Arab grave cairns and tombs

El Agheila

Steel-framed wind tower and water pump station

From maps drawn by Maj N. Plough.

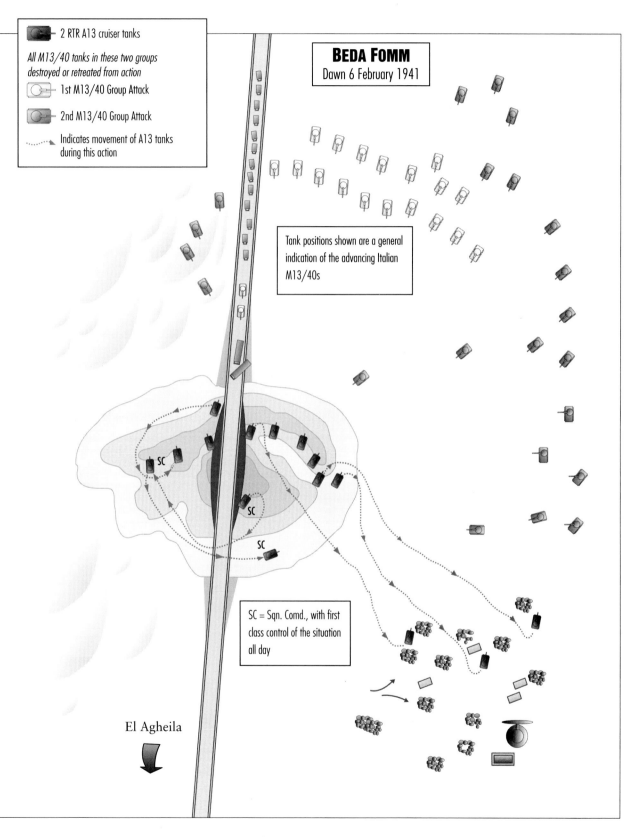

2 RTR A13 cruiser tanks

All M13/40 tanks in these two groups
destroyed or retreated from action

1st M13/40 Group Attack

2nd M13/40 Group Attack

Indicates movement of A13 tanks
during this action

BEDA FOMM
Dawn 6 February 1941

Tank positions shown are a general
indication of the advancing Italian
M13/40s

SC

SC

SC

SC = Sqn. Comd., with first
class control of the situation
all day

El Agheila

down the east side of the road and it was one of these that knocked out Henry Dumas' tank. I joined him for a few minutes while he took over one of his other troop tanks. This second group of M13s was also destroyed or withdrew from the action.

'There is no doubt in my mind that the Italian tank crews were "green" with little battlefield experience – their tactics were poor and they hadn't much knowledge of what they were up against. We were lucky, we had protection from the mound and road defile, they had none and had to advance across open ground.'

'Topper' Brown, Norman Plough's gunner, now takes up the story:

'We were hull down on a low rise and just as it began to get light, Lt Plough suddenly said,

"They're here, reverse!" While the driver (Cpl "Barney" Barnes) was reversing, I managed to get into my gunner's seat and the next thing I saw as I looked through my sights was an M13 about 30 yd away coming straight towards us. Without thinking I pulled the trigger of the two pounder, but as I didn't see any tracer I thought, "Oh my God I've missed". I gave it another one, but just then one of the crew climbed out of the top, so I shot him. Daylight shone through the hole in the turret made by my first shot – was I relieved! We were so close that the tracer hadn't had time to light up. Another M13 came up almost alongside the first, so I hit that one as well, knocking both out took less than a minute.

'Practically all morning we never stopped firing, at tanks or wagonloads of infantry. I haven't a clue how many enemy I killed, but it must have run into hundreds. We definitely

Bedouins rifling some of the knocked-out vehicles, which belonged to the retreating Italian Tenth Army and were destroyed at Beda Fomm. (Tank Museum)

had a score of about twenty M13s at the end of the day. . . . At times we were getting overwhelmed and had to keep withdrawing to the Pimple. One time we came around the right of the Pimple and stopped. My orders were to traverse left and I then saw at about 600 yd an M13 coming towards me on absolutely flat ground. Just as I was about to fire Taff Hughes (our loader/operator) said, "There are only two rounds left". I cursed him soundly, but fortunately hit the tank with both. Taff and I immediately had a good fall-out. We had started out with 112 rounds of two-pounder, 97 in the racks and 15 extra.[16] Hughes had let us get down to the last two. . . . We then went back for more ammo – I was also nearly out of machine-gun ammo as well, so you can understand the amount of firing that I had done. . . . When we pulled back after dark it was sheer relief. My right eye was aching with the strain of looking through the telescope for about 13 hours with hardly a break.'

Following the two group tank attacks, the A9s of 2 RTR appeared on the scene, with other elements of the brigade, and they followed up the retreating M13s, artillery and transport, doing considerable damage and capturing large numbers of prisoners.

While this was going on some Italians managed to clear the road-block in front of the mound defile and had started to move west again, so Norman Plough

'moved back to the road with two other A13s and machine-gunned the moving column, also putting in the occasional 2pdr shot. The column stopped again and the drivers hastily abandoned their vehicles, artillery guns, etc.

Another view of the knocked-out Italian convoy, with a KDG armoured car moving through the litter of vehicles, guns and tanks. (Tank Museum)

The action then moved out of our area and fighting continued north and south of us, while we spent the rest of the day with the LAD on tank repairs and recovery, clearing up the mess and making tea.'

Plough estimates that 2 RTR knocked out about seventy-nine M13 tanks during the action, of which his gunner, 'Topper' Brown, claimed nineteen, but accepted that several could have been joint efforts with other tanks. 2 RTR suffered just two A9 and one A13 casualties, but had no one killed or even wounded. The total casualties for 7 Armd Div were just nine killed and fifteen wounded, while the Italians' own estimate of the losses throughout Operation 'Compass' was well over 200,000 men, of which 120,000 were taken prisoner (including twenty-two generals and one admiral). Some 845 guns and 380 tanks were also captured – little wonder that Anthony Eden, then

Foreign Secretary, plagiarized Churchill by saying, 'Never has so much been surrendered by so many to so few!'

TANK ACES?
This was a monumental victory, but very much a one-sided battle. However, it should not have been so. The M13/40 was a perfectly respectable tank for the period. It had a larger calibre gun than the A13 (47 mm), was better armoured (up to 40 mm thick), yet over 100 were captured at Beda Fomm. The rest were M11/39s, yet they had gunpower comparable with A13 (37 mm) and armour up to 30 mm thick, so were supposedly on a par. Surely they should have been able to overcome the small number of British AFVs? The answer of course lies in the training and determination of the tank crews and of the other arms which made up the road-block.

As far as Norman Plough and his crew were concerned, undoubtedly they qualify as

Lt Norman Plough on radio watch outside his tank. (Maj N. Plough)

'aces', having knocked out a phenomenal number of enemy tanks in this engagement. The fact that these enemy tanks were better armed and better armoured is balanced to some degree by the fact that the British tanks were able to use the ground to gain further protection. Nevertheless it was a startling victory and one of which we can be justly proud.

NOTES TO BLITZKRIEG AND THE EARLY DESERT WAR

1. In German service they became known as the PzKpfw 35(t), the 't' standing for *tscheshich* (Czech).

2. *The 6th Panzer Division 1937–45*, Oberst aD Helmut Ritgen .

3. Gen Giraud had only just taken over command of the French Nineteenth Army, on the afternoon of 15 May, when its erstwhile commander, Gen Andre Corap, was dismissed.

4. The Dyle Line was basically a defensive line along the River Dyle to protect Brussels, but well behind the Dutch/Belgian borders with Germany. Allied planning was exacerbated by the fact that no Allied force could move into Belgium until invited to do so, and because the Belgians were scared of antagonizing the Germans, this could not happen until they were attacked.

5. Eben Emael was a vast concrete, seemingly impregnable fortress, the lynch-pin of a defensive line of forts built by the Belgians to defend Liège and the Albert Canal. It was captured in a few hours on 10 May 1940, by a daring German gliderborne force led by Hauptmann Walter Koch.

6. *Blitzkrieg in the West, Then and Now*, Jean Paul Pallud.

7. Ibid.

8. Ibid

9. *The Tanks*, Vol 2., Capt Sir Basil Liddell Hart.

10. Taken from Appendix A to 11 Indian Infantry Brigade Intelligence Summary No. 1, dated 6 December 1940.

11. *The Tiger Strikes*, Lt Col Hingston.

12. Extract from quote by Phil Wood, DADMS on Gen O'Connor's staff, in *The First Victory*.

13. Lt-Col Roy Jerram, later Brigadier, commanded 7 RTR throughout Operation 'Compass'. O'Connor, writing to him later, said, 'It has been a wonderful show, and you are more than ever responsible for the success'.

14. *Wavell, Scholar and Soldier*, John Connell.

15. Walter J. Christie was an irascible, brilliant American designer, whose revolutionary suspensions found little favour in the USA. However, they were bought by the British and Russians, the latter using it in their world-beating T-34 series.

16. 'Topper' Brown's memory must be failing slightly, because the full load (stowed) on the A13 was 87 not 97, so he either had 102 rounds in total, or 25 loose.

TOBRUK

THE GERMANS ARRIVE

February 1941 saw the British masters of the Western Desert, the Italians having beaten a hasty retreat back into Tripolitania, after losing vast numbers of troops, guns and tanks during the whirlwind campaign of Operation 'Compass'. The surrender of the Italian Tenth Army had apparently left the road to Tripoli wide open and all Wavell had to do was to continue his triumphal progress to drive the Axis forces completely out of North Africa. Two months later, however, the situation had changed dramatically. Once again the enemy was back on the Egyptian frontier, Tobruk was under siege and O'Connor was a prisoner, together with the newly arrived GOC of the 2nd Armoured Division (2 Armd Div). The cause of all this turmoil was of course the arrival on the scene of Gen Erwin Johannes Eugen Rommel and his Deutsches Afrika Korps (DAK), who started to arrive in Tripoli harbour on 14 February 1941. It lost no time in going onto the offensive, launching its first assault on 24 March. Just one month later, the Axis forces were back inside Egypt and Rommel, the Desert Fox as he was now called by friend and foe alike, had already become a legend.

The one stronghold which the victorious DAK had not been able to overcome was Tobruk. Here a determined garrison, mainly composed of Australians from the 9th Australian Division (9 Aust Div), plus one

When Oberst Johannes Kummel was a young captain serving with the DAK in North Africa, he was nicknamed the 'Lion of Fort Capuzzo' by his soldiers. They painted a roaring lion on one side of his tank, with the inscription underneath: 'The Lion of Capuzzo'. He was awarded his Knight's Cross on 9 July 1941 and his Oakleaves on 11 October 1942, having won both Second and First Class Iron Crosses in Poland. He was killed in a road accident in Italy in February 1944. (Panzermuseum)

brigade from the 7th, held out from 9 April until the siege was lifted on 10 December, when the Axis forces were pushed back westwards. The garrison included some British armour, namely: 1 RTR, less one squadron, with a total of 11 Cruisers (A9s and A13s) and 16 light tanks (Vickers Light Mk VIb); a composite squadron of 3rd Hussars and 5 RTR, equipped with 12 Cruisers and some light tanks from workshops, the remainder of 5 and 6 RTR being temporarily employed as 'dismounted infantry'; a squadron of 7 RTR, with, eventually, a total of 18 Matilda IIs.[1]

One of the squadron commanders of 1 RTR was Maj Gen (Retired) Rea Leakey CB, DSO, MC, then a young captain, who had already won a Military Cross during the Wavell campaign, when he destroyed all the Italian aircraft on the Martuba airstrip in a devastating raid. He writes about his experiences in Tobruk thus:

'Tobruk was full of soldiers but many were base personnel who had been trapped there by Rommel's rapid advance. 9th Australian Division, commanded by Gen Morshead, formed the bulk of the garrison. They were supported by British artillery and my Regiment provided the main tank support . . . . The perimeter was 30 miles in length and, unlike Bardia, the anti-tank ditch was shallow and provided little or no obstacle to tanks. Fortunately the Italian pillboxes and dugouts were in a fair state of repair and the Australians made full use of them.'

1 RTR Cruisers 'dug-in' within the Tobruk perimeter, May 1941. (Tank Museum)

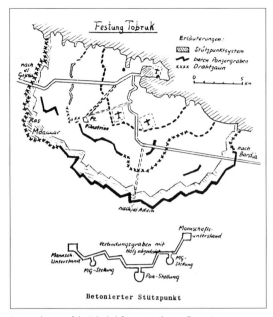

German drawing of the Tobruk defences. (Author's collection)

Rea Leakey goes on to describe how he was to use his cruiser tanks to deal with an incursion into the perimeter at Acroma by some Italian tanks and, finding that they were the little two-man tankettes, how he had no problem disposing of them. However, this done they were next ordered to move east to the area of the Tobruk–El Adem road, where more enemy tanks were closing in on the perimeter and the Australian infantry manning that area had no anti-tank guns. This was to be the first time that 1 RTR fought against German tanks, so it and the subsequent engagements are interesting battles to cover.

THE TANKS

1 RTR were equipped with a mixture of Cruisers and light tanks. However, as will be seen from Leakey's description of the action, the lights played little part, except as decoys. Leakey's Cruiser was an A9 (Cruiser tank Mk I), considerably different to the A13 manned by Norman Plough at Beda Fomm. It was originally designed in 1934 and went into

limited production in 1937. Weighing a little over 12 tons, it had a crew of six – the extra two men being machine-gunners in the sub-turrets. Its main armament was the 2-pounder gun (100 rounds stowed), with a coaxially mounted machine-gun. Its armour was only 6–14 mm thick, of riveted construction, so just like the other cruisers it had to rely on speed (maximum on roads 25 m.p.h., cross-country 15 m.p.h.) for most of its protection. It was, incidentally, the first British tank with hydraulic power-traverse.

The opposition was a mixture of PzKpfw II, III and IV, but clearly it was the heavier German Panzers which caused the major problems to the British cruisers, so while not describing all the DAK tanks in detail, it is perhaps worthwhile comparing their armour thickness, because it is upon this that survivability on the battlefield depends.

Armour Thickness

Tank	Min. armour (mm)	Max. armour (mm)
PzKpfw II (Ausf F)	5	35
PzKpfw III (Ausf E)	12	30
PzKpfw IV (Ausf E)	10	50

NB: This is just a selection to give a general idea. However, it is immediately clear that the A9 was seriously underarmoured as compared even with the smallest of opponents.

Together with the PzKpfw IV, the PzKpfw III formed the backbone of the Panzer divisions throughout the war. The original Ausf A had been produced in 1937 and the tank went on in production until the Ausf N in 1943. 531 Ausf E/Fs were built between December 1938 and July 1940. The majority were armed with

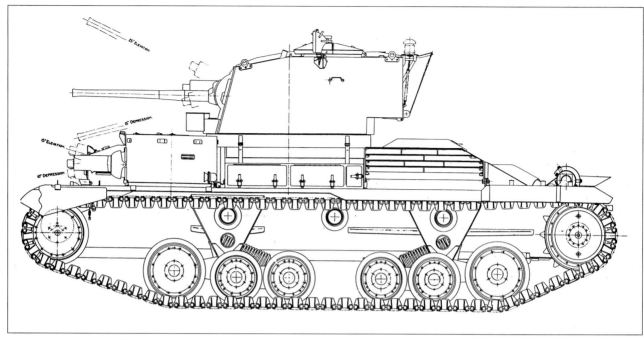

Cruiser tank Mk I (A9).

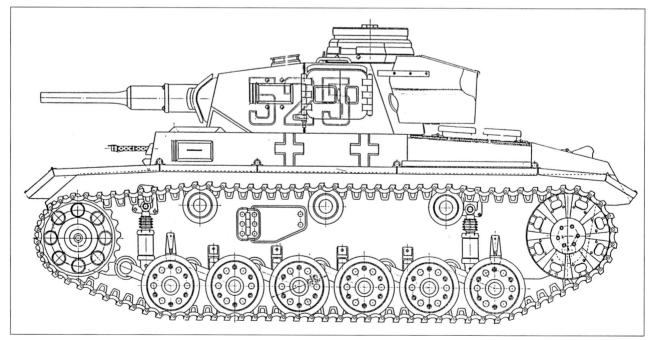

PzKpfw III Ausf E/F.

Excellent front view of an A9 Cruiser tank. It must have been taken fairly early on as the crew still have their Solar Topees. (Tank Museum)

the 3.7 cm KwK L/46.5 gun, although some 100 Ausf Fs had the more powerful 5 cm KwK L/42 gun. At 19.8 tons it had a crew of five, a speed of 25 m.p.h. and a radius of action of just over 100 miles. Some 131 rounds were carried for the 3.7 cm gun which could penetrate 34 mm of homogeneous armour sloped at 30° at a range of 500 m.

THE BATTLE
Rea Leakey describes the scene:

'This was the first time my Regiment fought against German tanks. There were about fifteen of them and we had about the same number of cruisers, but we also had an equal number of light tanks, which, although they were useless in a tank fight, could be used to distract the enemy and make him believe we were stronger than was in fact the case. We opened fire on them when they were within 800 yd of us and we were disturbed to see our two pounder solid shots bouncing off their armour. However, some of our shots found soft spots and the crew of their leading tank baled out. Then they opened fire on us and the battle was on.'

PzKpfw III Ausf E in the desert. Note the DAK symbol on the front plate – a palm tree and swastika. (Tank Museum)

The British tanks were on one side of the perimeter defences and the Germans on the other, with the Australian infantry in between cheering the cruisers on. Leakey continues his account:

'We were very relieved to see the Germans start to withdraw as they had already brewed up three of our tanks and we had only accounted for one of theirs. It was painfully obvious that we were outgunned by these tanks. When the action was over, I heard my gunner, Milligan, telling the other members of the crew that he had failed to brew up a single tank and yet he thought he was shooting as accurately as ever before. He had not seen his shots bouncing off the target and I did not enlighten him.'

Later the squadron went back to the Acroma area and spent the rest of the day firing at enemy tanks from hull-down positions, while enemy aircraft kept up a continuous bombing of Tobruk harbour. That night the tanks leaguered at Fort Pilastrino, some 3 miles inside the perimeter and settled down for their first night's sleep in 48 hours, only to be awakened by their next door neighbours – a British artillery battery. Gen Leakey comments that he turned over and went back to sleep, despite the noise and a stone sticking in the small of his back. But he was not left in peace for long. At midnight the duty wireless operator woke him – he was wanted on the set:

'I knew what to expect and all I had to be told was where the threat had now

Part of the German assault on Tobruk moving up to the wire. (Author's collection)

developed. It was a long move, at least 7 miles to the east and close to the Bardia road-block. I called up the tank commanders, gave out my orders and then we were on the move, slowly picking our way across the rough ground in the darkness.'

On this occasion, as before, the Australian infantry stood firm and the Germans withdrew, leaving a number of dead. Leakey's tanks were in action all that day, moving from crisis point to crisis point, losing a tank and having several men wounded through heavy shellfire. Another disturbed night followed and that became the normal routine day after day, night after night, as the enemy carried out probing attacks to discover a weak spot in the defences.

'We knew that very soon a major assault would be launched and it came on 14 April. At 1.30 a.m. I was called to the set and the CO gave me the news. The Germans had launched a heavy attack in the south astride the El Adem road and had breached the

defensive line. Tanks could be heard in this area and it was anticipated that at dawn they would advance north towards the town and harbour. My orders were to move east and be prepared to engage the enemy tanks as they attempted to get down the escarpment which ran east to west 3 miles south of the town.'

Leaving Rea Leakey giving his orders to his tank commanders, let us look at the enemy. They were Panzers belonging to Pz Regt 5 and one of their officers wrote down his account of the battle shortly after it took place. He began:

'At 00.10 I am called and ordered to report to the company commander at 01.00 hrs. Situation: machine-gunners and engineers have worked a gap through the anti-tank defences; 5 Panzer Regiment, 8 Machine Gun Battalion, anti-tank and anti-aircraft artillery will cross the gap under cover of darkness and overwhelm the position. Stuka attack at 06.45 hrs.

'07.15 hours. Storming of Tobruk. With least possible noise 2 Bn, RHQ Company and

A dawn patrol near Tobruk.

1 Bn move off completely blacked out. Bitterly cold. Of course the enemy recognizes us by the noise. . . . Soon artillery fire starts up on us, getting the range. The shells explode like fireworks. We travel 6 miles every nerve on edge . . . and then suddenly we are in the gap. Already the tank is nose down in the first trench. . . . We are through and immediately take up file in battle order. . . . Slowly, much too slowly, the column moves forward. We must of course regulate our speed by the marching troops and so the enemy has time to prepare resistance. The more the darkness lifts the harder the enemy strikes.

'Destructive fire starts up in front of us now . . . five batteries of 25-pounders rain shells on us. 8 Company presses forward to get at them. Our heavy tanks, it is true, fire for all they are worth, so do we all, but the enemy with his superior force and all the tactical advantages of his own territory makes heavy gaps in our ranks.'

Rea Leakey reached the junction of the El Adem and Bardia roads and was almost hit by a fighter plane (a shot-down Hurricane) as it crashed a few feet away from his tank. Then a lorry drove up and a gunner officer jumped out, shouting that his battery was being attacked by enemy tanks, only a few hundred yards away.

'He was right; some forty German tanks were now clearly visible and they were indeed busily engaged in destroying these guns. There would then be nothing to stop them driving down to Tobruk harbour, only 3 miles away. We swung right into battle line. I handed Milligan his cigarette and told him to start shooting. There was no need for me to indicate the target to him.

'"Loaded!" yelled Adams and away went another solid shot, tearing at the thick enemy armour. The fumes of burning cordite made us cough and our eyes water, and soon the turret was so thick with smoke that I could only just make out the figure of Adams as he loaded shell after shell into the breech. We were firing faster than ever before and so were my other four Cruiser tanks.

'It must have been at least a minute before the Germans spotted us and by then their tanks had received many hits from our shells. They appeared to panic, because they started to turn in all directions, many of them turning about and moving back the way they had come.'

Our German commentator confirms this moment of panic in his notebook thus:

'*Wireless.* "9 o'clock anti-tank gun – 5 o'clock tank!" We are right in the middle of it with no prospects of getting out. From both flanks AP shells whiz by. *Wireless* "Right turn, Left turn, Retire." Now we come slap into 1 Battalion, which is following us. Some of our tanks are already on fire. The crews call for medics, who dismount to help in this witches' cauldron.'

However, the firing was not all one-sided and Rea Leakey's tanks were soon under heavy fire:

'The tank on my left was hit several times and brewed up. I saw some of the crew bale out. Then another of my valuable cruisers went up in flames and there were just three of us left. I noticed one of the men of this crew dragging himself along the ground, badly wounded. I felt I had to give him cover. "Driver advance, turn slightly left", my tank moved across to give this man protection. It was a stupid move, because by turning I presented the German tank gunners with a

Lt Rea Leakey, 1939. Topees had to be worn in the summer before the war. (Maj Gen A.R. Leakey)

larger target and they took full advantage of it. As we were turning back head on to the enemy, the engine cut out and we were left slightly broadside on.

'"She's on fire Sir!" shouted Adams, but he went on loading shells. At the same moment Milligan's head fell back against my knees, looking down I saw that a shell had pierced the armour and removed most of his chest. He was dead. "Bale out!" I yelled and, as I pulled myself out of the turret, what few shells we had left in the turret started to explode and the flames were already licking around my feet. I saw Adams get out safely and we dashed round to the front of the tank to check on the others. As we got there the driver flopped out of his hatch and Adams grabbed him and helped him back. I opened up the first sub-turret gunner's hatch and looked in, but I knew what I would see, as there was a neat hole through the armour just opposite where the gunner's head had been. He was dead and his clothing was already burning fiercely.

'The other sub-turret gunner was lying on the side of the tank and looked up at me and smiled; his right leg was shot off just below the knee and the useless limb was attached by one small piece of skin. He was a big lad and how he got out of the hatch unaided and with only one leg has always remained a mystery to me. We were being machine-gunned. Somehow I got him over my shoulder and carried him back to where I found a shallow trench. The other two were there and we laid him down, but he straightened up, looked at his leg and said: "Cut it off sir, it's no use to me." I did so, and he then lay back smiling. At that moment up drove an ambulance driven by a large Australian. Within a few minutes this lad was in Tobruk hospital. I saw him a year later in a base hospital and he was as cheerful as ever, walking about on crutches.

'The two remaining cruisers survived this battle and the Germans fled out of the Tobruk perimeter. Only one of their tanks was left burning on the battlefield, but much later we learned that many others were put out of action for several months. Once again we were made conscious of our inferior gun and armour plating.'[2]

The German commentator reports the casualties in 2 Bn of Pz Regt 5 as being ten tanks, also five 7.5 cm guns of 8 Kompanie, while the anti-tank units, light and heavy AA were badly shot up and the 8th Machine Gunners cut to pieces. The regiment also lost all its doctors – presumably captured. He concludes: 'The Regiment is practically wiped out.' However, later in his diary he reports the arrival of reinforcements, and quotes his company strength as being the strongest in the regiment with just four PzKpfw II and four PzKpfw III.[3] Another source quotes the total German tank losses that day as sixteen, while in a captured report dated 9 June 1941, Pz Regt 5 summarized the casualties thus:

'38 tanks went into battle – 17 were destroyed by the enemy.

2 officers are missing and 7 wounded; 21 NCOs and men are missing; 10 NCOs and men are wounded. That is a total loss of 50 per cent.

'The regiment went into the fight with firm confidence and iron determination to defeat the enemy and take Tobruk. Only the enemy's great superiority, our great losses and the total lack of support caused us to withdraw.'[4]

A TANK ACE

Rea Leakey is a soldier of legendary bravery of whom the Royal Tank Regiment is justly proud. Undoubtedly a tank ace, he was to fight many more battles and to have many more hair-raising escapes. His second Military Cross was won during the period of the Tobruk siege, when, not long after the battle I have just described, he was serving (as an honorary Lance Corporal) with one of the Australian infantry battalions, aggressively patrolling against the enemy. It was widely rumoured that he was in fact recommended for the Victoria Cross, when he won this Military Cross. He went on to be awarded a Distinguished Service Order and the Czechoslovakian Military Cross (while supporting their independent brigade) in north-west Europe, where he commanded 5 RTR. After the Second World War he commanded the 1st Armoured Car Regiment in the Arab Legion and later, the 7th

Capt Rea Leakey on his way 'up the blue'. (Maj Gen A.R. Leakey)

Armoured Brigade in BAOR. He was then Director General Fighting Vehicle Research and Development, and later, GOC British Troops Malta and Libya, his last Army appointment.

In this particular battle, on the Tobruk perimeter, honours between the British and German tank crews were probably even, both sides losing far more heavily than they might have expected. The A9s do appear to have given as good as they got, and caused many more casualties among the better armoured German Panzers than might have been expected.

ALAM HALFA

A WATERSHED

The Battle of Alam Halfa was undoubtedly a major turning point in the Desert War and the first of a long series of defeats for Rommel, which would eventually see the end of the Axis forces in North Africa. The Eighth Army had some 700 tanks available and plenty of time to prepare for the German attack, so a co-ordinated defence plan had been carefully worked out. However, it was not an easy battle, especially at lower level, as Rommel had managed to amass over 240 Italian and 200 German tanks, including a goodly proportion (75) of the later model PzKpfw III, mounting the long-barrelled 5 cm KwK L/60 gun, and some thirty PzKpfw IV Ausf F2s, with the even more powerful 7.5 cm KwK40 L/3 gun. This latter weapon was far superior to anything the Allies could field, although by now there were a fair number of American-built M3 mediums (Grants) in service. However, as the table below shows, even its 75 mm gun was still outclassed by the formidable new long-barrelled weapon on the Ausf F2.

Weapon type	Type of ammunition	Muzzle velocity	Penetration in mm of armour at 30°			
			500	1,000	1,500	2,000 yd
KwK40 L/3	APCBC	2,300	84	72	62	53
Gun 75 mm M3	APC	2,030	70	59	55	50

Part of the British force defending the Alam Halfa Ridge was 22nd Armoured Brigade (22 Armd Bde), commanded by Brig 'Pip' Roberts. This brigade had been given most of the available Grant tanks and made up to strength with a motley collection of combined units, viz: C Sqn, Royals (armoured cars); Greys, 1 RTR [comprising 1 and 6 RTR], 5 RTR [comprising 5 RTR and Royal Gloucestershire Hussars (RGH)] and the 4th County of London Yeomanry (4 CLY) [both 3rd and 4th CLY] (armoured regiments); 1 RHA and 104 RHA (artillery); 1 RB (motor bn); 20 Fd Tp RE (engineers); plus 98 Fd Regt and one medium battery in support. Each of the armoured regiments consisted of two squadrons of 12 medium tanks (Grants) each and one light squadron (either Crusaders or Stuarts). The only exception was 4 CLY who had just one Grant squadron of 15 tanks.

The tank commander concerned is Sgt (later Lt) Bob MacGregor, DCM, MM, who was then commanding a light tank troop in A Sqn of 1 RTR. He had already made his name as a fearless tank commander and would go on to become one of the most revered members of 1 RTR, tragically losing his life towards the end of the war in a tank gun accident. At Alam Halfa, 1st was commanded by Lt Col G.C. Webb, MBE, with Maj Holliman, MC as OC A Sqn, Maj Pink as OC B and Maj Pedraze as OC C. A Sqn was equipped with American-built light tanks, known by the British as 'Stuarts', by the Americans as the 'M3 light', but by the desert tank crews as 'Honeys' because they

Instruction taking place in Cairo on the newly issued Honeys. The .30 Browning machine-gun is still in service worldwide. (Author's collection)

were so easy to maintain and so reliable. B and C Sqns had Grants. C Sqn crews included an American tank crew who were gaining battle experience, plus a secretary from the Belgian Embassy in Alexandria, who was serving as a Grant 75 mm sponson gunner because 'he wished to fight the war with a gun not a pen'.[5]

The whole of August was spent preparing for the Axis attack and these preparations intensified with the arrival of the new Eighth Army commander, Gen Bernard Montgomery. Final positions were not recced until 18 August. Before that date, however, much had happened, including test and range firing of the new 75 mm guns on the Grants, and visits by Montgomery and other VIPs. Churchill visited on 20 August, and two days later the first warning was issued that a full-scale Axis attack could be expected within 48 hours. The codeword 'Pepsodent' was given at 01.30 hrs 31 August, which ordered the immediate occupation of the Alam Halfa positions. Soon all were on the move, and at 02.30 hrs 1 RTR reported they were all in position.

THE TANKS

Sgt MacGregor's tank was an M3 light – 'a honey of a tank' despite the fact that its 37

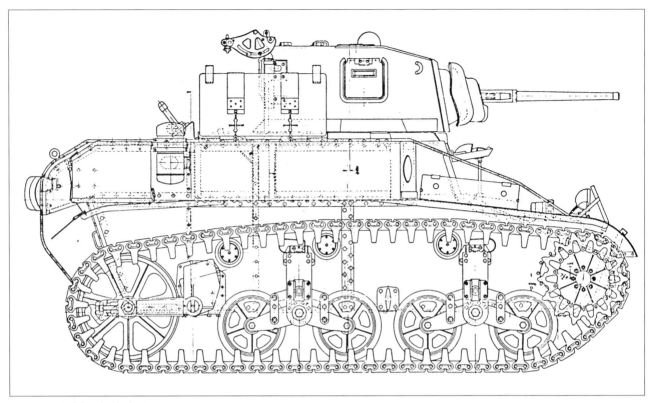

M3 light tank, side elevation.

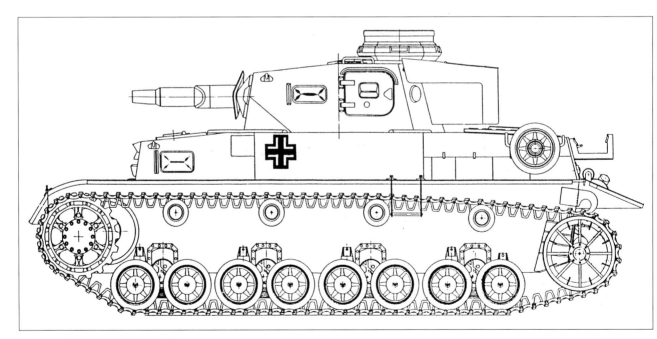

PzKpfw IV Ausf F2, side elevation.

Happy Christmas to all! The crew of a Stuart get ready to eat their Christmas pud in the middle of the desert. (Tank Museum)

mm main armament was inferior to the British 2-pounder. The reliability and ease of handling of this 'great little tank' soon made it a firm favourite with the British tank crews, who were the first to try it out in action. The first shipment of eighty-four had arrived in the Middle East in July 1941 and were used to re-equip the 8th Hussars, subsequent shipments going first to 3 and 5 RTR, then to other armoured regiments. Weighing 12.3 tons, with armour 10–51 mm thick, the Honey had a top speed of 36 m.p.h., a road radius of 70 miles and a crew of four men. The major drawback inside the tank was the fact that there was no turret basket, so the two-man turret crew (commander and

gunner) had to move around with the turret as it traversed. This was rectified in the M3A1 and later marks, but in solving one problem it created another as the basket obstructed the vital escape route between the driving and fighting compartments. The turret had only one hatch (on top of the commander's cupola), a drawback which was also rectified in the M3A1, by fitting hatches for both commander and gunner.

The second main Allied tank taking part in the battle was the Grant. The Grant was the British version of the M3 medium, differing from the American standard M3 (known as the Lee) in that it had a slightly lower but larger turret, with a rear bustle to provide

Grants moving into action in the desert. (Tank Museum)

room for the radio,[6] and no machine-gun cupola. Essentially a stopgap AFV, soon to be superseded by the M4 Sherman, the Grant did, nevertheless, play a significant part in the battles in North Africa. We shall be describing the Lee in detail in the section on the Far East (see pp. 204–5), so a photograph of a desert Grant of the period will suffice here.

The third tank involved was the German tank the PzKpfw IV Ausf F2, which had such an great impact on British armour. It was known by the British as a 'Special' in view of its obviously much longer and more powerful gun. Weighing 23 tons, with a crew of five and armour 10–50 mm thick, the Ausf F2 was produced in relatively small numbers, although the production of PzKpfw IV G, H, and J tanks was continued almost to the end of the war. The major reason for the PzKpfw

IV's longevity was that its turret ring was wide enough to accept larger, more powerful guns, while 'add-on' spaced armour could be fitted to enhance its armoured protection, without materially affecting its performance. The F2 had a top speed of 25 m.p.h. and a range of 125 miles. Its reliable Maybach HL120TRM engine and excellent suspension gave it a good all-round performance in desert conditions.

THE BATTLE

Gen Montgomery rightly appreciated that Rommel would never willingly bypass the Alam Halfa Ridge or the other Eighth Army positions on the Ruweisat Ridge some miles to the west, and leave them behind him on his way to conquer Egypt. On the western slopes of the Alam Halfa Ridge, 22 Armd Bde was some distance away from the initial fighting,

A captured PzKpfw IV Ausf F2 'Special'. Its improved 7.5 cm KwK 40 L/43 gun had a superior performance to contemporary British AFVs. (Tank Museum)

but at about 17.00 hrs on the 31st, 1 RTR saw a large number of enemy tanks 'in review order' advancing towards them. As Basil Forster, then Regimental 2IC of 1 RTR, later recalled:

'It was a very frightening sight. At this hour the head of a large tank column of Mk III Specials and Mk IV Specials approached the position in a northeasterly direction and aimed on the Brigade's eastern flank. They were about 2,000 yd from our tanks and not a shot was fired from the whole brigade position. The wind deadened the noise of their engines and they came on in silence. Our tanks, where possible, were turret down with the commanders standing in their turrets.'

This all took about half an hour, and as the enemy got nearer the infantry of 90 Leichte

Division could be seen, moving by bounds, in their half-tracks, accompanying the tanks. The column was now advancing due east across the brigade front and one enemy tank, which had taken a more northerly route than the others, approached the exact position of Maj Pink's (OC B Sqn 1 RTR) tank. He had no alternative but to move into his hull-down position or be caught behind the bank. But before he could reach it he was seen by the enemy. Both tanks stopped, but neither could depress their guns sufficiently to engage, the two tank commanders 'eyeballing' each other at a range of under 30 yd. After what must have seemed a very long time, the Panzer reversed and rejoined the main body of enemy AFVs.

Basil Forster again:

'At 18.00 hrs the whole column was halted with about fifty tanks directly opposite the

103

Regiment at a range of 1,500 yd and intense enemy fire was brought to bear on the squadron of 4 CLY who were positioned between the Regiment and 5 RTR on the left. At 18.10 hrs Brigade ordered fire to be opened and all tanks adopted hull-down positions and started firing. The clouds of dust resulting from the muzzle blast made observation extremely difficult. At 19.30 hrs the enemy broke off the engagement, leaving thirteen tanks behind, opposite the Regimental position. Our casualties had been nil as the enemy fire had been AP with very little HE landing on the position. . . . As dusk fell, motor patrols from 1 RB were sent out beyond the area of the battlefield and behind them RE working parties blew up those Axis tanks that were considered repairable. The Regiment slept in its battle positions with double guards mounted.'

With tanks, anti-tank guns and artillery all able to engage the enemy heavily in a co-ordinated defence, 22 Armd Bde's position was a strong one. However, the Germans were making a determined effort to break through, aiming their main thrust at 4 CLY as Basil Forster has already explained. The Greys had initially been in reserve, but when 4 CLY was heavily engaged and many of its tanks destroyed ('Our A Sqn bore the first shock of the battle,' wrote the Earl of Onslow later, 'losing ten of their twelve Grants before darkness fell.'[7]), the Greys were ordered forward to plug the gap. As their history tells:

'The Regiment arrived at a critical moment when the issue of the tank battle appeared to be in doubt; but the fire-power and the sight of a fresh Regiment charging down the hill into action to fill the gap they had battered, prevented any further progress by the Germans. The battle went on until nightfall, by which time the Regiment had two Grants

knocked out. . . . The battlefield was littered with wrecked German transport and the hulls of twenty-six German tanks lay helpless on the plain below.'

Clearly, despite the 'Specials', the DAK had paid a terrible price for taking on such a strong defensive position.

It was on the following day, 1 September, that Bob MacGregor won his Military Medal. His troop of Honeys was sent out on a wide recce of the area to the west of the Alam Halfa Ridge, along the southern slopes of Bare Ridge. His citation tells how an enemy column, which included ten tanks, moved north between the patrol and the Alam Halfa positions. MacGregor, displaying great gallantry, fought his way back to the regiment, without losing any of his troop, and even succeeded in making the enemy believe that his tiny force was far stronger than it actually was, forcing them to take cover and to remain there for the rest of the day.

After failing to make any real impression on the 22 Armd Bde position, Rommel tried an attack on both flanks, but was thwarted by the New Zealand Division on the right and 23rd Armoured Brigade (23 Armd Bde) on the left. By 3 September the Germans had shot their bolt and went onto the defensive, being hammered both from the ground and the air. Permission was then given to carry out ground raids against the enemy and the ubiquitous Bob MacGregor was again sent out with his troop at about 10.00 hrs on the 3rd. After initially making good progress, they were engaged by a screen of well-hidden anti-tank guns, and lost two Stuarts, but KOed two 50 mm anti-tank guns. Long-range fire was then brought to bear from the Grants in both 1 RTR and the Greys, and most of the anti-tank guns were silenced.

There were similar raids on the 4th and

Bob MacGregor is on the end of this row of heroes, all from 1 RTR, taken at their Buckingham Palace investiture. Left to right: T. Harland, DCM, H.A. Bennett, MM, J. Maconnachie, MM, F.J.W. Williamson, MM and R. MacGregor, DCM, MM. (A.W. Green)

5th, the Stuarts of A Sqn being boosted with Grants from B Sqn, but they were held up by a number of 'Specials' and forced to give ground after suffering casualties. As Basil Forster rightly comments:

'The ground as always dominated the battle . . . the Regiment, because it was well sited and well prepared, could afford to let the enemy do the manoeuvring and, in a purely defensive role, inflicted great loss on them without loss to itself. . . . It was only when the Regiment moved off its chosen ground and went looking for trouble, that it

suffered casualties. . . . Finally, it will be noted that once the enemy realized he was denied the vital ground, he had no alternative but to withdraw right back to where he had started. Further, he had received such a mauling in his attempts to take the vital ground that he was incapable of making further attacks.'

Final German losses were of the order of more than fifty tanks, sixty guns and many hundreds of lorries, which was a serious blow in view of the fact that Rommel was so far away from his main bases. While the Eighth

Lt Bob MacGregor receiving the DCM ribbon from Field Marshal Montgomery. (A.W. Green)

Lt Bob MacGregor's grave. (A.W. Green)

Army had suffered similar casualties, there now were replacements available, which meant that Montgomery was in a better position than Rommel at the end of the day. Alam Halfa thus prepared the way for the launching of the most well-known battle of the Desert War, Montgomery's attack at El Alamein, some weeks afterwards.

Two years later, SSM Bob MacGregor was awarded the Distinguished Conduct Medal in north-west Europe for an attack on Middelrose village near S'Hertogenbosch, during which he knocked out two anti-tank guns, two MG nests, took twenty prisoners and forced a numerically superior enemy to withdraw from the village. Commissioned in the field and recommended for a Military Cross a year later, he was killed in an accident on 9 April 1945, before it could be awarded. One of his contemporaries told me that Bob MacGregor was the best tank commander in 1 RTR during the war, and, as the photograph on the previous page shows, there was plenty of competition.

THE BATTLE OF TEBOURBA

Alam Halfa was followed by the Eighth Army's major assault at El Alamein on 23 October 1942. After many days of hard fighting Rommel was forced to withdraw across Cyrenaica, following the well-trodden paths through Tobruk, Benghazi, Agedabia and on across the Tripolitanian frontier. The Afrika Korps fought tenaciously every inch of the way, becoming masters of the fighting withdrawal, which they continued westwards across North Africa and into Tunisia. As the Allies pressed on towards Tunis, the Eighth Army linked up with both the First Army and the Americans who had landed in Algeria and Morocco on 8 November 1942 (Operation 'Torch'). But it was by no means all over and there were many hard battles still to be fought. The Axis was determined to fight on and continued to send reinforcements over to Tunisia. These included 10 Panzer Division (10 Pz Div) and two Panzer Abteilung (501 and 504) of the new and formidable Tiger PzKpfw VI tanks. 10 Pz Div was commanded by Gen Wolfgang Fischer, a field commander of considerable energy and merit, who immediately began planning a counter-attack on the Allied forces, who had recently captured the important road junction of Tebourba (see map overleaf) while on their way to attempt to take the important bridge and communications hub of Djedieda on 29 November. They failed and this left them drawn out in a long salient, ripe for a counter-attack.

Gen Walther Nehring, the German commander in Tunisia, gave Fischer the following orders: 'You will attack and destroy the enemy in and around Tebourba.' Gen Fischer moved his forces to an assembly area to the north-east of the town and prepared for the coming battle. Part of the German force was Kampfgruppe Hudel, based upon the 1st Battalion of Panzer Regiment 7 (Pz Regt 7), commanded by Hauptmann Helmut Hudel, who was to be awarded the Oakleaves to his Knight's Cross for his part in this action.

Opposing 10 Pz Div was the British 78th Infantry Division (11 and 36 Bdes, 78 Inf Div), under Maj Gen Vyvyan Evelegh, who also had elements of both the British 6th Armoured Division (6 Armd Div) and the American 1st Armored Division (1 (US) Armd Div) working with them. The former comprised 'Blade Force', based upon the 17th/21st Lancers (17/21L) and commanded by Col Richard Hull, late 17/21L, who would win a Distinguished Service Order in the battle, then go on to command both a brigade and division in action and finish his army career as a Field Marshal and Chief of the Defence Staff. The latter, the American element, was Combat Command B of 1 (US) Armd Div, under the command of Brig-Gen Paul M. Robinett.

THE TANKS
The British Blade Force tanks were mainly Valentines (each squadron had three troops

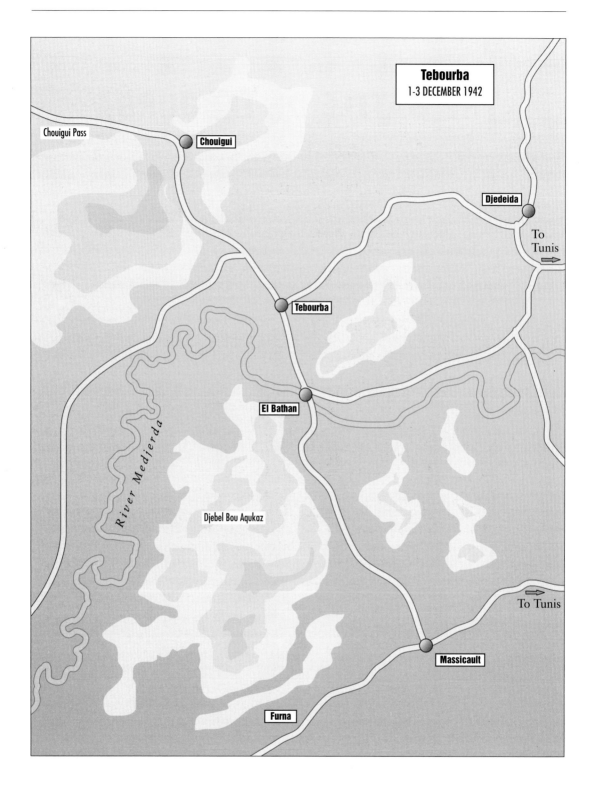

Chouigui Pass

Chouigui

Djedeida

To Tunis

Tebourba

El Bathan

River Medjerda

Djebel Bou Aqukaz

To Tunis

Massicault

Furna

Tebourba
1-3 DECEMBER 1942

Valentines at Gabes Gap, Tunisia, April 1943. (Tank Museum)

of Valentines and one troop of Crusaders); the Americans had M3 mediums and M3 lights; the Germans, mainly PzKpfw IIIs and IVs but, as already mentioned, there were a small number of PzKpfw VIs.

The Valentines in Blade Force were Mk IIs/IIIs, which had an AEC diesel engine in place of the original petrol engine of the Mk I. They were still armed with the 2-pounder gun – the 6-pounder not being introduced until the Mk VIII. Valentine was a 'private venture' infantry tank, designed and produced by Vickers Armstrong Ltd as a replacement for the Matilda II. It went into production in 1939, after the plans had supposedly been drawn up and submitted to the War Office on St Valentine's Day in 1938. However, its name was more likely evolved from Vickers Armstrong Ltd Engineers, Newcastle upon Tyne. Production went on until 1944 and over 8,000 were built – a quarter of the total British tank output, the last model (Mk XI) mounting a 75 mm gun. It was also built in Canada and many

Valentine Mk 2s in the desert. (Tank Museum)

Valentines were sent to Russia. It had a three-man crew (four from Mk III onwards), weighed some 16 tons, with armour 8–65 mm thick. Its cross-country speed was only about 8 m.p.h. and its range 90 miles. Although undergunned until fitted with the 6-pounder, the Valentine was a well-liked tank, with a stable gun platform and good mechanical reliability. The main drawback was the small turret (Mk II), which meant there was no room for a loader/radio operator, adding to the commander's workload.

The 'big punch' was supposed to be provided by the Crusader troop in each squadron of six tanks. These were Mk IIIs which mounted the 6-pounder gun. However, the Crusader's armour was only 7–51 mm thick and only sixty-five rounds were carried for the 6-pounder, compared with seventy-nine for the Valentine 2-pounder. Within each SHQ there were two Crusader Close Support

tanks, equipped with a 3 in howitzer. This weapon had a range of about 3,000 yd, could fire either HE or smoke, and proved invaluable in battle.

CCB of 1 (US) Armd Div had both light M3 Honeys and medium M3 Grants, while the Germans were equipped with mainly PzKpfw IIIs and IVs. I shall be describing Tiger in a later section.

THE BATTLE

The aim of the German force was to capture the two passes at Tebourba and Chouigui, as by doing so they could block any attempt by the Allies to reinforce their salient, which could then be destroyed piecemeal. The Allied force had the bulk of Blade Force at Chouigui village and the infantry brigades between Tebourba and Djedeida, roughly in a triangle. Gen Fischer had four battlegroups (BG):

110

The Crusader Mk III, mounting the 6-pounder gun, gave each squadron in Blade Force a 'big punch'. (Tank Museum)

Gruppe Luder: one Kompanie/Panzer Abteilung 501 (20 tanks)
11/Panzer Grenadier Regt. (infantry)
Pioner Zug (engineer platoon)
Flak Zug (AA/anti-tank platoon)

They were located some 3 miles north of Chouigui and their initial task was to block the road from the pass.

Kampfegruppe Hudel: two Panzer Kompanien (40 tanks)
two Panzerjaeger Kompanien (anti-tank guns)
one Kradschutzen Kompanie/Kradschutzen Bn 10. (motorcycle infantry)

They were located on the left flank of BG Luder, with the task of destroying the Allied armour in Chouigui by drawing it into an ambush, then, in conjunction with BG Luder,

attacking Tebourba and blocking the gap there.

Kampfegruppe Koch: Fallschirmjaeger Regt. 5 (paratroops)
2 Panzerjaeger Abteilung 90 (anti-tank guns)
Infanterie-Bataillon A24
11/Panzer Artillerie Regt. 90 (two field guns)
one Leichte Flakbatterie (2 cm)

Located to the east, with the task of advancing north-west towards Tebourba, cutting off the Allied escape routes.

Gruppe Djedeida: 3 PzKpfw III, 2 PzKpfw VI (Tiger)
one Panzerjaeger Kompanie (anti-tank guns)
one Fallschirmjaeger Kompanie (paratroops)
one Infanterie Kompanie (infantry)
one Flak Batterie

111

Hauptmann Hudel commanding a PzKpfw III Ausf N in Tunisia. (Panzermuseum)

18 mm x 20 mm guns
one Zug/Kradschutzen Kompanie (motor-cycle platoon)

Commanded by Gen Fischer himself, this group was to act as reserve for phase one and then pursue the Allies westwards.[8]

The German attack started in the north, BGs Luder and Hudel advancing on Chouigui in the early morning in the usual wedge-shaped formation, which allowed all tank gunners to engage targets, and smashing their way into the Blade Force positions. 17/21L counter-attacked and were caught in the flank by a hidden platoon of Panzers, which quickly knocked out five tanks as the 17/21L history recalls:

'B Squadron and RHQ advanced to meet the attack, but could only find a bare ridge for

fire positions. The enemy were in vines and olive trees, and outranged the 2-pounders and 6-pounders completely at 2,000 yd. Five tanks were soon knocked out.'

The Germans pressed on towards Tebourba, but were halted by heavy artillery fire. Fischer then switched his attack to the Djedeida BG, under his personal command, and advanced towards Tebourba from the east, the armoured column spearheaded by his two Tigers. Capt Nikolai Baron von Nolde, who was commanding the leading Tigers, had been warned to expect American tanks and he was not disappointed. He was able to knock out the American tanks from 1 Tank Bn, but could not dislodge the British infantry (2 Hamps) from their positions on the ridge above Djedeida. Capt von Nolde was killed by shellfire while directing his Tigers from an open *Kubelwagen* (the German equivalent of the Jeep).

While this thrust was taking place, BG Koch was beginning to infiltrate into the Allied positions from the south, thus encircling the Allied force. This is how the first day ended, with the Germans having inflicted many casualties on the Allied armour, but with the vital ground still in Allied hands.

The following day, instead of making further abortive assaults, the Germans went onto the defensive and waited in good positions to see what the Allied force would do. Clearly the Allies had to try to break out. However, instead of gathering together all their armoured forces and making a determined thrust, they chose to attempt a series of isolated and unsupported 'cavalry charges' and suffered accordingly. The first of these was launched by a company of American light tanks at the Djedeida BG about 11.00 hrs on 2 December. Unfortunately they did not know that, during the night, a battery of dreaded 88s had been brought up and was now sited in camouflaged positions on their flank. As 1 (US) Armd Div's history recalls:

'Mayshark's company which had been on the way most of the night was sent at mid-morning in a direct frontal attack over unfamiliar terrain against an enemy force of uncertain strength. It advanced generally parallel with the railway line, which was on the south flank and over ground which was bare except for a few clumps of trees and scattered farm buildings well ahead and for some woods to the north. About 1½ miles to the north-east of the start line some enemy tanks were plainly visible on a knoll, but within 500 yd of the line the attacking formation came under heavy anti-tank fire from much closer, and as they rolled forward, one after another of the tanks was hit and began to burn.

'After seven tanks were lost, the attack fell

apart, with most of the remaining tanks risking hits in their vulnerable rears as they withdrew as ordered, while others continued to search for defilade.'[9]

This type of futile attack was unfortunately repeated, until the Americans had lost at least half their tank strength. Then the Germans took the initiative again and began to fight their way forward, eventually forcing the British infantry to withdraw from the vital ground, back into Tebourba and then on the 3rd, from the entire area. The Germans captured Tebourba on the 4th, then pursued the Allies westwards back along the road to Medjez el Bab.

This was undoubtedly a German victory, the Allies losing an estimated 55 tanks, 29

Oberst Helmut Hudel. (Panzermuseum)

guns, 300 assorted vehicles and over 1,000 men taken prisoner. The immediate Allied threat to Tunis was averted and the Germans could breathe again, while they established a new defensive line in the mountains around Tunis.

A TANK ACE

Helmut Hudel fought on with 10 Pz Div until by 21 April 1943 they had only twenty-five tanks left. However, he was transferred out of the African theatre before the final surrender. In 1944 he commanded Schwere Panzer Abteilung 508 in Italy, then in February 1945 he was given command of the Panzer Lehr Regiment, which fought in Holland in March 1945 and later, against the American bridgehead at Remagen. By the end of this battle the Regiment had just fifteen tanks left. Hudel survived the war and died in 1985, aged sixty-nine.

A close-up of a 6-pounder Crusader Mk III.

THE BATTLE OF STEAMROLLER FARM

Just over two weeks after El Alamein, the Germans had to face another threat in the shape of the Allied landings on the coast of Algeria and Morocco on 8 November 1942. Later, the war moved into Tunisia and the British First Army's Churchill tanks were in action for the first time since their disastrous debut in August 1942 on the ill-fated Dieppe raid. Comprising 51 RTR, the North Irish Horse (NIH) and the 142nd RAC Regiment (142 (RAC) Regt), the 25th Army Tank Brigade (25 Armd Bde) was the First Army's 'secret weapon', its presence in North Africa initially being kept a close secret.[10]

Its first major action took place some miles to the north of El Aroussa and has been described as being one of the most remarkable stories in the history of the Royal Armoured Corps. It was a reconnaissance in force by an all-arms group, which included A Sqn 51 RTR and resulted in the immediate award of a Distinguished Service Order for tank ace Capt (later Maj) E.D. 'Gin' Hollands, to add to the Distinguished Conduct Medal which he had already won in France in 1940.

THE TANK

The A22 Infantry was one of the most successful British tanks of the Second World War, although, as already mentioned, its début at Dieppe was a disaster. By early 1943, however, many of its problems had been overcome and the tank, now the Mk III, was fitted with a larger, welded turret containing a 6-pounder gun. Weighing 38½ tons, with armour 16–102 mm thick, it had a crew of five (the extra man being the co-driver/hull gunner), a top speed cross-country of only 8 m.p.h. and a radius of action of 90 miles. It was later upgunned (Mk VII onwards) with the British version of the 75 mm gun and adapted for many specialized armour uses (e.g.: armoured engineer vehicle, armoured recovery vehicle, bridgelayer) due to its roomy interior and good armoured protection. Despite its slow speed, it did well in Tunisia, being able to negotiate the hilly country with ease.

Hollands was commanding 1 Troop of A Sqn in 51 RTR. However, on this particular operation he was riding in *Adventurer*, a 5 Troop tank, to which he had transferred after losing a track.

THE SETTING

Early on 26 February it became clear that the Germans had cut the El Aroussa–Medjez el Bab road, isolating a force of No. 6 Commando in some scrub-covered hillocks near Steamroller Farm. The enemy force comprising some six Panzerjaeger companies

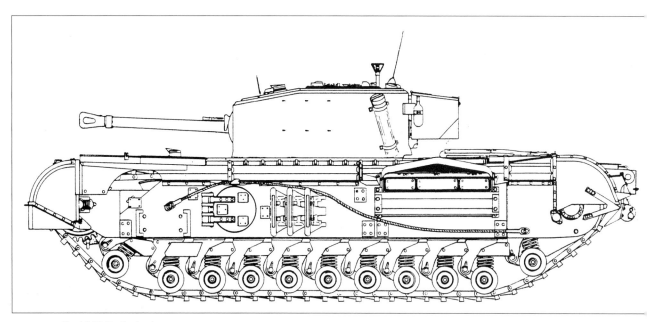

Churchill Mk III, side elevation.

of the Hermann Goering Regiment, supported by seven PzKpfw IIIs and IVs of 6 Kompanie, Pz Regt 7, plus armoured cars and anti-tank guns. They had occupied the farm and poured heavy fire onto the commandos, who, by midday, had been scattered with heavy losses.

On the 27th it was decided to send out a strong reconnaissance in force the following day, to advance the 5½ miles north from El Aroussa to Steamroller Farm to discover what was happening. The force comprised a company of 2nd Battalion Coldstream Guards, A Sqn 51 RTR, a troop of 12 RHA with 4 x 25-pounder guns, plus an engineer detachment to deal with any minefields found en route. The operation was under command of the Coldstream Guards, who had direct radio contact with the tanks via a scout car of the Derbyshire Yeomanry. Just as they crossed the start line some Ju 87s appeared, but instead of dive-bombing the column, they dropped supplies to the Germans in and around the farm.

Gin Hollands later wrote:

'Maj Ted Hadfield, OC A Sqn, deployed his dozen-plus Churchills in the usual two waves, with the infantry riding on the tanks in the second wave. Probing slowly forward in the close country, it was not until 16.00 that the force came into the area of Steamroller Farm, where the valley opened out. Pushing 1 and 4 Troops forward to take up suitable fire positions, Maj Hadfield deployed 2 and 3 Troops from the second wave on the left to protect that flank of the attack and avoid bad going. Suddenly, the Tuesday afternoon quiet was noisily dispelled by the whiplike crack of anti-tank guns sited in the farm and surrounding wadis. The infantry hastily deployed and went to ground. 1 Troop opened up in reply and soon a heavy fire-fight was in progress. Tracks clattering and clanking, 2 and 3 Troops waddled forwards to take the infantry onto their objective as they had done in so many exercises back in Britain.

Churchill Mk IIIs in Tunisia. Note the camouflage pattern and colours, which were very different to the plain sand-coloured livery of the Western Desert. (Tank Museum)

'Suddenly and without warning the air was filled with noise, as Stukas came hurtling out of the sky to release bombs that burst in an irregular pattern around the tanks; simultaneously, the German anti-tank gunners redoubled their fire. When the dive-bombers left it was seen that two tanks had been knocked out – they were Capt G.C. Franklin (2IC A Sqn) and tank one in 2 Troop. The anti-tank guns had accounted for more, so only nine tanks remained; 1 and 2 Troops had one each, SHQ and 3 Troop had two each and 4 Troop was intact but badly held up by wadis.'

The tanks had knocked out some of the enemy anti-tank guns and mortar positions beyond the farm. However, the British force was clearly in some difficulty and the German defenders could rightly have felt they were winning the battle. At this point Maj Hadfield was told that he must get on at all costs, force a way past the farm and destroy the enemy on the high ground beyond. He therefore ordered 1 Troop to move forward, despite the fact that Hollands had only his own tank, *Adventurer*, left. So the single Churchill, without any infantry support, began to move forward, making for the head of the pass.

The tank was being driven by Tpr John Mitton, who later recalled:

'Dropping feet first through the cupola and nearly massacring the rest of the crew, Capt Hollands gave the order to advance. Moving forward I found the ground pretty difficult, scrub, rock and very little if any cover. After moving on half a mile or so, I stopped, not by an order, but because on passing through a patch of bushes, the ground fell away, heavily bushed, farther than I could see through the visor, and then rose to the opposite slope, which seemed miles away. Clearly impassable. Could I get down? Over the intercom, "No, driver reverse!" Inch by inch I backed away. The German "ants" opened fire from across the wadi. I wished for four reverse speeds at that moment. "Driver, right. Speed up." Now we were broadside onto the wadi and the "ants".

'I was told the next day that the German gunners hit all around us. I didn't know it then. I just kept moving as fast as possible, crossing the road, round through the trees of a farm. Out into the open on to the road. Follow it uphill, then weave left and sharp right. Taking this corner in third gear, I drove round and stopped dead.

'I appeared to be facing a barricade of greenery blocking the road, surmounted by a large black hole. It was in fact an "88", not more than 30 yd away, if that, set up on the left verge. Peering through the visor, I saw a flash of white faces and the hole vanished in the red sheet of flame, blinding me for the moment. The tank rocked, a sound of falling kit in the turret. The right-hand junction box and roof fan had dropped, as the shell grazed the turret, taking half of the back bin with it. "We're hit! Traverse right! Right not left!" The turret was at 20-to-6 and Mick, the gunner, was struggling to free a jammed 6-pounder round which had slipped out of its rack.

'Once again the hole vanished in another sheet of flame, but they missed completely this time. During these hectic few seconds Hank Howson, the front machine-gunner, was calmly reloading his Besa with a new belt as though on range practice. Closing its cover carefully, he cocked the gun, laid and fired. The tracer streaked through the greenery, then climbed lazily in the air and vanished.

The dreaded 88 mm anti-tank gun in action. Gin Hollands and his crew knocked out two of these at point-blank range. (Tank Museum)

The gun crew ran. We had knocked out our first 88! The intercom was deafening as Capt Hollands shouted for the Bren gun, so I pulled past the 88 muzzle – just in case – and waited. The Bren fired one round then stopped! "Tommy gun!" – with which he fared no better, firing one burst and jamming. Hollands was now fighting mad. Throwing the Tommy gun after the fleeing Germans, he shouted for grenades and stood half out of the turret throwing them. Again I moved forward as ordered. Directly in front was a running mass of grey figures. All guns fired, bowling them over until nothing moved.'

Hollands then saw a second 88, to the right of the road below the crest of the hill and quickly knocked out the crew. He then moved forward, reaching the top of the pass and radioed for tank and infantry support, but was told that neither was able to get through. However, Lt Jock Renton, who had been listening to Hollands' request on the radio, asked for permission to join him and did so successfully. The two Churchills then sat at the top of the pass, picking targets.

John Mitton continues his narrative:

'Directly in front of us was a slit trench covered by a camouflage net and from it emerged a German helmet, face and shoulders, with a rifle and grenade-thrower attached. Taking a snap-shot upwards, he ducked back into the trench. A muttered curse over the intercom, then "Who the **** is firing at me?" from Hollands. I pointed out the German in the slit trench. "Mick, traverse left, on, see him, right, fire!" The Besa burst was right on target. "Stop, traverse right, continue firing. . . ." During the next few minutes the German fired three times at Hollands and twice at the tracks. After each shot Mick swung back and fired, using two full belts of Besa and four armour-piercing rounds. On the fourth AP the trench seemed to vanish in a cloud of smoke and dust.

As it settled, the German crawled out, stood dazedly looking at the tank, turned slowly, dropped his rifle and staggered away. Hollands ordered: "Stop firing! He deserves to live!"

'Two tanks (Panzer IIIs) came into view lower down the valley and although we both used our "special" AP, we were unable to set them on fire, but the crews bailed out and were given a burst of Besa fire. Inside the tank was pretty thick by this time having been closed down from 10.00 and it was now 19.00. During this time we had fired twenty-one rounds of AP and twenty-three boxes of Besa. Most of the empty cases remaining with their attendant packing strips and loose rounds, Hank and myself half deaf by blast.'

At this point they were ordered to withdraw because the infantry were held up and the squadron was in bad shape with two tanks burning, so they were unable to consolidate. Gin ordered: 'Destroy everything!'

'Here was a gunner's dream. The echelon of soft vehicles, twenty-seven in all, laid out in orderly array, backs down towards us. Mick rang up on the intercom: "see that staff car Johnny, watch me let its tyres down." He was good to his word; next a 3 ton Bedford, a burst of Besa into the petrol tank, a lick of flame up the cab, igniting the camouflage net and seconds later a roaring inferno. Lt Renton was up alongside, also firing and adding to the general din of explosions and crackling flames as petrol and ammunition blew up. To get further gun depression I was ordered to swing left, sideways to the slope, the gun moving to 3 o'clock. The vehicle park was now well ablaze and we commenced to retire, well satisfied that Jerry would not be able to use that lot again. Starting downhill we came up in rear of the second 88 and fired two rounds of AP into the breech at point-blank range, fixing it good and proper.

'Down the reverse slope, the wireless failed

completely. Hollands, seeing I was moving away from the road, jumped out of the turret and sat on the front. Guiding me with his hand in front of the open visor, shouting directions through the open driver's hatch. On again in third gear, then the engine stalled. I pressed the starter, the lights grew dim, but no engine roar. Stalled with flat batteries in the middle of enemy positions.'

The other Churchill was now safely on its way and Renton saw Hollands' frantic hand signals as he came round a bend. Dismounting, the two crews struggled to connect a tow rope, under enemy machine-gun and mortar fire, which wounded Lt Renton. However, they managed to attach the rope and fortunately *Adventurer* started at the first tug. They then couldn't stop to undo the tow rope, but managed to snap it by revving hard and then braking sharply. At the bottom of the hill they halted opposite a burning Churchill and took two badly wounded men onto the back decks (one each), but from then on it was a straight run back to the squadron lines, where their story was greeted with disbelief. However, three days later when the infantry finally got through, they confirmed even greater damage than had been claimed. The final 'bag' was confirmed as: two 88 mm, two 75 mm, two 50 mm and several smaller calibre anti-tank guns; two PzKpfw III; two 3 in mortars; 25 wheeled vehicles and about 100 Germans.

The Germans at Steamroller Farm had been badly shaken by the two Churchills. An intercepted radio message from their commander, Hauptmann Schirmer, to Oberstleutnant Walther Koch, CO of the Hermann Goering Parachute Jaeger Regiment, said that they were being attacked by a 'mad tank battalion', whose tanks had scaled impossible heights and caused him such heavy losses, which made it imperative for him to withdraw.

TANK ACES

As a direct result of this remarkable action, Gin Hollands was awarded an immediate Distinguished Service Order, Lt Renton the Military Cross, Sgt Rowlinson, commander of the burning tank at the bottom of the hill, the Distinguished Conduct Medal, and Tpr Mitton and another crewman both received Military Medals. Only one other RTR officer was awarded both the Distinguished Service Order and Distinguished Conduct Medal during the Second World War, so Gin Hollands was definitely a tank commander of considerable merit. His medals are now on display at the Tank Museum, Bovington.

One last comment from Gin Hollands:

'Any reader of this action would no doubt be entitled to ask: "How could a seasoned

Capt (later Maj) Gin Hollands at his Buckingham Palace investiture. He was one of only two RTR officers to be awarded both the DSO and DCM in the Second World War. (Maj E.D. Hollands)

German gun crew of an 88 mm anti-tank gun fire two rounds at a range of about 30 yd and fail to destroy a 40 ton Churchill tank and its crew of five?" Here I would remind the reader of how Hank Howson (the front machine-gunner) reacted when, coming round the bend in the road, he was confr̶ ... ̶at us. He kept a cool

and

wer

cau

his

in

all

N

T

1

T

l

assault on Tobruk by Pz Regt 5, held by the Tank Museum Library (RH (43). 8 5 PANZER REGT 6010).

5. Quoted in an officer's winter study report on the Battle of Alam Halfa, written by Capt B.C. Forster. (Copy held in Tank Museum Library.)

6. Standard American practice at that time ̶as to mount the radio in the hull, while the ̶ritish preferred theirs in the turret, thus ̶aving one crew member as the 37 mm loader ̶could then act as radio operator.

7. *Men and Sand*, Earl of Onslow, KBE, MC, TD.

8. Information extracted from *Uniforms, Organization and History of the AFRIKA KORPS*, R.J. Bender and R.D. Law.

9. 1 (US) Armd Div's light tanks had met the German Panzers before Teboura, namely on 26 November 1942, when Lt Col John K. Waters' light tank battalion was in reserve near the Tine Valley entrance to the Chouigui Pass. An enemy detachment of three plus PzKpfw IIIs and at least six PzKpfw IV Specials approached from the north. In the ensuing fire fight, although Company A, which had deliberately attacked the enemy's west flank, lost six of its twelve tanks, it did manage to keep the enemy's full attention, while Company B took them from the rear. It knocked out six Mk IVs and at least one Mk III before the enemy withdrew.

10. I am reliably informed that, in order to keep their presence secret, the men of the brigade had to hide their black berets in their kitbags and sailed out wearing khaki side-caps and plastic Royal Artillery badges.

ALWAYS A STRATHCONA: LT EDWARD J. PERKINS AND THE MELFA RIVER BRIDGEHEAD BATTLE

24–5 MAY 1944

BREAK-OUT FROM THE HITLER LINE

By 15 May 1944 the Allied armies summer offensive in Italy had breached the Gustav Line and established a base from which to mount an attack on the next German delaying position – the Hitler Line. On 16 May I Canadian Corps (I (Can) Corps) took over the southern sector of the Eighth Army front and the following day the Corps Commander, Gen Burns, ordered an attack to be launched on the Hitler Line, followed by exploitation on to Rome. During an early phase in the battle that followed, Lt Edward J. Perkins and nineteen men of the Reconnaissance Troop of Lord Strathcona's Horse took and held a small bridgehead over the Melfa River. They repelled repeated tank and infantry attacks, until reinforced by A Company, Westminster Regiment (a motorized infantry battalion), commanded by Maj Jack K. Mahoney, who arrived with about forty all ranks. Perkins and Mahoney were an inspiration to the bridgehead defenders as they beat off countless enemy attacks, extricated several men under fire and

brought down artillery so expertly that they were able to break up all the enemy counter-attacks that night and to silence all enemy mortars. The next day, the 5th Canadian Armoured Division (5 (Can) Armd Div) poured through the bridgehead and the enemy withdrawal turned into a rout. Rome fell a few days later.

THE AFVS

The Strathcona's Reconnaissance Troop which Perkins was commanding had been re-equipped a couple of months earlier with the American-built M3 light tank from which the turret and 37 mm gun had been removed, being replaced by a .50 Browning machine-gun. So in most respects the 'tank' had a similar performance to the M3 light Honey tank already described in the last section (Alam Halfa, pp. 98–106). The main armament was different of course, being a single .50 Browning M2HB (Heavy Barrel) machine-gun, an air-cooled version of the M2, which was used for fixed installations such as AFVs, where sustained fire was

Turretless Honey tanks like this one were the main AFV in Canadian armoured regimental reconnaissance troops. (Tank Museum)

required. It was – and still is for that matter – a first-class weapon, with a muzzle velocity of 884 m/sec and a rate of fire of 450 to 575 rounds per minute (rpm). It was fed by a 110-round metal link belt. More of these guns were produced than any other American machine-gun used during the Second World War, as they were fitted into aircraft (nearly 1½ million produced of this type alone), used on ships and on land as AA guns, used on AFVs and in other ground roles by all three Services. Other weapons carried in the Honeys were a .30 MG mounted in the bow and (stowed on board) a Bren, four Thompson sub-machine-guns, a PIAT,[1] grenades and HE charges for demolition work. It had a crew

of five and was light, fast and reliable – an ideal recce vehicle.

The enemy tanks which were involved in the action included the PzKpfw V, the Panther, a first-class medium-heavy tank, which owed its development directly to the shock which the Panzertruppen received when they first met the Russian T-34 in October 1941. Panther Ausf D was the German answer to T-34 and was put into production in 1942–3. It weighed 43 tons, had a crew of five and mounted the 7.5 cm KwK 42 L/70 gun which had an excellent performance, being able to penetrate 80 mm of armour plate at 1,000 yd. It could knock out T-34 (head-on) at 875 yd and Sherman at over 1,000 yd. Types of ammunition fired were:

This Panther was knocked out in a town in Italy. It is a Model G, the final production model which took over from the Model A. (Tank Museum)

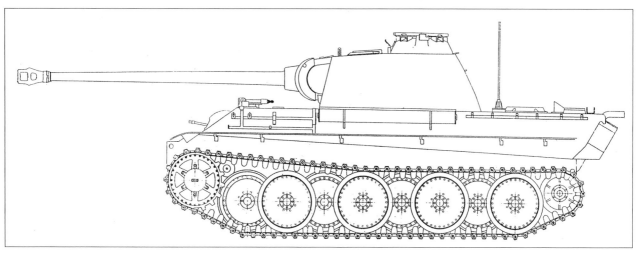

Panther Ausf G, side elevation.

Type	Muzzle velocity (m/sec)
AP 40 (Pzgr Patr 40)	1120
APCBC (Pzgr Patr 39)	935
Hollow Charge (Patr 38)	N/A
HE (Sprgr Patr 42)	700

Seventy-nine rounds were carried for the main armament. Panther also had two x MG 42 (one coax, one for co-driver). Powered by a Maybach HL230P30 700 b.h.p. engine, it had a top speed of about 30 m.p.h. and a range of 125 miles. Panther was a formidable AFV which could outperform most Allied armour of its generation.

The Ausf D which first saw action at Kursk in July 1943 was followed by the Ausf A, which was most probably the model used in this action. It had a new cupola for the commander and improved running gear over the Ausf D. A ball-mounting was also introduced for the hull MG42 to replace the 'letter-box' MG flap.

The final model was the Ausf G which continued in production almost right up to the end of the war. In total some 6,000 Panthers were built, plus a further 500 plus of other derivatives (e.g.: Jagdpanther tank destroyer and Bergepanther recovery vehicle).

THE BATTLE

The 'break-in' battle breached the Hitler Line by nightfall on 23 May and the stage was now set for the armoured advance. A two-phase operation had been planned by 5 (Can) Armd Div:

Phase 1: Vokes Force (based on the British Columbia Dragoons (BCD)) was to establish a firm base 2,000 yd plus of the breach.

Phase 2: Griffin Force (based on the Strathcona's and Westminster Regiment) would pass through the firm base and seize a crossing over the Melfa River.

Phase 1 was successfully achieved by 12.00 hrs 24 May and although resistance was not strong, there was some contact with enemy Panther tanks. Griffin Force passed through at about 13.30 hrs and deployed for battle. Leading the Regimental Group was the Headquarters of the Recce Troop plus one section of four light tanks, commanded by Lt Perkins. A Sqn tanks followed, then RHQ and behind it A Coy Westminsters. B Sqn was off to the right and C off to the left. Everyone on the regimental wireless net heard the CO, Lt Col P.G. Griffin, urging them to push on regardless, but it was not easy country. To quote from a small pamphlet issued by the Beaver Valley Military Museum of Clarksburg, Ontario:

'The attack over the dusty, flat plain was made difficult by innumerable irrigation ditches, vineyards, lack of roads and the fine powder-like dust churned up by hundreds of vehicles of all types. The dust hung like a pall over the valley. The few meandering farm tracks were frequently below the level of the fields. Here and there were patches of woods, small stone farm houses and numerous outbuildings.'

Perkins and his small command raced ahead of the main body of Vokes Force. Their first encounter with the enemy was when they spotted a half-track parked beside a farmhouse. Perkins later explained:

'My troop opened fire, and the crew tried to escape. Five enemy soldiers were hit, two got away. Next we encountered a Panther tank, the first that we had seen in Italy. It suddenly appeared on my right front about 300 yd away. The crew commander was standing up in the turret. I fired at him with the .50 heavy machine-gun and saw him slump over. With its commander hit the Panther kept going and made no attempt to retaliate. We kept going as fast as we could.'

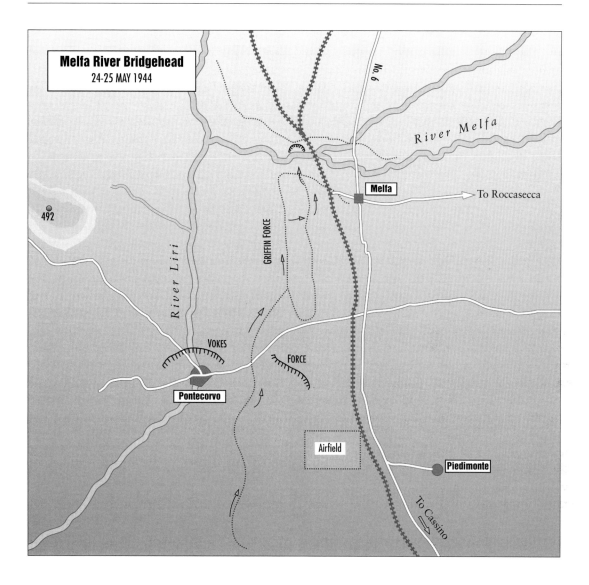

Perkins de-turreted light tank broke down and he had to move to another, leaving a sergeant to make repairs. As they approached the Melfa River, Perkins saw movement in a farmhouse and engaged it with his three tanks. A white flag appeared at one of the windows and eight German soldiers surrendered. He handed the POW over to an infantry scout car which had arrived on the scene and then pressed on down to the riverbank, reaching it at about 15.00 hrs.

Perkins's account continues:

'I parked the three tanks under cover, dismounted, posted three men with Bren LMGs to cover us and, with Sgt C.N. Macey, searched for a crossing. About 75 yd to the right was a narrow track leading down to the river bed. It was steep and difficult to negotiate but passable. Sgt Macey and I crossed the river and as we came up the far bank we came under fire from one of A Sqn's tanks that had reached the river. I contacted them by radio and the fire stopped. I then got into cover on the far side and remained there, trying to find a route for the tanks to climb the bank on the enemy side of the river. The enemy was still unaware of our presence. I sent Sgt Macey back to guide the tanks down the track on the opposite side and cross the river one at a time. Macey and I decided that a track up the enemy side could be made with some explosive charges and some pick and shovel work.'

After blowing the charges and some fast digging by all ranks, they completed a rough track and moved two light tanks over to hull-down positions below the top of the slope, their .50s just clearing the crest. There was another farmhouse about 100 yd away and Perkins spotted signs of the enemy in it, so, together with Sgt Macey and three men, carrying two Thompson sub-machine-guns and a Bren, he crept down the river under cover of the bank and approached the house from the rear. The group rushed in and captured eight well-armed, burly German paratroopers without firing a shot. Having disarmed them Perkins sent them to the rear with one man, also sending Sgt Macey back to guide the Sherman tanks of A Sqn across. That left thirteen men to hold the bridgehead.

A sniper in a tree some 150 yd away opened fire, so Perkins shot him with a PIAT, then sized up the situation:

'It was 30 minutes since we had reached the river. We had seized the bridgehead and now expected to be reinforced by the Westminster's A Coy. But the route we had taken proved impracticable for the infantry's half-track White scout cars. They had to feel their way over difficult ground in the face of artillery and small arms fire. It was apparent that we would have to hold on until they arrived.'

Perkins then had a nasty shock. Two Panthers and a self-propelled 88 mm gun appeared some 400 yd away to his left and began to fire at the house they had captured. The enemy tanks also began to engage the Strathcona tanks on the far bank, who were soon suffering heavily. Sgt Macey then brought the fourth Honey which had been repaired, across into the bridgehead and Perkins stationed it below the riverbank, to be a rallying point and to cover the bridgehead if they were forced to withdraw.

'The situation was becoming very difficult, heavy machine-gun fire was now being directed at us from a farmhouse about 150 yd away to our left, where a group of about twenty German infantry were forming up to attack. We kept up heavy small arms fire to confuse the enemy as to our real strength and caused a few casualties. I decided not to use our PIAT weapons for anything but a tank attack. I now realized that only with the Westminster's infantrymen could we expand the bridgehead, move A Sqn's tanks across the river and continue the advance. They were heavily engaged and not able to give me much support.'

It was a hell of a fire fight. The numerous enemy tanks and SPs which had been on the Strathcona's side of the river were all eventually destroyed, but there were many casualties to A and C Sqns, who lost about half their Sherman tanks, with most of their senior officers killed or wounded. The south bank of the Melfa was littered with the wreckage of war – some seventeen Shermans and five enemy SPs were in flames.

It was now about 16.00 hrs and Col Griffin, realizing the critical situation, ordered Perkins to withdraw, but the young Recce Troop commander was able to persuade him to let them hang on and, about an hour later, A Coy of the Westminster's began to arrive on foot.

Surveying the scene a member of one A Sqn tank crew later wrote:

'As far as one could see through the trees and hedges to the south of the river, the eerie light from burning tanks blended grotesquely with the glow of the setting sun; smoke from burning oil and petrol mingled with the dust that hung over the valley to give the effect of a partial eclipse. Now and then, as the ammunition in the burning tanks caught fire, the sharp staccato crackling of the small arms and the loud reports of the 75 mm shells seemed as an echo of the afternoon's tumult, punctuated by the steady whine and explosion of "Moaning Minnies" landing in the river bed, by the sickening "carumph" of heavy shells landing. . . . Hot and tired, and confessedly stunned by the ferocity of the battle through which they had come, the tank crews dug slit trenches, set out dismounted machine-guns in defensive positions, brewed tea and wondered "What now?" as they listened to the fire fight on the far bank of the Melfa. Each could hear the conversations on the radio, each knew that, although ordered to come back, "Perky" had persuaded the Colonel to let him stay on.'

A Coy, Westminster Regiment, commanded by Maj J.K. Mahoney, had suffered several casualties since its arrival in the bridgehead, so Mahoney quickly organized an attack on the house still in enemy hands to its left and captured it, taking twenty prisoners. Perkins goes on:

'The SP 88 mm on our left was still firing at A Sqn's tanks, and Tpr J.K. Funk of my troop offered to volunteer to destroy it with a PIAT, covered by two Bren gunners of the Westminster's A Coy. He crept to within 100 yd of the SP gun and hit it with his fourth shot. The Bren gunners shot one of the SP crew and the rest were captured. The two Panther tanks withdrew to positions about 800 yd from the house, which Maj Mahoney now occupied as his Company HQ.'

Gen Bert Hoffmeister, who was probably the best Canadian armoured commander of the Second World War, commanded the 5th Canadian Armoured Division in Italy. (CFPU)

Shortly before dusk, the bridgehead was attacked by three Panthers and about 100 infantry. The garrison: '. . . fired everything from .50s to Tommy guns. We also fired PIAT, although the range was too long, to persuade the enemy that we had heavy anti-tank weapons in position.' The enemy tanks broke cover about 400 yd away, firing HE as they came forwards. Fortunately their aim was high, and although two aerials on the Honeys were clipped by shells, there were no casualties. The PIAT fire caused the Panthers to turn away at about 175 yd. They then attacked again, but were once more held off. Visibility was becoming limited and PIAT ammunition was running low. Then for some unaccountable reason the enemy tanks withdrew some 1,000 yd. About this time C Coy Westminsters crossed the river and took up positions on the right of A Coy, then B

Coy crossed and dug in on the left of A. During the night the bridgehead was subjected to continual bombardment by Nebelwerfers.[2] Perkins and Mahoney personally rescued a section of infantry, carrying one wounded man out and '. . . somehow brought their charmed lives and their burden through the fire that was being pumped into the smoke-screen by enemy tanks'. Perkins, who had some pre-war militia experience with the 74th Field Battery RCA, then acted as FOO for the artillery and managed to direct their fire accurately onto enemy targets, which undoubtedly saved the garrison from being overrun.

Daylight saw an attack by the Irish Regiment of Canada scheduled for first light, then delayed until 09.00 hrs and later moved forward to 11.30 hrs, due to difficulties in organizing the necessary fire support. Perkins continues:

'At 08.00 hrs, my CO again ordered me to return to the other side of the river. The situation was still uncertain and I felt the heavy machine-guns of my Honey tanks would be badly needed in the event of another enemy attack. I therefore requested permission to remain until the infantry attack was completed. This was granted and as the

Canadian tankmen prepare their Shermans for action some weeks after the Melfa River battle. (Tank Museum)

infantry moved forward we fired our remaining ammunition to support their attack. At about 12.15 hrs we returned after an extremely eventful 24 hours.'

By the end of the battle, although the Strathcona's had lost 17 Shermans and sustained 21 killed and 34 wounded, their 'bag' was: 7 Panthers, 4 PzKpfw IV, 9 SP guns, 1 field gun, 5 Nebelwerfers, 4 multi-barrel AA guns and 24 assorted soft-skinned vehicles.

A TANK ACE

Maj Mahoney was awarded the Victoria Cross, Lt Perkins the Distinguished Service Order, Sgt Macey the Distinguished Conduct Medal, and Tpr Funk the Military Medal. Their gallant action was later described as being the event that '. . . really broke the German resistance and turned his defence into a rout'. Perkins went on to distinguish himself again in the Battle of the Torrice Crossroads on 30 May, leading his Recce Troop in the regiment's drive to cut Highway 6, the enemy's main escape route from Cassino. He was wounded early in the action, but stayed with his men for some 6 hours, observing and directing artillery fire, always cheerful, an inspiration to all. Promoted to captain and then, after the war, to major, he left the Canadian Army in 1965, after completing thirty-one years, to become an apple farmer in Ontario. He died in July 1986.

Perkins showed that, even with very little –

Lt (later Maj) Edward J. Perkins DSO, hero of the Melfa River bridgehead battle. (Museum of the Regiments, Calgary)

and you cannot get much smaller than a de-turreted Honey with a .50 machine-gun as its main armament – much can be accomplished against seemingly overwhelming odds. It is such spirit and determination that makes a good tank commander, which Perkins undoubtedly proved that he was; he justly deserves his place in this book.

Cpl Alfie Nicholls, a tank gunner of B Sqn, 9 Queen's Royal Lancers, won his Military Medal at El Alamein when he knocked out nine German tanks in one day and a total of fourteen during the entire battle. (Author's collection)

The legendary 'Skip' Rycroft, photographed here as a WO2 in 6 RTR, wearing his DCM and MM ribbons. He was later commissioned and won the MC with 46 RTR. He was killed in action at Anzio on 4 February 1944. (A.W. Green)

Lt Tom 'Conky' Harland, DCM of 1 RTR. Commissioned in the field in the late autumn of 1944, he had been awarded the DCM in April 1943, soon after breaching the Mareth Line, for his leadership, tactical skill and devotion to duty. He was also awarded the Belgian Croix de Guerre 'Order of Leopold'. (A.W. Green)

Sgt Douglas A. Browne, MM of 44 RTR fought in every action from Normandy onwards. On the outskirts of Bremen, for example, when the advance was held up by a battery of 88 mm guns, which had knocked out three tanks, he managed by a perilous foot recce to find a suitable fire position, then guided his tank on foot over boggy ground to reach it. His first shot knocked out one 88 and, after dealing with two more, he caused the entire battery to surrender. (A.W. Green)

VILLERS-BOCAGE: A LIVING LEGEND

BREAK-OUT IN NORMANDY

No book about tank battles and tank aces would be complete without mention of one of the most remarkable tank commanders of all time – Michael Wittmann, the man who held up an entire British armoured division with three Tigers and one Panzer IV, knocking out 20 Cromwells, 4 Fireflies, 3 light tanks, 3 scout cars and a half-track belonging to 4 CLY (Sharpshooters), together with numerous other vehicles of 1 RB and 5 RHA. In fact Wittmann and his small force practically annihilated the entire vanguard of 7 Armd Div, before they were themselves knocked out in this bloody encounter.

The battle took place in the close bocage country of France as the Allies sought to break out of the Normandy beachhead. The main aim of the British Second Army at the time was to capture Caen and a pincer movement had been launched with 51st Highland Division (51 Highland Div) to the east of the town and the 50th Infantry (50 Inf Div) and 7 Armd Div to the west. Neither arm of the pincer was particularly successful, the opposing SS Panzer Corps proving a really tough nut to crack. Meanwhile, however, the Americans, had made good progress in their break-out at the other end of the beachhead, pushing inland some 20 miles, to form a salient around Caumont. It was

therefore decided that 7 Armd Div should wheel behind 50 Inf Div and strike south, so as to be advancing parallel with the Americans; then it would turn due east again to take first Villers-Bocage and then Caen from the flank. Leading 7 Armd Div was a vanguard composed of 4 CLY, A Coy 1 RB and B Bty 5 RHA.

As the history of 4 CLY recalls:

'The next day, the 12th, the Regiment continued the advance with the Reconnaissance Troop leading, then B Squadron, followed by Regimental Headquarters and A and C Squadrons, but movement was difficult, partly because each little village was still strongly held. In the afternoon of this day, new orders were issued which, as will be seen, were to involve 4 CLY in the bloodiest battle it was to fight as an independent Regiment in the European theatre.'

THE TANKS

SS Untersturmführer Wittmann was commanding 2 Kompanie of the Schewere (heavy) SS Panzer Abteilung 101, the Tiger battalion of I SS Panzer Corps which had been formed in the spring of 1944 in France. Tank companies should have had a complement of fourteen Tigers, although at the time of this battle Wittmann had just three available and

The Tiger 1, PzKpfw VI, the 56 ton heavy tank, with its 8.8 cm gun, was probably the most feared tank of the Second World War. Note the Panzerfaust on the ground in front of the Tiger (marked with 'X'). (Tank Museum)

battleworthy, including his own, plus a single PzKpfw IV. His Tigers were of course the PzKpfw VI Ausf E, undoubtedly one of the most feared tanks of the Second World War. At 56 tons, with armour 25–100 mm thick, it was capable of taking enormous punishment, yet its five-man crew could generally expect to remain unscathed, certainly against the vast majority of Allied AFVs, except at point-blank range. It mounted the 8.8 cm KwK 36 L/56 gun, probably the most feared anti-tank weapon of the war, capable of defeating 103 mm of homogeneous armour at 30° at 1,000 m and 84 mm at 2,000 m. Ninety-two rounds were carried for the 88 mm and 4,500 rounds for the three MG 34s (one coax, one ball-mounted on the front plate and one on the cupola – demountable). Top speed was some

23½ m.p.h. and its range was about 120 miles.

Opposing the Tigers were mainly British Cromwells, the five-man Cruiser tank Mk VIII, with which the armoured regiments of 7 Armd Div had somewhat unwillingly been re-equipped when they came back to the United Kingdom from Italy, leaving their beloved Shermans behind them. Cromwell was light (27–8 tons) and fast (top speed on roads of 40 m.p.h.), but its armour was only 8–76 mm thick – so a Tiger could knock it out through its frontal armour at 2,000 m. It was armed with a 6-pounder (Mks I to III) or 75 mm (Mks IV to VII), except for Mk VI, which had a 95 mm howitzer. Sixty-four rounds were stowed for the 75 mm. The 75 mm was an adequate

Cromwells of 22 Armd Bde, like these lined up ready for the Orne River crossing in July 1944, were easy pickings for Wittmann and his Tiger at Villers-Bocage. (Tank Museum)

gun but, as this engagement will show, it did not have an anti-tank performance comparable with the Tiger's 88 mm, even at short ranges. Secondary armament comprised two Besas (one coax and one for the co-driver). Cromwell was numerically the most important British Cruiser tank of the war and formed, with Sherman, the main equipment of British armoured formations in 1944–5, until it was replaced by the Comet.

THE TANK ACE
Born in 1914, Wittmann began his military service with 10 Kompanie, Infanterie Regiment 19 at Freising in 1934, then three years later he joined the Allgemeine SS and was swiftly accepted as a recruit for the élite SS guard regiment: Leibstandarte–SS Adolf Hitler (LAH).

At the outbreak of war he was a sergeant in the armoured car platoon of the LAH in France and the Low Countries. Re-equipped with SP assault guns, young Wittmann got his first taste of tracked AFV commanding in Greece in 1941, with a Stug III. Operation 'Barbarossa' followed, with the LAH well to the fore, and Sgt Wittmann quickly distinguished himself. The Iron Cross Second and First Class followed, the latter awarded for a battle against eighteen Soviet tanks, in which he brewed up six of them, despite the fact that he was commanding a turretless assault gun, with minimal traverse. In early 1943 he changed his Sturmgeschutze assault gun for the Tiger in which he would become the world's most successful tank commander.

By the autumn of 1943 he had knocked out a total of sixty-six enemy tanks, ten in a single engagement which brought him his Knight's Cross, presented on 13 January 1944. Three weeks later, with his personal 'bag' now at eighty-eight, he was awarded his Oakleaves and his gunner, SS Rottenführer Woll, the Knight's Cross. By the time Wittmann and his Tigers moved over to France, his phenomenal tally of tank kills amounted to 117. And there were more to come.

THE BATTLE

The Tiger company had reached the Villers-Bocage area on 12 June, having had a difficult journey via Paris, where on 8 June, near Versailles, it was caught in an air raid during which several tanks were damaged. It leaguered that night in a small wood north-east of Villers-Bocage, and in the morning Wittmann decided to go and have a look at the village, having heard a rumour that the

British had pushed into the SS Corps' left flank. As his small force approached the village, he saw an enemy armoured column leaving the built-up area and moving slowly up the N175 road towards the high ground at Point 213. It stopped at the top of the hill, just past the Tilly road junction and, as no opposition had been encountered, some of the crews dismounted to stretch their legs – the little town of Villers-Bocage had been full of cheering villagers and there were no signs of enemy except for a report of an armoured car being seen observing from the top of the hill north of the town. 'With A Sqn on the objective and all seemingly quiet, RHQ moved over the River Seulles and into the main square. Recce sent a patrol to the south on the road to Aunay, perhaps the deepest penetration into France that had been made up to that time. . . . For a short time all seemed quiet. . . .'[3]

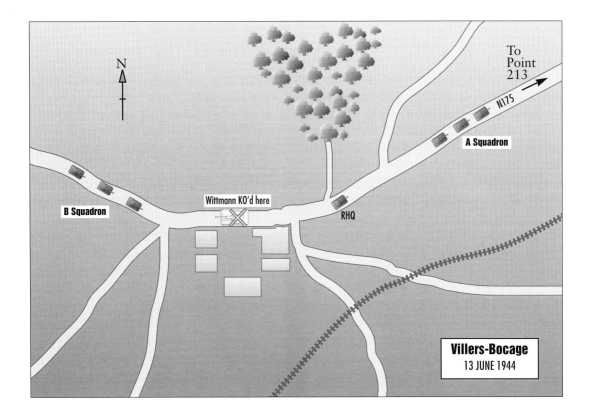

Artist's impression of part of the Villers-Bocage battle, with a British tank firing at a Tiger through the side of a building. The tank looks rather like a Covenanter, which is odd as they never saw action. Fanciful stuff, but presumably meant to portray the eventual ambush of Wittmann in Villers. (*Illustrated London News*)

Wittmann, having seen the stationary tanks, decided to leave the rest of his force and cut around behind the enemy in his Tiger, in order to take a closer look at Villers-Bocage and size up the situation. Entering from the east, he immediately spotted the four Cromwells of RHQ 4 CLY, parked in the main street, knocked out three of them – those of the CO (who was away on a recce), the 2IC and the RSM – but the fourth managed to escape by getting off the road into the garden of a house. To continue the Sharpshooters account:

'. . . and then the most indescribable confusion broke out. Up the street in front, Lt Ingram's Honeys and a dozen half-tracks of the Rifle Brigade were burning. The RHQ tanks started to move backwards down the main street. As they did so spandaus opened up from the windows above and the street began to fill with smoke and the noise of falling slates, punctuated by the sharp crack of an 88 mm. Out of the smoke trundled a German Tiger tank. Maj Carr, 2IC, fired at it with his 75 mm but, heartbreaking and frightening, the shots failed to penetrate the side armour even at this ridiculous range. Almost immediately his tank was on fire, he himself seriously wounded and other members of his crew killed and wounded also.'

Having dealt with RHQ, Wittmann carried on up the road, meeting and engaging the leading tanks of B Sqn. The Tiger received at least one hit and, realizing that he was heavily outnumbered, Wittmann turned round and moved back eastward. He then met the fourth RHQ tank which had been stalking him, hoping to get a shot at the Tiger's rear. This tank fired twice, but the shells did not penetrate and Wittmann fired back and knocked out the Cromwell.

Leaving Villers, Wittmann joined his other tanks, replenished his ammunition and then turned his attention onto A Sqn on Point 175, shooting up the entire squadron and the accompanying Rifle Brigade infantry. This was done very systematically, first knocking out the end Rifle Brigade half-track to block the road so that no one could escape, then traversing down the column hitting tanks, lorries, half-tracks, Bren carriers, etc.,

including a total of twenty-five armoured vehicles. Those tank crews who were not killed were captured by German infantry supporting the German heavy tanks. One of the very few lucky enough to escape was Maj (then Capt) Christopher Milne, MC of the Rifle Brigade, who managed to get back to British lines that night.

Replenishing again, Wittmann decided to return to Villers-Bocage but did not know that, while he had been busy with A Sqn, the situation had changed. Four Cromwells and a Firefly (a Sherman mounting the British 17-pounder gun), commanded by Lt Bill Cotton, had been despatched by B Sqn to contact A Sqn, but having found this to be impossible, had set up an ambush in the main square, together with a 6-pounder anti-tank gun of

The end of a Tiger. Even the great PzKpfw VI was not immune to enemy fire. (Tank Museum)

the 1/5th Queen's. Thus when Wittmann, plus the other two Tigers and the Panzer IV, motored in they were heavily engaged. Lt Cotton wrote later:

'When the Tigers were about 1,000 yd away and were broadside on to us I told 3 Troop and my gunner to fire. The Firefly did the damage, but the 75s helped and must have taken a track off one which started to circle out of control. They shot back at us, knocked the Firefly out, as its commander was hit in the head. However, at the end of a very few minutes there were three "killed" Tigers.'

The PzKpfw IV initially escaped unscathed but was later also knocked out, by a shot up its rear. Michael Wittmann and his crew escaped on foot, evaded capture and lived to fight another day.

Soon after Villers-Bocage, Wittmann was promoted to SS Hauptsturmführer and awarded the Swords to his Knight's Cross, making him the only tank commander to be awarded the Knight's Cross, Oakleaves and Swords in the space of five months. His tally now stood at 138 tanks and 132 guns, plus countless other soft-skinned vehicles. He was then offered a staff posting at a training school but refused, choosing to stay with his regiment. This decision cost him his life.

Wittmann's luck did not hold for very much longer and, on 8 August 1944, while fighting alone against eight Sherman tanks

SS Hauptsturmführer Michael Wittmann poses on the front of his Tiger. (Tank Museum)

east of Clintheaux in the Falaise area, he met his end. He had managed to knock out three of the Shermans, but the combined fire of the other five, attacking from all sides, finally blew his Tiger to smithereens – there were no survivors.

US Armor in North-west Europe: A Quartet of 3rd Armored Division Aces

To add some variety to the pattern of this book, I'm now going to include a brief résumé of the exploits of four American tanker aces, all of whom were nominated in the 1980s under the US Armor Association awards programme, designed to honour the very best of America's tankers and troopers.

A TEXAS TANKER: SSGT LAFAYETTE G. POOL

'Beyond the Siegfried Line in Germany. Here in the mud and wind of approaching autumn, in a town which is clamorous with the crump of enemy mortars and the sigh of our own shells passing overhead, elements of an élite American unit, the 3rd Armored "Spearhead" Division [3 (US) Armd Div], were poised, waiting for the word that would send them slashing into greater Germany. In the new attack, tankers of this striking force would have one regret: that SSgt Lafayette G. Pool, lanky one-time Golden Gloves boxing champion, from Sinton, Texas, could not be there to lead the assault.'

That is how an article by reporter Sgt Frank Woolner began in *Yank*, the Army weekly. It went on to explain that the 'Texas Tanker' had just been wounded[4] on a windy hill in the Siegfried Line, after taking part in the great armoured drive across Europe, during which time he and his tank crew had been

The 'Texas Tanker', Sgt (later WO) Lafayette G. Pool, 1 Company, 3 Bn, 32 Armd Regt of 3 Armd Div. (Thurman C. Smith via Col Haynes Dugan)

credited with knocking out a total of 258 enemy armoured vehicles, capturing 250 prisoners and killing over 1,000 German soldiers. 'Pool is the tanker of tankers,' said his CO, Lt Col Walter B. Richardson. 'He can never be replaced in this regiment.' Pool's latest Sherman, nicknamed *In the Mood*, mounted a 76 mm gun. (It was in

The Sherman M4A2, with 75 mm gun and twin GMC diesel engines, November 1944. In service from 1942, this tank was built in larger numbers (8,053) than any other model. This one has been fitted with 'Duck Bills' on the outside of the tracks to give them better traction in muddy conditions. (US Army)

fact *In the Mood III*, the other two having been lost in action on the way across Europe.)

The article continues:

'Pool's crew was ideal for the task, besides Richards and Close (driver and co-driver) there was Cpl Willis Oller from Morrisonville, Illinois, the gunner, and T/5 Del Boggs, of Lancaster, Ohio, the loader.

Boggs fought with a special fury: he had a brother killed in the war. Oller, gunner of *In the Mood*, is alleged to have seen all of Normandy, France, Belgium and the Siegfried Line through the sights of his gun. He was always quick and alert, such as on the night when the spearhead had driven deep into German lines from Origny in France. It had become quite dark when the order came to halt and coil. Pool opened his mouth to say

The advent of the 76 mm gun considerably increased the fire-power of the Sherman. This one, an M4A3E8, belonged to Capt (later Col) James H. Leach DSC, who was CO B Company, 37 Tank Bn, 4 Armd Div. (Col J.H. Leach)

"Driver, halt", but found himself looking at a big Jerry dual-purpose AA gun in the gloom ahead. He said: "Gunner fire!" And Oller, with his eye perpetually pressed into the sight, squarely holed the enemy weapon before the crew could recognize the American tank.'

Clearly the most important requirement to improve the Sherman after its initial successes was to upgun it, so the Ordnance Department developed the 76 mm gun T1. This was

similar to the 3 in gun M7, but not so heavy. It had a muzzle velocity of 2,600 ft/sec as compared with 1,930 ft/sec for the 75 mm M2 gun and 2,030 ft/sec for the 75 mm M3 and M6 guns. 'Our morale went up when we began to receive the Shermans with the long barrel 76 mm,' wrote Col Bill Lovelady of 3 (US) Armd Div, '. . . the gun had more fire-power and greater muzzle velocity.' Its main advantage was that it would penetrate one more inch of armour plate than the 75 mm,

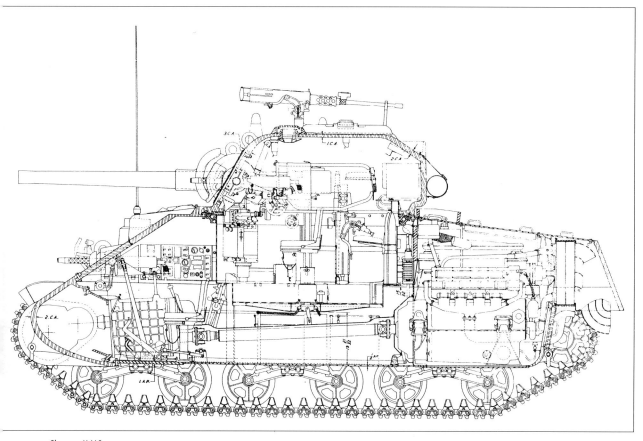

Sherman M4A3.

although its HE performance was not as good. Soon after D-Day, 138 Shermans with the new gun were sent to Normandy.[5]

To return to the *Yank* article:

'Night actions were commonplace to the crew of *In the Mood*. At Colombier, in France, Pool's leading tank almost collided with a Jerry Mk V Panther, pride of the Wehrmacht. The Panther fired twice, and missed, Pool's single projectile tore the turret off the big German vehicle. Again, at Couptrain, the armored column reached its daily objective in the night. Besieged on all sides, unable to send help forward, Colonel Richardson listened to the radio report of the battle from Pool's vehicle. He heard the Sergeant say joyously: "I 'ain't got the heart to kill 'em . . ." And then, over the airways came the mad rattle of the .30 calibre bow gun. And again the fighting Sergeant's voice "Watch them bastards run. Give it to 'em Close!" Surrounded by dismounted enemy troops, Pool and his crew fought steadily until morning brought reinforcements.

'The amazing score compiled by the Texas tanker and his gang is fully authenticated. At Namur, Belgium, they knocked out a record twenty-four hour bag of one SP Sturmgeschutz gun and fifteen other enemy armored vehicles. It was great stuff for Pool. He was proving to himself and to the world, that the American soldier is more than a match for Hitler's "supermen".

This American crew of an M26 Pershing named *Fireball*, commanded by Sgt Nick Mashlonik (second from left), of E Company, 33 Armd Regt, 3 Armd Div, knocked out a Tiger and two PzKpfw IVs near Elsdorf in February 1945 during one of the first combat actions of a Pershing in the Second World War. (Author's collection)

'Again at Dison, in Belgium, as the spearhead neared the great city of Liège, Pool distinguished himself. Acting as platoon commander, he characteristically decided to use one tank, his own, to clean out an annoying pocket of resistance on the left flank of the route they were travelling. After finding and destroying six armored infantry vehicles, Pool discovered that the head of his column had been fired upon by a German Panther tank. Hurriedly he gave orders to his driver to regain the column. Upon arriving at the scene of action he immediately observed the enemy tank, gave a single estimate of range to Oller. The gunner fired one armor-piercing projectile at a range of 1,500 yd to destroy the Panther. The column went forward again, Pool at his accustomed place in the lead.'

Pool was awarded the DSC, the Legion of Merit and the French Croix de Guerre with Gold Star. He was also twice nominated for the Congressional Medal of Honor. The US Armor Association made him a Distinguished Knight in the Order of St George in recognition of his wartime record.

SHELTON C. PICARD AND HIS PERSHING: A 'TASK FORCE' OF ONE TANK

Picard of D Company, 2nd Battalion, 33rd Armored Regiment (2 Bn, 33 Armd Regt), had received a battlefield commission during the latter part of the St Lô breakthrough, and took part in the Mortain counter-attack and the Falaise gap actions in Normandy, the advance through northern France, Mons, the Siegfried Line campaign, the Bulge and the capture of Cologne. On reaching Marburg in

First Sergeant (later commissioned) Shelton C. Picard of D Company, 2 Bn, 33 Armd Regt was described as a 'one tank Task Force'. (Shelton C. Picard via Col Haynes Dugan)

Germany, Picard was assigned one of the new M26 Pershing tanks (see p. 224). Because the tracks of the new tank were too wide to cross the normal pontoon bridges, Picard was told to detour on his own from the unit to an intact bridge and then rejoin the task force for the assault on Marburg. The detour took several hours and Picard felt certain that the task force must be well ahead of him on the main route. He and his crew continued on until they reached the outskirts of Marburg. The task force was nowhere to be seen.

Picard took his tank into the middle of the town and radioed the task force commander, Col William B. Lovelady. He discovered that the task force had been held up in a battle with some anti-tank guns and had had to change routes. Picard was given the new route and told to make his way to rejoin the task force, clearing the anti-tank guns on the way, so that the task force could then continue to Marburg as planned. Picard found the road and as he came around the first bend he could see some Germans behind a log barricade with an anti-tank gun zeroed in, just waiting for the column to come close enough. Picard recalled that he told his gunner to:

'Put an HE in the gun and just let them have it, which he did. You could see logs and guns and Germans flying all over. Then we kept going. Anyway, we met about two or three of the road-blocks and we finally cleared all the anti-tank guns and met up with the column. This is one day that comes to mind every time I discuss the European operations because it was something to remember, taking an objective with a Task Force consisting of one tank!'

Picard was awarded a Silver Star for this action.

CLINTON E. REID: A REMARKABLE SINGLE-HANDED ACTION

On 22 September 1992 three former officers of the 703rd Tank Destroyer Battalion (703 TD Bn) – the OC of 2nd Platoon C Company, the OC of C Company, and the CO of 703 – all signed a resolution recording the heroism of one member of 2nd Platoon, C Company, 703 TD Bn, during the Battle of the Bulge in December 1944. This was Clinton E. Reid and their resolution reads:

'On December 16, the 703rd, detached from its parent unit, the 3rd Armored 'Spearhead' Division near Stolberg, moved promptly to the Ardennes where it was attached to the 1st Infantry "Big Red One" Division in the Butgenbach, Belgium area. German SS and Panzer divisions made repeated attacks to

Lt Col Creighton Abrams (centre), CO of 37 Tank Bn, 4 Armd Div, with Lt Col Harold Cohen, the CO of 10 Armd Inf Bn, also of 4 Armd Div. Abrams was one of the brightest young American commanders of the Second World War, who went on to five star rank and to have the M1 Abrams named after him. (Patton Museum)

break through and outflank US forces defending the Elsenborn ridge. On December 20, Company C's 2nd Platoon was attached to Lt-Col Daniel's 2nd Bn, 26th Infantry. Its front was so wide and the infantry so few that three out of every five TD crewmen had to be employed outside the TD as outpost security.

'That night Clinton Reid's crew was suddenly reduced to only himself, when Frank Glod's hip was broken by the gun's recoil. Reid then single-handedly had to load, climb back into the gunner's seat, select a target, aim, fire, return and reload (always taking care to avoid stepping on his injured companion). Once he even had to back up his TD to improve its field of fire. Although his TD was hit, a tank knocked out the enemy tank before it could finish the kill. The

An M10 'Wolverine' tank destroyer in a good ambush position, 'bombing-up' prior to an enemy attack during the winter of 1944/5. This was the type of tank destroyer manned by Clinton Reid. The officer on the right is Lt Owen McDermotte, OC 1 PLt, C Company, 644 TD Bn. A Silver Star winner, McDermotte and his platoon knocked out two Panthers, two PzKpfw IVs, a half-track and 40–50 enemy on the morning of 17 December 1944. All his crew received Bronze Stars. (US Army)

number of enemy vehicles destroyed by Reid's actions is estimated at five to seven tanks, half-tracks and other armored vehicles. This action appreciably assisted the "Big Red One" in its successful defense of this critical area.'

Clinton Reid's TD was the M10 Wolverine, which used the standard M4A2 or M4A3 chassis from which the turret and its 75 mm

gun had been removed. In its place was fitted an open-topped turret with a 3 in M7 gun. The gun was originally an AA weapon which had had its normal 42 in recoil shortened to about 19 in, and this made for problems. One TD crewman told me that the vehicle would rock so badly every time they fired, that they would have to wait some time before firing a second round. They tried to offset this by placing two 500 lb weights on the back of the

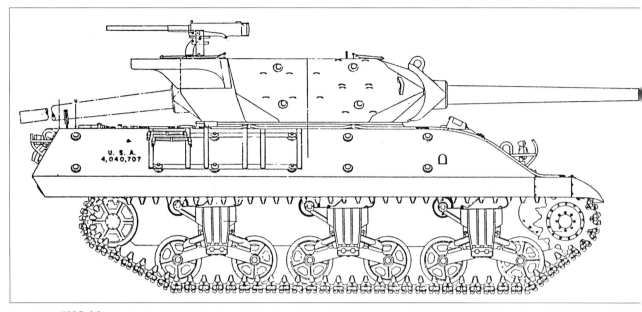

M10 Tank Destroyer.

turret. However, it was an accurate weapon, with a good performance out to at least 1,500 yd.

CLIFFORD L. ELLIOTT HAS 'QUITE A DAY'

'I am outlining one day's action,' wrote Lt Clifford L. Elliott to Col Haynes W. Dugan, 3 (US) Armd Div's historian, in April 1988. 'I was on "point" so many times that I do not remember the day-to-day action, but I can remember action that stood out as an extraordinary day. One such day was 26 August 1944. It started at Meaux and ended at Soissons. My tank and crew destroyed two PzKpfw IVs, two 88 mm dual-purpose guns with their prime movers and crews (about twenty men), two other anti-tank guns and seventeen large trucks. When we reached Soissons we had four rounds of ammo left and my gunner had not missed a shot during the entire drive.'

At Soissons, Elliott was responsible for even more slaughter, writing later:

Lt Clifford T. Elliott of 3 Armd Div, who had a field-day at Fieron on the way to Liège. (Col Haynes Dugan)

The eight-wheeled armoured car, which mounted a 5 cm KwK 39/1 L/60 gun, was known as 'Puma' and fought in Panzerspahwagen companies of twenty-five vehicles, on both the Western and Eastern Fronts. (Tank Museum)

'When we reached the outskirts of Soissons we were on a high ridge overlooking the South road leading into the town. The road made a bend and was hidden by a hill. Up the road and behind the hill was a large German column. We did not see them at the time, but they thought they could get to Soissons. The equipment started roaring down the road. I had my tank platoon in line formation and as the vehicles came down the road the platoon took turns firing at them. It was like shooting ducks in a barrel. One large black truck loaded with ammunition ran the gauntlet without being hit. I told my platoon that the "SOB" was not going to get away from me.

'Down the hill, over the railroad tracks and onto the road taken by the truck. When I reached the first building I gave Cpl Roberts, my gunner, the fire command, at that moment, the truck turned a corner and exposed an anti-tank gun. One of these hard-tyred choke bore 75 mm jobs that we referred to as a "Puma".[6] I yelled: "Down two fire". I don't know whether Cpl Roberts ever adjusted or not, but I know we hit the gun. It was completely enveloped in smoke and flame.'

However, just as he hit the Puma, Elliott's Sherman was hit with four rounds of HE and he and his crew had to bail out. Fortunately the damage was not serious and two days later the tank was back on the road again.

Another very similar battle for Clifford Elliott was at Fleron, on the way to Liège, where an independent observer estimated that Elliott and his platoon were responsible for knocking out at least 150 assorted enemy vehicles. The observer was Robert J. Casey, a well-known newspaper reporter and war correspondent from Chicago, who included a detailed description of the action in his book, *This is where I came in*. Casey had arrived in Fleron to find the street covered with dead horses, dead men and smashed transport. He had managed to find two American officers of whom Elliott was one, the other was his OC Maj Walter McCahan. There were two

Sherman tanks 'actively at work' on the corner, but no other friendly forces anywhere to be seen. Casey found this a puzzle as, looking at the debris scattered along the road towards Liège, it appeared to him that there had obviously just been a major engagement.

' "Where are the rest of the tanks?" Casey asked.

' "What tanks?" countered the major. "The two you see down there are the only ones we've got here. They belong to Lt Elliott."

' "But the battle," Casey persisted. "Who fought it?"

' "It isn't a battle," said the major. "It's a road-block and a very good one. It belongs to Lt Elliott, too."

'Casey looked at the lieutenant – a thin, tired-looking young man – incredulously. "Did you knock off all this stuff?" he asked him.

' "Well," he said, "I suppose I did, or rather my two tank crews did. I'm just a little surprised at it myself." '

Casey comments that Elliott had every reason to be surprised as he could count at least 150 German vehicles burned out or demolished. Only 50 yd from the nearest Sherman was an SP 88 mm, still smoking, plus a number of other ack-ack guns piled up further on under some trees. 'It didn't look to me as if there could be any explanation under the law of averages why Lt Elliott was still alive, and as I got the details of the story the impression became firmer.' He was told how the night before, Elliott and his two tanks had come into Fleron and, acting on a hunch, had set up a road-block, with the tanks in side lanes facing the road and then had sat down to wait. Nothing had happened until nearly midnight, when they suddenly heard the noise of tracks, wagon wheels and horses' hooves – 'I knew it was a big column,' said Elliott, 'it

wasn't coming very fast but it was making a lot of racket.'

First to arrive were the horse-drawn vehicles, with the SP guns travelling in the middle of the road alongside them. Elliott heard them, but still held his fire. The convoy did not see the two Shermans and Elliott didn't fire until an 88 mm SP was almost directly opposite his tank. However, his first shot just bounced off the enemy gun. Luckily the gun wasn't in a position to fire back and before it could swing round Elliott fired again and destroyed it. After that the slaughter went 'according to plan' – a few rounds at each end of the convoy to immobilize it, then the tanks blew everything to bits at their leisure.

Elliott's platoon spent a fairly traumatic night, even being visited by some German infantry in the late evening, who sat round the tank eating their supper – 'My hatch was open and I didn't dare close it,' recalled Elliott. 'The Heinies were so close I couldn't depress any guns far enough to get at them. I just sat there looking at a patch of sky and praying.' After they had eaten, the Nazis got up and left, without realizing that they had been with the enemy.

Clifford Elliott's most satisfactory single engagement came the following night when he knocked out a formidable 65 ton tank destroyer – the Sturmgeschutz mit 8.8 cm PaK43/2, known as Ferdinand or Elefant, only ninety of which were ever built. The armour thickness was up to 200 mm on the front of the superstructure, so Elliott was indeed fortunate to have been able to knock it out with his Sherman. However, it was at point-blank range as he explains:

'After we had intercepted the German column at Fleron we perceived that there were probably more Germans in Liège and that they would try to get out through the main road at Fleron.

'I set my tank in a cross street in Beyne

Maj Gen Bob Grow, CG 6 Armd Div, receives the French Légion d'Honneur, 28 April 1945. Bob Grow was the S 3 (Adjutant) of US Mechanized Force in 1930, and did much good work in the early days of the 1930s and '40s. He typified the brave, energetic American armoured commanders of the Second World War. (US Army)

The 65 ton *Elefant*, also known as *Ferdinand*, was a formidable tank destroyer, of which only ninety were ever built. They mainly served in Russia. (Tank Museum)

Heusay. It was still light and I told my crew to boresight the tube. We set the elevation at about six feet. I did not want to hit the front plate of a German tank, especially if it was a Panther. My tank was about four feet from the left buildings, the street was about 25–30 ft wide. This gave me an angle of 30 degrees, but it also would put the tank or vehicle about 40 ft from our tank before we could fire. My crew and I mounted our tank and sat to wait. We had an extra crew member in the tank. My platoon sergeant's tank had been knocked out so the rest of my platoon each had an extra crew member. Sgt Jones was in my tank.

'We waited for 5 or 6 hours. It was as black as the ace of spades, you could hardly see your hand in front of your face. We then heard the steel tracks on the cobblestone street. We knew that we had some worrisome times. A tank, and not some soft-shell vehicle. The German tank would come a little further and stop. I could follow the sound on the street. I believe the German tank commander knew there was an American tank up the street. He just did not know where.

'He made one more stop and I believed I could see a darker shadow. I yelled at my gunner to fire. I could see the sparks fly. Steel on steel. We fired three more times. The end of the *Ferdinand*!'

In the eight months that Lt Clifford Elliott served with 3 (US) Armd Div, his tank

Gen Jacob Devers, CG 6 and 12 Army Groups, presents 4 Armd Div with a Presidential Unit Citation for their outstanding combat performance in France and Germany. (US Army)

destroyed over 250 pieces of German equipment, including tanks, trucks, artillery pieces, anti-tank guns and even a train. He was wounded four times, knocked out of eight tanks and received the Bronze Star and four Purple Hearts. Discharged in 1946, he was recalled for the Korean War 1950–2, and sadly died in 1993.

SGT FRED KITE MM AT LE GRAND BONFAIT

3 AUGUST 1944

During the Second World War there was only one British soldier to have the unique distinction of winning the Military Medal three times and that was tank commander Sgt Frederick 'Buck' Kite of the 3rd Royal Tank Regiment (3 RTR). All three awards were immediate, the two bars both being awarded within the space of two weeks of hard fighting in France in 1944, when the 11th Armoured Division (11 Armd Div) showed its excellence in the break-out and subsequent advance across France from the Normandy beachhead area.

THE TANK

During the action which took place in a orchard near a farm in the vicinity of the small hamlet of Les Grands Bonfaits (also spelt Le Grand Bonfait on some maps), Sgt Kite was commanding a four-tank troop comprising three 75 mm Shermans plus one Sherman IIC (Firefly). The Firefly was there to provide Sherman- and Cromwell- equipped tank troops with a 'Sunday Punch', mounting as it did the British 17-pounder anti-tank gun. This made it the most powerfully armed British tank of the war, giving it gunpower on a par with Tiger 1 and Panther. The OQF 17-pounder Gun Mk 2 had a muzzle velocity of 1,204 m/sec when using the recently introduced Armour Piercing Discarding Sabot (APDS)[7] round capable of defeating homogeneous armour at 30° at the following ranges and thicknesses:

Range (in yd)	500	1,000	1,500	2,000
Penetration	187	170	153	135
	(in mm)			
(Compare with the 75 mm APC)	70	59	55	50)

Fireflies were only issued on the scale of one per troop because of a shortage of 17-pounder guns. There were in all three models viz:

Sherman IIC (Firefly) based upon an M4A1
Sherman IVC (Firefly) based upon an M4A3
Sherman VC (Firefly) based upon an M4A4

Prime Minister Winston Churchill later said in a Parliamentary Statement about British tanks:

'As the House knows, we succeeded in mounting the 17-pounder gun in the Sherman tank, a remarkable feat, and many hundreds of these are either in action in Normandy or moving thither in a steady stream. . . . I saw with my own eyes an example of the work of its 17-pounder. It was on the approaches to Caen where there was an expanse of fields of

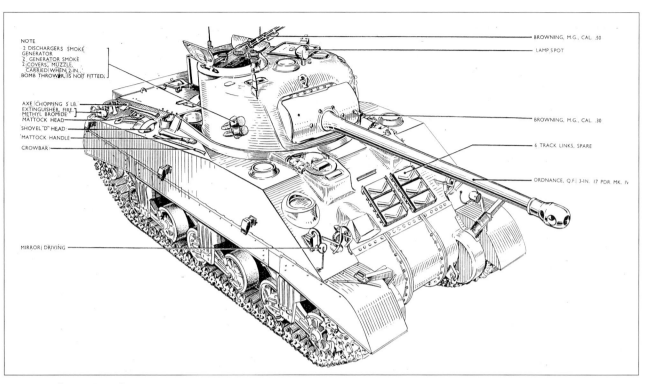

NOTE
2 DISCHARGERS SMOKE GENERATOR
2. GENERATOR SMOKE
2 COVERS, MUZZLE
CARRIED WHEN 2-IN.
BOMB THROWER, IS NOT FITTED

AXE CHOPPING 5 LB.
EXTINGUISHER, FIRE,
METHYL BROMIDE
MATTOCK HEAD
SHOVEL "D" HEAD
MATTOCK HANDLE
CROWBAR

MIRROR DRIVING

BROWNING, M.G., CAL. .50
LAMP SPOT

BROWNING, M.G., CAL. .30

6 TRACK LINKS, SPARE

ORDNANCE, Q.F. 3-IN. 17 PDR. MK. IV

Sherman IIC – Firefly.

waving corn. Gen Montgomery and Gen Dempsey took me there and invited me to count the broken-down Panthers lying about. I counted nine and the General told me that all had been shot by the 17-pounder from one British tank.'[8]

THE ACTION
11 Armd Div had been pushing south-east, as part of Operation 'Bluecoat' through Le Beny Bocage and on to the Vire–Conde–Tinchbray area, south of 7 Armd Div's thrust through Villers-Bocage, with an initial aim of establishing positions on the Perrier Ridge which dominated the Vire–Estry road. 11 Armd Div's task was right flank protection and to keep in contact with the Americans on its right.

'The next day, 3 August, a very annoying thing occurred. A determined, but small force

of all arms managed to infiltrate into Presles, a small village in the valley between the two ridges in the 29th Armoured Brigade area . . . eventually the Germans withdrew, much to everyone's relief.'

That is how Maj Gen 'Pip' Roberts CB, DSO, MC, the superlative commander of 11 Armd Div, described the events of the day on which Kite would fight his last battle of the Second World War, against one of the aggressive enemy battlegroups.

Sgt Kite's troop was part of A Sqn 3 RTR, supporting part of 4 KSLI, with whom it had just completed a rigorous and dangerous march on a pitch black night, through the difficult, close bocage countryside. He had taken up position with another troop in an orchard, near to a farm in the hamlet of Les Grands Bonfaits and later wrote: 'My Sherman was right under a tree. The OC and

It was Panthers like these (pictured near Bayeux) which made for problems in tank battles with allied Shermans and Cromwells. The front one is an Ausf D, while to the rear is the later Ausf A, with the ball-mounted machine-gun in the front glacis. (Tank Museum)

the others were about 400 yd away. I had a Firefly and three 75 mm Shermans with me and there were a couple of RA OP tanks with us.'[9]

The infantry had dug their slit trenches into the edge of an enormous field of corn which bordered the orchard. They had spent a quiet night, had a leisurely breakfast and were just getting down to some 'interior economy', sorting out their tanks, etc, when suddenly all hell broke loose. The orchard and adjacent field were struck by shell and

The Sherman Firefly, with its 17-pounder, was the only tank that was capable of competing with the gunpower of Tiger and Panther, until Challenger (17-pounder on a Cromwell chassis) and the M26 Pershing (90 mm) appeared. This Firefly is leading a column of 75 mm gun Shermans. (Tank Museum)

mortar explosions, heavy machine-gun and tank fire. Kite managed to get himself and his crew into their tank and began to engage an enemy tank on the far side of the cornfield. Some crews were not so quick, having to seek shelter under their tanks, unable to risk getting on board, while others were even worse off – two tanks were already hit and on fire (one Sherman and one artillery OP). Having managed to halt the first enemy tank, Sgt Kite then saw three more and engaged them as well, firing continuously at the Panthers until he ran out of armour-piercing ammunition and had to start to use HE.

His opponents in the orchard battle were probably part of a 10 Pz Div battlegroup, which had been formed from Schwere SS Panzer Abteilung 102 (Tigers) and the Hohenstaufen's armoured reconnaissance group, led by SS Sturmbannführer Hans Weiss. There was at least one Tiger and four Panther tanks in the enemy force that counter-attacked at Les Grands Bonfaits, plus a company of infantry. In *Panzers in Normandy, Then and Now*, Eric Lefevre talks about the operations of this battlegroup in the area north-east of Vire and says that on 3 August its attack on the hill (presumably the one on which the orchard was located) had failed, because the close-in fighting was brutal, but that it had managed to destroy seven enemy tanks, for the loss of only one Tiger (Tank No. 233) which was hit seven times at close range. For the whole Abteilung, the tally of kills for the day was 17 Allied tanks, 2 recce vehicles and 2 anti-tank guns.

Kite writes, '. . . we were in a bit of a mess really. Then I remembered the Firefly.' He had no idea where the crew was, but the tank looked to be in one piece. So Sgt Kite and his gunner, Herbie Barlow, ran across to it and got on board – Barlow into the gunner's seat, and Kite standing on the back decks. He shouted to another member of his troop (Tpr Shaw) to come over and load the gun. They fired a few shots, then the Firefly was hit and later caught fire, so it had to be abandoned. Back in his own tank with Barlow and Shaw, Buck Kite started using the rest of his HE against the mass of enemy targets. He also organized other members of his troop, whose tanks had been knocked out, to fetch some armour-piercing ammunition from the knocked-out Sherman OP some 50 yd away. The tank crewmen together with some of the infantry, who had left their slit trenches, formed a chain and handed up ammunition so that Kite could keep on firing. 'And there was no shortage of targets, as by this time there were about seven Jerries firing at a range of a few hundred yards. I think we hit a couple of them as they stopped and ceased firing.'[10]

They say you never hear the one that gets you, but that was certainly not the case with Sgt Kite. He was concentrating on engaging one Panther when he saw another one swinging its gun towards him. He started to give a correction to Herbie Barlow, but before he could complete the fire order saw the flash of the German tank gun firing and the corn bending as the round sped towards him and he thought to himself, 'This is it. Goodbye!' When he came to, he was lying on the back of the tank, wounded in the head and left hand. He was carried back to a trench where some wounded infantry were lying, but was wounded again as he was being lowered into the trench and this turned out to be the worst wound of the lot. With typical professionalism Kite comments that he thought the German gunner must also have run out of AP ammunition, because he

was using HE. The shell which had wounded him had burst on the front of the tank and had done no damage to the tank or to Barlow and Shaw. If the Panther had hit the same spot with AP everyone would have been killed and the tank destroyed.

A TANK ACE

Frederick Kite had won his first Military Medal in the Western Desert on 20 January 1943, his second at Bras in Normandy, when he had knocked out one PzKpfw IV and one 88 mm gun while holding his position under extremely heavy fire over a period of two days – 18 and 19 July 1944. His third Military Medal was won as just explained, but it is also worth noting that he was

Sgt 'Buck' Kite, MM and two bars, seen here outside Buckingham Palace before his investiture. (Tank Museum)

recommended for the Distinguished Conduct Medal on both the last two occasions. 'The King will get tired of pinning medals on you,' commented one of his comrades. Certainly Sgt Kite was a tank ace of whom the Royal Tank Regiment can be justly proud.

NOTES TO ITALY AND NORTH-WEST EUROPE

1. The Projector Infantry Anti-tank was a small anti-tank weapon that fired a hollow-charge grenade and could knock out a tank at about 100 yd, or fire HE and smoke shells to a far greater range (max. 750 yd). However, it was unpopular because it weighed 32 lb and cocking it was quite difficult.

2. Known also as 'Moaning Minnies', they were six-barrelled mortar projectors, mounted on two wheels.

3. *Sharpshooters at War*, Andrew Graham.

4. Pool was medically evacuated to the States after losing a leg.

5. It was still not as good as it needed to be and it was soon discovered that it would not penetrate the frontal armour of either Tiger or Panther. 'You mean our 76 won't knock these Panthers out?!' Gen Eisenhower exclaimed angrily. 'Why, I thought it was going to be the wonder gun of the war.' (*A Soldier's Story* by Gen Omar Bradley.)

6. The Puma was actually the name given to the heavy eight-wheeled armoured car (Sd Kfz 234/2), which mounted a 5 cm gun, not the more lightly armed 7.5 cm version (Sd Kfz 234/3 or 234/4), but the chassis were identical.

7. The APDS round comprised a sub-calibre round of dense material (e.g.: tungsten), enclosed in a lightweight carrier – known as a sabot (shoe) – which was discarded at the muzzle, leaving the shot travelling on by itself at a much higher muzzle velocity, because the weight of the core plus carrier was less than that of a full calibre solid shot.

8. *The Tank*, August 1944.

9. *Panzer Bait*, William Moore.

10. Ibid.

AN ARMOURED ROAD-BLOCK

THE FATAL MISTAKE

Without doubt Hitler's greatest mistake of the war was to think that he could overwhelm his erstwhile ally, the Soviet Union. His Panzers' dazzling successes in Poland and France must have helped to cloud his judgement, causing him to make the same mistake as Napoleon had made and appreciate neither the size of the country he was invading nor the severity of its climate. He also underestimated the will of the Russian people to resist and their ability to produce battle-winning tanks, although at the start of the Great Patriotic War, as the Russians call it, their armoured forces, though vast, were of inferior quality and design. Much has been written about the tank battles between the German and Soviet armoured forces, which culminated in the greatest tank battle of all time, at Kursk in July–August 1943. In choosing a few examples of low-level actions I have deliberately tried to select those which involved different types of tanks, rather than concentrating upon the Soviet war winner, the T-34.

OPERATION 'BARBAROSSA'

When Hitler launched his surprise attack on Russia on the morning of 22 June 1941, he let loose some 3,350 German tanks spread between three Army groups (North, Centre and South), against an enemy who had a massive 20,000 tanks, although many were obsolete and nothing like that number were actually with front-line units. As in Poland and France, the German blitzkrieg sliced through most of the opposition and cut deeply into Soviet territory, destroying large numbers of Russian AFVs – one estimate was put as high as 17,000. Therefore it is of interest to look at one battle where the Panzerwaffe did not have the upper hand and a lone Russian tank held up their advance for 48 hours.

The engagement took place in southern Lithuania, where, on 23 June, 6 Pz Div (part of von Leeb's Army Group North) was ordered to capture the town of Rossienie, then seize two road bridges over the Dubyana River to the north of the town (see sketch map). The town was captured successfully, and two Combat Teams (CT R and S) were sent forward to take the two bridges. This also was achieved and contact established between the two bridgeheads. Mopping-up operations then took place, which netted some twenty prisoners (including a lieutenant at the most northerly bridgehead, taken by CT R), who were subsequently put onto a lorry and sent back to Rossienie, with a German sergeant in charge.

About half-way to Rossienie, the truck driver was suddenly confronted by a large Russian tank on the road and braked sharply. In the confusion which followed the prisoners tried to overpower their guards, but were unsuccessful, most of them being killed when

Hero of the Soviet Union, Lt D.F. Lavrinienko (first left) with his tank crew from 1 Guards Tank Bde. In the battle for Moscow they destroyed fifty-two enemy tanks (see p. 177). Lavrinienko was killed in December 1941. (Central Armed Forces Museum)

(see p. 177)

Tank gunner Vedeneyev knocked out seven enemy tanks in the first month of the Great Patriotic War, July 1941. (Central Armed Forces Museum)

Guards Junior Technical-Lt G.V. Tyulayev, winner of three classes of the 'Order of Glory'. During the winter of 1945 at Jaroslaw in Poland, he broke into enemy positions and neutralized enemy strong points, personnel and equipment. His tank was knocked out but he fought in the burning vehicle until more Russian troops arrived. (Central Armed Forces Museum)

Right: Guards Capt Konstantin Samokhin commanded a battalion of medium tanks in 1 Guards Tank Bde. During five months of unabated savage battles, he and his crew destroyed 69 German tanks, 13 other AFVs, 82 guns, 48 earth and timber pillboxes, 15 prime movers, 3 bowsers and 117 motor vehicles. Decorated with the Orders of 'Lenin' and the 'Red Banner', he was killed in action on 23 February 1942. (Central Armed Forces Museum)

Guards Junior Lt (later Col) Alexander Oskin, Hero of the Soviet Union, knocked out three enemy Tiger tanks, captured three Panthers in full working order and killed dozens of enemy soldiers at Staszow on the banks of the River Vistula, 12 August 1944. (Central Armed Forces Museum)

Hero of the Soviet Union, Capt (later Col) Alexei Grigorevich led a tank battalion in the crossing of the River Spree, destroying 4 artillery batteries, 5 mortar batteries, 10 APCs and many other weapons, killing their crews. Severely wounded in street fighting in Berlin, he was awarded the title 'Hero of the Soviet Union' on 31 May 1945. (Central Armed Forces Museum)

the sergeant opened fire with his machine pistol. The truck returned to the bridgehead where the sergeant told his CO that the only supply route to the bridge was now blocked by a heavy tank of the KV type. Meanwhile the Russian tank crew had cut the telephone line between the bridgehead and the divisional command post.

Anticipating a counter-attack, the commander of CT R organized all-round defence and moved artillery and anti-tank units into suitable covering positions, while a neighbouring tank battalion got ready for a counter-attack. However, no attack came, and the next morning the division sent twelve supply trucks from Rossienie to resupply the bridgehead. They did not get through, all twelve being destroyed by the Russian tank. Thus, the bridgehead could not be resupplied and in addition, wounded could not be evacuated. Every attempt to bypass the tank

failed, any vehicle attempting to get off the road quickly sank into the mud and became easy prey for the Russian partisans hiding in the nearby forests. It was clear that something had to be done with the tank, even though it was definitely not part of a general Russian counter-attack, but apparently operating completely on its own.

THE TANK

The KV-1 heavy tank was named in honour of Marshal Klimenti Voroshilov, head of the Russian Army in 1936, who had been responsible much earlier for ensuring the development of the Russian tank industry. Unfortunately, Voroshilov was then taken in by the theories expounded by the so-called 'tank expert' Gen Dmitry Pavlov. The latter's findings, based upon the use of tanks in Spain, suggested that tanks were only suitable in support of infantry. This, in turn, led to a

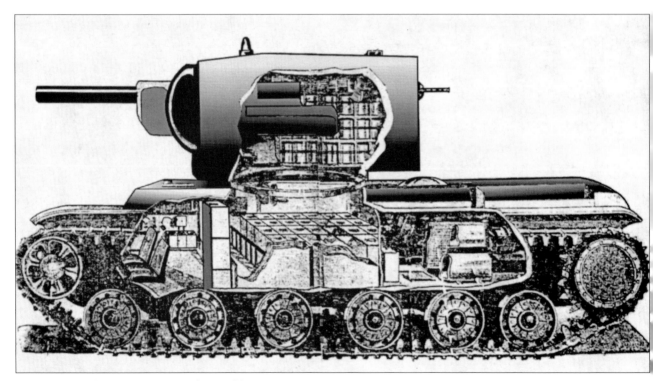

KV-2A, close support version, 1940 production model.

The KV-2, with its monstrous slab-sided turret, was the close-support version and mounted 152 mm howitzer. This one is being inspected after its capture by the Germans. (Tank Museum)

disastrous 'penny-packeting' policy of spreading tanks too thinly across the entire front (cf: French Army), making the German blitzkrieg, when it came, all the more effective.

Powerful and very well armoured, the 46½ ton tank had a crew of five, mounted a most effective 76.2 mm gun and had armour up to 77 mm thick. Prototypes were tested under combat conditions in the war against Finland. It had the same 550 hp diesel engine and numerous other components in common with the T-34. Improved models included KV-1A

(1940), KV-1B (1941) and KV-1C (1942). It had a top speed of 22 m.p.h. and a range of 156 miles. In 1943 it was upgunned to 85 mm, using the same turret as for the T-34/85. The KV-2A was the close-support version, mounting a 152 mm howitzer in a large, unwieldy box-like turret, which put the weight up to 53 tons and proved to be of limited tactical value only. However, its armour thickness was now up to 100 mm which, in a semi-static battle such as this one, made it a formidable foe.

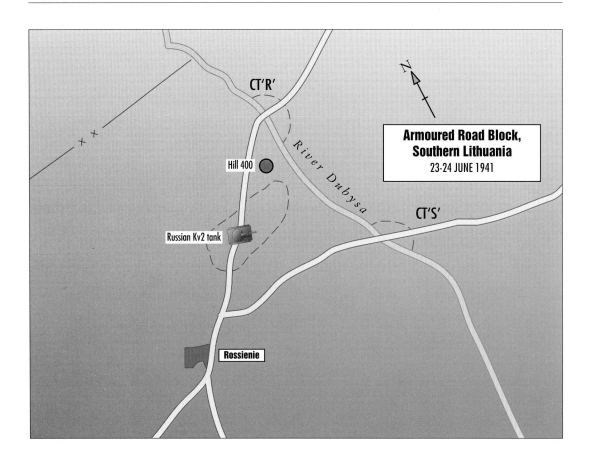

Armoured Road Block,
Southern Lithuania
23-24 JUNE 1941

THE BATTLE

The 50 mm Anti-Tank Artillery Try

An anti-tank battery of 50 mm guns was ordered to work its way forward and destroy the tank. The battery confidently accepted this mission, approaching within 1,000 m without the tank apparently realizing what was happening. Half an hour later, the entire battery was ready to fire and the engagement began. The first round was a direct hit and was followed by a second and a third hit. 'The troops assembled on the hill near the combat team's command post cheered like spectators at a shooting match. Still the tank did not move.'[1] The battery commander was certain that the tank had been abandoned, but he was wrong! After the eighth direct hit, the Russian tank crew had worked out the correct position of the battery. Then, with a few well-placed howitzer shells, it silenced the entire battery, completely destroying two guns and damaging the rest. Having suffered such heavy casualties the gun crews were withdrawn, but the damaged guns could not be rescued until nightfall.

The 88 mm 'Flak' Try

As the 50 mm had failed, it was now the turn of the dreaded '88', with its highly effective AP shells. One such weapon was pulled out of its defensive position near Rossienie and carefully manoeuvred to within 900 yd of the tank, which was then facing towards the bridgehead. Carefully camouflaged with branches and hidden by the knocked-out lorries, the German gun crew was just getting ready to fire, when the

5 cm Pak 38 L/60 anti-tank guns like this one made no impression on the KV-2 turret, except for scorch marks. (Tank Museum)

A captured 88 mm anti-tank gun in Russia is guarded by a Soviet rifleman. Most dreaded of all anti-tank guns, it might well have penetrated the KV-2 in our story, but it did not get a chance to try. (Tank Museum)

tank traversed its turret round and fired, blasting the 88 mm into the ditch and killing many of its crew. Neither the gun nor the bodies could be retrieved because of heavy machine-gun fire from the KV-2. Clearly the tank crew had allowed the 88 Flak to get close, knowing that it was no threat while in motion and that the nearer it got the more likely they were to be able knock it out first shot.

The Engineers Try

At the bridgehead supplies were running low and the troops were having to eat their emergency rations. A staff meeting was held to decide what to do next and it was eventually agreed to send an engineer detachment to blow up the tank that night. All 120 men in the engineer company volunteered, but only twelve were needed. They were carefully briefed and issued with the necessary explosives, etc. Led by the company commander the detachment moved off under cover of darkness, down a sandy path leading past Hill 400, into the woods to its south and on to the tank. Soon they could make out its contours clearly. Removing their boots, they crawled forwards to the edge of the road, so as to observe the tank more closely. They then had to wait, in silence, for about an hour while partisans brought food to the tank crew and talked to them, but eventually all was quiet and the tank turret was tightly closed. At about 01.00 hrs the engineers got down to work, attached an explosive charge to one of the tracks and then withdrew after lighting the fuse. 'A violent explosion ripped the air. The last echoes of the roar had hardly faded away when the tank's machine-guns began to sweep the area with fire.'[2] The tank still did not move and, although the track appeared to have been damaged, the machine-gun fire prevented a close inspection. The engineer detachment then returned to the bridgehead, reporting that one of their twelve men was missing.

Just before daylight there was another explosion from the area of the tank, followed by more machine-gun fire. Later that morning, the missing soldier turned up and explained that he had been detailed as the observer for the detachment. He had watched everything and then waited until he could observe the effects of the explosion clearly. The machine-gun fire had kept him pinned down, but eventually he had crept up to the tank and examined it, to find that the track had only been partly damaged. While looking for his boots he had come across another explosive charge, which he had fastened to the barrel of the gun, then crept under the tank and detonated it. More machine-gun fire had kept him pinned down yet again, and once more he saw that, to his annoyance, the tank had not been badly damaged. He then made his way back.

So all three attempts had failed. A fourth, an attack by dive-bombers, had to be cancelled because none were available, but eventually a fifth plan was formulated. This involved getting a tank formation to make a feint frontal attack on the KV-2, while another 88 mm was brought up behind it. This plan worked, the KV-2 being hit seven times by the 88 mm, while its crew tried desperately to bring their gun to bear. The tank did not burn and following the last hit, the gun elevated straight up '. . . as if even now to defy its attackers'.[3]

The Germans nearest the Russian tank dismounted and went to examine it more closely. They were amazed to discover that *only* two of the 88 mm AP rounds had penetrated, the other five just making deep dents. Eight blue marks were found, made by the direct hits of the 50 mm anti-tank guns, while the results of the engineer attack was only a partially damaged track and a dent in the gun barrel. *No trace of any of the fire*

Top left: Oberstleutnant Bruno Kahl saw action in Poland and at Narvik before transferring to the Panzer arm, joining Pz Regt 21. He took part in 'Barbarossa' with 20 Pz Div and was awarded his first Iron Cross (Second Class) on 8 July 1941. Just three months later he received the Iron Cross First Class and German Cross in Gold. On 8 February 1943 he received his Knight's Cross, and six months later his Oakleaves for his exploits while commanding Panzerjaeger Regt 656 during the Kursk offensive. (Gordon Williamson) Top right: Leutnant Rolf Due served in 19 Pz Div in 'Barbarossa', winning the Iron Cross Second Class. In November 1941 he was awarded First Class. In May 1944 he was promoted to Hauptmann and five months later qualified for the General Assault Badge for twenty-five engagements. In March 1945 he was awarded his Knight's Cross, while commanding a Panzer battalion in the ferocious battles during the Soviet advance. After the war he reached the rank of Oberst in the reformed German Army. (Gordon Williamson) Bottom right: Maj Josef Rettemeier was a gallant soldier and a fine leader of men who won his Knight's Cross on 5 December 1943, near Smolensk, and just three months later was awarded his Oakleaves. He was also a member of the famous Pz Lehr Div in Normandy, being posted to the Officer Cadet School at Erlangen when the division was all but annihilated. After the war Oberst Rettemeier spent three years as military adviser to the Nationalist Chinese forces in Taiwan when the Germany Army was reformed in 1956. (Gordon Williamson)

from the German tanks could be found! Some Germans climbed on board and tried to open the turret but to no avail. Suddenly the gun barrel began to move again and everyone scattered. A quick-thinking engineer dropped some hand grenades through the hole made in the lower part of the turret by the 88. There was a dull explosion and the turret hatch cover blew off, revealing the mutilated bodies of the brave tank crew who had fought to the death and single-handedly held up the strong German force for 48 hours.

In a wood behind the front lines, members of a Soviet tank squadron listen to an address by their commanding officer as they prepare for their next attack, 3 November 1942. The tanks are KV-1As.

EIGHTEEN-TO-ONE AT NEFEDEVO

The previous section demonstrates how much punishment the KV could take before being knocked out. This section presents an example of the punishment which the KV could itself give to the enemy. It concerns a battle in a small village near Moscow in December 1941 and was written up on 8 December 1941 by E. Vorob'ev, a correspondent for the newspaper *Krasnoarmeiskaya Pravda*.[4]

The tank commander's name was Lt Pavel Gudz; he was new to the tank platoon and needed to prove himself to his crew. His principal theory for combat was simple. 'When the German wants to lay a shell on us,' he told his crew, 'then we must have already fired on him. Whoever is first to fire is the winner of a duel.' He went on to say that he did not want the Germans to set the tone for combat; they must be able to do this themselves.

This KV-1 is now on show at the Tank Museum, Bovington. It is seen here at the Lulworth Gunnery School, *c.* 1943. (Tank Museum)

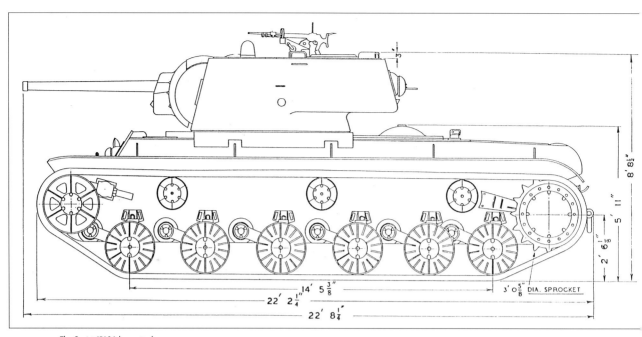

The Soviet KV-1A heavy tank.

His tank was the KV-1A Model 1940, which was very similar to the KV-2 already described, but with the smaller turret which mounted the 76.2 mm F-32 gun. The Model 1939 had been armed with the L/11 gun as a stopgap measure.

He soon had a chance to put his theory into practice because, that morning, 5 December 1941, once the early morning fog had cleared, it was possible to count eighteen enemy tanks in the nearby village of Nefedevo getting ready to move out towards the Russian positions. Lt Gudz arranged for the artillery to put down a noisy barrage, underneath which he managed to move his tank, unheard and unseen, into a suitable ambush position. Now the enemy began moving out of the village and Lt Gudz decided to take on the lead tank, reasoning that 'a burning tank at the head of their column would be visible to all of those following it'. He gave the command: 'On the leader, armour piercing, aim for the joint, FIRE!' The tank shuddered and rocked on its

suspension, while commander and gunner watched anxiously through their sights. The gunner, Lt Starykh, made a few minor corrections then fired again and they saw the lead tank lit up by a brilliant flash, then, less than 15 seconds later, it burst into flames. Starykh immediately engaged the next one in line. The second tank also began to smoke without having fired a shot and no one baled out.

Now the enemy were firing back, but their fire was not aimed, clearly they could not see the big KV in its ambush site. The crew watched the results of their handiwork in the streets of the village, where panic now ensued. The Germans ran from the houses they had occupied and several of them dived into trenches, as the tank crew opened up with their machine-guns. However, this finally gave away their ambush position and shortly afterwards the tank '. . . rang with a terrible noise and Gudz felt as though someone had hit his tanker's helmet with a sledge hammer, after which the lights went out'. A shell had struck the glacis plate and bounced off. 'Blessed were the hands of those steelworkers who had made this shell-proof steel!'

Lt Gudz and his crew kept on firing at the enemy until, after firing some three dozen rounds, the smoke and fumes inside the tank became almost unbearable. The fan was doing its best but could not cope. They were now continually hit by enemy fire, but not one round penetrated. Five enemy tanks were on fire in the village, illuminating it from end to end. Three more tried to leave the village, but as they left the cover of the houses, Lt Gudz and his crew knocked them out. 'Eight cheery bonfires, eight glowing torches!'

With his supporting infantry then putting in an attack, Gudz moved forward with them, engaging the enemy tanks as they entered the village. He blasted another two at the edge of the village, while the remaining eight frantically tried to escape. By now the KV was almost out of ammunition and had been hit on its side armour, blowing off one of its road wheels. Gudz ordered the tank to be pulled back, slowly, so as not to lose a track and

'when it returned to its starting position it did not appear to be the same machine. It was missing fenders, fuel tanks, tool bins and spare track links. . . . Two days later Pavel Gudz and his battalion commander showed the front newspaper correspondent the tank, where he could personally count twenty-nine hits on its armour.'

For his part in the battle on 5 December 1941 in the village of Nefedevo, Lt Pavel Danilovich Gudz was awarded the Order of Lenin.

THE T-34S FIGHT A BATTLE

6 OCTOBER 1941

The main aim of the German Army Group Centre in the late autumn of 1941 was to capture Moscow before the onset of winter. Both 3rd and 4th Panzer Groups (3 and 4 Pz Gp) would take part in Operation 'Taifun', together with Guderian's Second Panzer Army. Marshal Zhukov explains in his autobiography how the Germans had assembled a vastly superior force for this operation with 40 per cent more men, 70 per cent more tanks, 80 per cent more mortars and guns, and twice as many planes as the Russians. Initially, the battle went well for the Germans, and by late September 1941, Guderian's Second Panzer Army had broken through in the area of Orel and was moving on Tula. However, they were starting to run out of steam and to suffer heavy casualties.

A T-34/76D hammers away at an enemy position. This was the improved model with the new hexagonal turret and wide mantlet/mount for the 76 mm gun. Note also the jettisonable external fuel tanks for extra range. The new turret put the weight up to nearly 40 tons. (Tank Museum)

174

Zhukov quotes Guderian as saying how the battles near Orel and Mtsensk failed because

'. . . a large number of T-34s was engaged in the battle, causing considerable losses to our Panzers. The superiority that our Panzers had so far was now lost and seized by the adversary. This wiped out the chances of a rapid and unintermittent success.'

One of the reasons for this change of fortune was of course the onset of winter. As Steven J. Zaloga and James Grandsen explain in their book *The T-34 Tank*:

'The thick mud of September was starting to congeal and solidify and promised a hard and early winter to follow. . . . The Panzers started acting capriciously. Oil in delicate gun sights jellied; other parts froze solid; and the tracks stuck to the ground. . . . It was an inauspicious start for an army so ill-equipped to handle the cold winter of the endless steppe.'

THE TANK

On the other side of the hill, the Russians had just produced a tank which was not prone to such problems, and its appearance on the battlefield came as a decided shock to the Panzerwaffe. 'The best tank in any army up to 1943' is how Guderian rated the Russian T-34, which owed much of its conception to the brilliant but irascible American engineer/inventor J. Walter Christie, whose T3 'fast tank' gave rise to the Russian BT series and then to the fast medium tank series. The T-34 was the first of a highly successful line of main battle tanks (MBTs) and is still to be found in many of the world's armies.

At first T-34 did have its problems, early production batches had serious transmission defects and it is estimated that, in 1941, more T-34s were lost to mechanical problems than to enemy action. With a crew of four men, the 26.3 ton T-34/76A went up to 28 tons with the 76B and 30 tons with the 76C. Apart from the 76A all had the longer

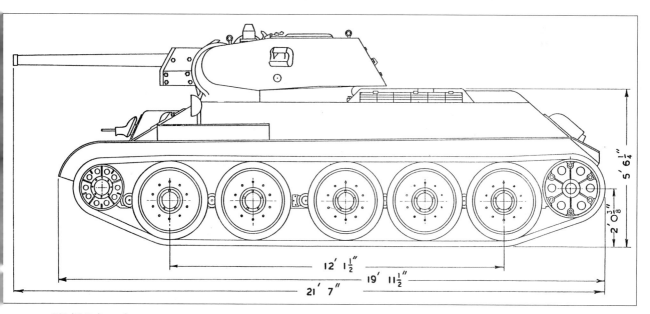

T-34/6B Medium tank.

Into the attack! T-34/76Bs, plus assault infantrymen, move into the attack through the snow. (Tank Museum)

barrelled L/40 gun (L/30 on the 76A), plus two or three MG. Armour was initially 14–45 mm thick, going up to 18–70 mm on the 76D. Powered by a 500 hp diesel engine, it had a top speed of 31 m.p.h. and was extremely manoeuvrable over most terrain.

One of the Russian tank formations opposing Guderian was the 4th Tank Brigade (4 Tank Bde), led by Col M.E. Katukov. One of his major problems was how to prevent the enemy from discovering how outnumbered the Russian forces really were:

'. . . Guderian had two Panzer divisions and one motorized division in his army. Our brigade had but a single battalion of T-34s. The remaining tanks were BT-5s and BT-7s. . . . On the morning of 6 October nearly 100

enemy tanks and APCs with infantry began their offensive in the direction of our brigade, which was straddling the Orel to Tula highway in the vicinity of Mtsensk.'[5]

The brigade was deployed in ambush positions in the groves of trees and bushes that lined the highway. Katukov impressed upon all his tank commanders that manoeuvre was the most important element of the ambush. 'You see,' he told them, 'if you open up first, then you must swiftly change position and carry the battle to the Fascists in such a manner that they have no idea what hit them or where it came from.'

Fifty plus Panzers, belonging to 4 Pz Div, approached the ambush position during the night of 6/7 October together with Panzergrenadiers in half-tracks. They caught the full force of the ambush, the T-34s acting on their commander's orders and manoeuvring, as well as firing. For example, the T-34 of Lt Kukarin broke out of its ambush position and headed straight for a group of PzKpfw IIIs and half-tracks.

'The Fascist tankers opened fire on him. But his driver-mechanic, Fedotov, skilfully urged the machine forward. When he was 600–800 m from the enemy, the tank halted. Sgt I. Lyubushkin opened fire. His fire was very precise and accurate. Four shots – four destroyed enemy tanks! One of the enemy shells struck the side of the '34. The driver-mechanic was wounded. The tank commander gave the command for the tank to back up. Fighting his pain, Fedotov managed to guide the vehicle backwards. When the tank stopped again, Lyubushkin opened fire once more and proceeded to destroy four more enemy tanks. Having used the fire-power, protection and mobility of the

T-34 with great skill, this one single tank crew was eventually to destroy sixteen Fascist tanks in a single battle!'[5]

And they were not the only tank to be so successful. In the same engagement Lt Lavrinienko with his platoon of four T-34s, supported by three KV-1s under Sgt Antonov, knocked out eleven enemy tanks plus a pair of artillery guns, which the KVs squashed flat. By the time the battle was over (not until noon on the 7th) the Germans had lost 43 tanks, 16 guns and 6 trucks – for the loss of 6 T-34s, only 2 of which were damaged beyond repair. As the German advance moved slowly onwards, 4 Tank Bde continued to decimate the enemy, putting a total of 133 tanks out of action. Several of the Soviet tank men became aces – Lyubushkin was among the first to be awarded the distinction of 'Hero of the Soviet Union', while Lavrinienko, who was killed two months later at Volokolanski, knocked out a staggering fifty-two enemy tanks in his short two-month battle career.

MARIA'S TANK

A WOMAN TANK DRIVER

Although the next example could not be called a tank ace as she occupied the driving seat of a T-34 for most of her career, the story is sufficiently remarkable to warrant inclusion. This is how it was told in a wartime issue of the magazine of the Royal Tank Regiment, *Tank*:

'Maria Oktyabrskaya, 38 years old, was hard hit by the war. Her husband, a Regimental Commissar, had been killed in action, her two sons had perished and her old parents were left behind in German-occupied territory. On top of all this Maria had to evacuate her beloved Sebastopol. Without home or family she had but one thought and that was to take revenge on those who had broken her life. She sold her trinkets and embroidered linen (her own fine work) and donated the proceeds to the Red Army Aid Fund. Then she decided to sell everything she had and to

Maria's tank. Mariya Vasilyevna Oktyabrskaya, posthumously awarded 'Heroine of the Soviet Union', was one of a small number of Russian women who commanded a tank in action. (Central Armed Forces Museum)

use the money to build a tank. She wrote a letter to Stalin asking permission to drive this tank into battle. Her request was granted.

'Maria zealously studied to become a tank driver and mechanic. In a difficult 1,350 kilometre try-out she showed that she had become an expert. By this time the tank she ordered was completed. A brand new machine bearing the inscription "Maria's Tank" was delivered to Sergeant Maria Oktyabrskaya. Henceforth the tank was her home. She decorated its steel walls with photographs of her loved ones, on whose behalf she was going out to fight the enemy.

'In the forward lines Maria became a mother to her crew, which was made up of young people, and took care of them all. She got up before the rest, prepared their meals, and when necessary, helped them wash and mend their linen. Many long evenings during lulls in fighting they would sit together round the camp fire, or in a bunker, talking about their past lives and the suffering of the people. In her first battle, when her tank broke through German infantry, Maria displayed marvellous composure and endurance.

'Battle followed battle. Attacks, reconnaissance thrusts, ambushes, all became part of everyday life and Maria soon became a seasoned tank man. Hardships and dangers at the front seemed to make her younger and to endow her with greater energy. One day the machine was damaged by an enemy shell. For three days the crew lived in the crippled machine, Maria was wonderful. With shells bursting all around she kept up her cheerful banter and seemed concerned with only one thing – what her new 'sons' planned to do after the war. After the attack on Maria's tank, among others, she took cover in a small wood, but the Germans suddenly opened up artillery fire, damaging the tracks of Maria's tank. The crew jumped out to repair them. "Keep inside Maria," said the turret commander, "we'll get along without you." But Maria wouldn't hear of it. Two shells burst nearby and the intrepid tank driver fell wounded.

'I met Maria recently in hospital. She was well on the way to recovery and for her courage has received the Order of the Patriotic War.'[6]

Sadly, this was not the end of the story. Maria went on to become a tank commander, but was badly wounded near Kyrnka on 18 January 1944, after knocking out two enemy guns. She died of her wounds two months later and is buried in the 'Wall of Glory' in Smolensk.

A 'Winter Tank Ballet' at Workers' Settlement No. 5

During the Russian offensive on the Leningrad and Volkhov fronts in January 1943 a surprising action took place near Workers' Settlement No. 5, in the vicinity of Leningrad. The Germans had been working on the settlement for some time, turning it into a veritable fortress, with trench lines, anti-tank ditches, berms and wire obstacles. Within the garrison were a number of Tiger tanks belonging to 502nd Heavy Panzer Battalion (502 Hy Pz Bn), which had helped to drive back some of the most determined Russian assaults. However, on 16 January, during yet another attack, the Tigers were outmanoeuvred and defeated by a much smaller opponent. This particular engagement involved some recent Russian reinforcements, which included a battalion of light 'Baby' T-60 tanks from the 61st Light Tank Brigade (61 Lt Tk Bde). One of its companies, commanded by Lt Dmitry Osatyuk, was supporting the attack against Workers' Settlement No. 5, leading the advance, when his command tank was hit by enemy artillery fire, damaging one of its tracks. With the help of the company fitters the damage was soon repaired and Lt Osatyuk hurried to catch up with the rest of his company. He had only gone forward a short distance when he spotted three Tigers coming out of a nearby wood. The Tigers were forced to move slowly, following one behind the other,

as the swampy ground did not allow them adequate room to spread out into proper combat order. They did not appear to notice the little Russian tank just in front of them, but if they had done so would hardly have been bothered by its presence. However, Osatyuk realized that if he did nothing the Tigers would be able to carry on unchallenged, and attack the assaulting Russians from the rear with disastrous consequences.

THE TANK

The T-60 scout tank weighed just 5.8 tons, had a crew of two men – in this case the driver-mechanic was Starshina (Sgt Maj) Ivan Makarenkov, who, like Dmitry Osatyuk, was an absolute expert on the 'Baby' and loved it dearly. The tank was armed with a 20 mm cannon and a machine-gun. The cannon was an aircraft-type automatic cannon, known as the TNsh in its tank version, for which 780 rounds were carried. Its armour was 7–20mm thick, so it would only keep out small arms fire. Built in the early 1940s as a replacement for the then obsolescent T-26 series, some 6,000 were built by 1943. A highly manoeuvrable little vehicle, it had a top speed of nearly 30 m.p.h.

THE BATTLE

'Lt Osatyuk had to make a quick decision – he must save the infantry and his tank

The tiny T-60 light tank weighed just 5.8 tons and was armed with a 20 mm gun, so it was no match for any of the German tanks, let alone the formidable Tiger. However, Lt Osatyuk 'danced' his way to success. (Tank Museum)

company but how? Make a ramming attack? Start a fire fight? Firing shells from his fast-firing 20 mm cannon at these beasts would be like shooting peas at an elephant. . . . But there was one other thought that came to him. . . . 'The lieutenant commanded the driver-mechanic: "Reverse!"

' "We can't show our tail to them!" exclaimed Makarenkov, "or they'll pick us off with the first shot!"

' "But you Vanya, back so well, even courteously. Let's dance before them, so that, if luck is with us, they won't be able to draw a bead on us. Dance and dance, and try to make it back into the grove of trees where our artillery is located."

' "Got it!" answered the driver-mechanic. "Let's hope that our artillery boys don't make a mistake!"

' "Never happen – our artillerists are a race of keen-witted people," the lieutenant exclaimed to his subordinate. "Now, dance Vanya!" '7

And that is just what the little tank began to do. Turning in circles and pirouettes so quickly in front of the leading Tiger that its crew were mesmerized. The Tiger halted, while the commander tried to decide what to do next. Eventually he opted to attack, but the T-60 was never still long enough for him or his companions to satisfactorily draw a bead on it in order to carry out a successful engagement with their fearsome 88 mm guns. The T-60 and the Tigers followed one another into the peat bog and clambered out again. The enemy tanks continually interfered with each other's line of sight while 'Baby'

Tigers in Russia. Was there ever a more menacing sight than the great bulk of Tiger, silhouetted against the sky? (Tank Museum)

adroitly eluded them, Makarenkov throwing the little tank about so much that none of them were able to engage it. Osatyuk was continually firing his 20 mm cannon to keep the German tank crews buttoned up inside their turrets.

' "Enter the woods over there and then circle around to the edge again," ordered Osatyuk. Makarenkov had never worked the steering levers with such speed and skill. Swerving from side to side, the T-60 shot into the trees in a cloud of flying snow. "Turn left!" ordered the lieutenant after about 10 metres and the little tank responded to his commands. The Tiger hard on their heels did the same, presenting its side to the waiting artillery guns, who had fortunately guessed what Osatyuk was trying to do in his game of 'cat and mouse' and were ready and waiting.

'Two 76 mm shells slammed into the side of the enemy tank. Seconds later there was a tremendous explosion, followed in a few moments by another, as the second tank suffered the same fate. The third Tiger wisely turned around and left the battlefield. "There it is, Vanyushka, that is what you get with courtesy!" exclaimed Osatyuk. The tank then rejoined its company and went on with the assault, which this time was successful.'

Hero of the Soviet Union, Col (Retired) Dmitry Ivanovitch Osatyuk survived the war to tell of how his 'Baby' played the game of cat and mouse with the Tigers.

THE DEFENCE OF THE VIENNA BRIDGEHEAD

12 APRIL 1945

THE ASSAULT ON VIENNA[8]

On 6 April 1945 Soviet forces launched an all-out assault on Vienna. They had to fight for every street, for every building, for every room and for every cellar. The German garrison defended tenaciously and there were many remarkable small unit actions, in which a handful of defenders held off far greater numbers of assaulting forces. However, the pressure was inexorable, and by 12 April only one bridge in the vicinity of Vienna was left standing over the Danube. This was the Florisdorf Bridge, in the 21st District, where a mixed bag of elements of various SS units – about two battalions in total and supported by a handful of tanks – held a small area some 1 to 2 km wide, on the southern side of the bridge. It was essential for the Germans to retain the bridge, in order to buy time so that a properly co-ordinated defence could be set up on the northern bank. The Russians wanted the bridge intact to aid their advance, so were prepared to spend time and effort on capturing it unblown. The Germans hoped to impose as much delay as possible, then blow the bridge, which was fully wired for demolition, before the Soviet Army could take it.

On the afternoon of 12 April, the Regimental Commander of Das Reich Panzer Regiment, SS Obersturmbannführer Enseling, visited an area where some tank crews were resting or working on their vehicles. These included tank number 227, a replacement tank, which now belonged to SS Obersturm-führer Arnold Friesen. Although only nineteen, Friesen was a veteran tanker, having fought at Kursk, in Normandy, the Ardennes and more recently, in Hungary. At the time he had a remarkable ninety-seven tank kills to his credit,[9] while his Panther crew were equally experienced – Sgt Gert Ehegotz, the gunner, had been with the unit since 1943 and was twenty-three years old, Cpl Fritz Sprieg, the loader, was nineteen, Sgt Guenter Rau, the radio operator, was twenty, while the oldest member of the crew was the driver, Sgt Alwin Sternauth, aged forty-four, who had been driving tanks for years and was a master mechanic. He was like a father to the younger members of the crew, calling them all (Friesen included) by nicknames.

Enseling called the crews around him – there was a battery of Hummels[10] firing nearby, so the noise was considerable and he had to shout to make himself heard. He explained how the situation at the bridge was critical. The tanks supporting the infantry were nearly out of ammunition, but no resupply trucks could get across the bridge because of the intense enemy fire. He wanted a volunteer tank crew, therefore, to take the ammunition across in their vehicle. The men, who knew very well that it was a suicide mission, were initially silent, but then Sternauth raised his hand, nudged Friesen and said 'Baby, we're going!'

That afternoon the crew worked hard, loading up ninety-two rounds of ammunition for the Panthers 75 mm main armament, plus machine-gun ammo, insulated containers of hot food, cigarettes and even two bottles of brandy. In addition, they would tow a trailer with a further fifty rounds of main gun ammo. Late in the afternoon, Friesen said goodbye, shook hands with Enseling and set off towards the bridge. They arrived about 17.00 hrs, parked in a covered and concealed position, then Friesen, accompanied by Sternauth, went forward on a foot recce.

On the friendly side was a battery of 88 mm Flak/anti-tank guns and Friesen talked to the commander, Lt Struwe, a Luftwaffe officer, who told him that there was a bomb crater in the middle of the bridge, making driving difficult. He asked them what they were going to do and when told said, 'Not for a million marks would I drive across that bridge, only the Waffen SS could be so crazy!'.

Friesen's plan was to drive across the bridge at top speed under cover of darkness. The Panther has seven forward gears and, in order to get up to top gear for the rush across the bridge, he decided to start some 2 km away. While some of the crew watched the bridge, Sternauth and Friesen walked the route and then tried to memorize every foot of the bridge, so that they would be able to swerve out of the way of the shell hole in the pitch darkness. Friesen had also requested covering fire from the Hummels as they began their run and this came down together with fire from the German units on the northern bank. Small arms fire ricocheted off the turret, but they crossed safely to the southern side and drove off the bridge into an open plaza (see map).

THE BATTLE

No sooner did the Panther reach the plaza than the battle began in earnest, as an artillery barrage raked the area, rounds landing dangerously close to the tank. They were quickly guided off the plaza and into a position in the front line. Down the street was another Panther[11] and Friesen drew up behind it, as close as possible, and dropped the ammunition

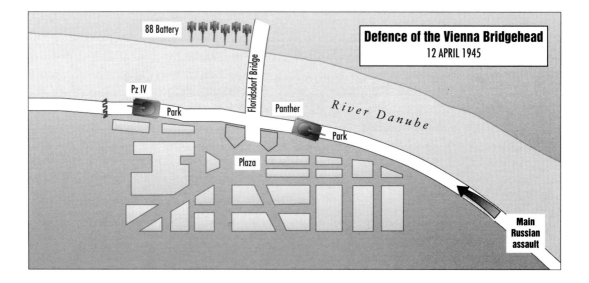

trailer. The other Panther crew then transferred the much needed ammunition; they had been constantly in action for several days and were down to their last five rounds. They also enjoyed the rations which Friesen had carried over the bridge.

The replenishment safely completed, Friesen backed his Panther into a building for the night and then went to talk to the other tank commander, who told him that the situation was still confused, but that the Russians had been kept away from the bridge by well-positioned, experienced German infantrymen. As they were talking, a tank suddenly appeared behind them and the infantry screamed that it was enemy. Friesen rushed back to his tank, while the other commander traversed rear:

'The street was bedlam. German infantry and half-tracks were in the line of fire. A flare went up, illuminating the street. The Russian tank crew, realizing their situation, flew past the Panther towards their own lines, before it could engage. The Russian tank escaped.'[12]

Order was quickly restored, the half-tracks were taken off the street, the infantry went back into cover, all was quiet again.

Suddenly the other Panther exploded – hit by a bazooka, fired by an urban guerilla from a building across the street, the entire tank crew was killed. The German infantry were quick to exact retribution, clearing the building room by room, with grenades and satchel charges. All inside, civilian or military, were killed. Friesen then took control and restored order. The ammunition in the blazing Panther continued to explode while he radioed back to RHQ. He was told to hold the bridgehead until the following night.

At 04.00 hrs he moved his tank to the infantry command post in control of the bridgehead, where he met the commander, Sturmbahnführer Schmidt. He told Friesen

that the only other operational tank in the bridgehead was a PzKpfw IV. Four others had been knocked out by guerillas during the night. The infantry had dealt comprehensively with the surrounding buildings and streets, blocking them with dynamite charges and covering them with automatic weapons. However, the major problem was the riverside road, which could not be blocked on the east side. It was decided that the Mk IV would be sited to protect the western approach, behind a barricade of steel railway lines, while Friesen's Panther, plus two 75 mm anti-tank guns, would defend the eastern approach.

Friesen was worried about guerillas, so Schmidt promised to occupy or guard all the waterfront buildings in the German sector. This was done and all settled down to what was to be, for the Panther crew anyway, one of the busiest days of the war. They were positioned in a riverside park and had made use of the natural foliage to camouflage their tank. At about 08.00 hrs the first T-34 appeared, coming round a bend in the road about 900 m to the east. Friesen let the enemy tank get to within a few hundred metres, when it made a sharp left turn into a side street. Gunner Ehegotz fired immediately, hitting the T-34 in the right rear. The tank exploded, the first of their fourteen 'kills' that day. During the morning four more tanks appeared and were swiftly knocked out. Then around noon a Russian jeep appeared, its occupants, who appeared to be drunk, were waving a large Soviet flag and drinking vodka. Both Rau and Ehegotz fired at them with their machine-guns (Rau firing the hull MG), killing them all.

Meanwhile, Russian infantry were crawling forward, building by building, towards the bridge and soon rifle grenades started to hit the Panther, but could not penetrate its thick frontal armour. Backing the tank into a hull-down position, Friesen hosed all the surrounding buildings with machine-gun fire, then collapsed them with main gun fire. No more rifle grenades were fired.

Early that afternoon Russian fighter-bombers flew overhead and dropped their bombs indiscriminately from a high level, so none landed near the tank. The IL-2s returned many times that afternoon, but never bombed with sufficient accuracy to worry the Germans.

Then around 14.00 hrs, Obersturmführer Weber, commander of the German infantry along the river front buildings, told Friesen that a Russian heavy tank had been spotted, sitting just outside the German perimeter. This was identified as a Josef Stalin IS-III, probably the most powerful Soviet tank to see action in the Second World War. Friesen immediately dismounted and together with the infantry commander carried out a careful foot recce to observe the enemy tank. They found it quite easily, in a side street, facing north, some 75 m from the river front road and covered in infantrymen, who were smoking and drinking: '. . . taking a rest from the war!' Friesen asked Weber to have a squad of men ready with Panzerfausts and automatic weapons. Once the Panther had knocked out the tank, they could deal with any survivors.

Going back to his Panther, Friesen got out his enemy AFV recognition information, in order to determine the exact height, etc. of the IS-III. He wanted to ensure that he got a perfect first-round hit, as his opponent was both better armed and better armoured than T-34. He was confident that his long-barrelled KwK 42 gun could penetrate its armour, provided he hit it in the right spot. He then carefully briefed his crew. Sternauth would drive forward until Ehegotz could get a clear shot at the enemy, then, once the round had been fired, quickly reverse and get away back into cover. The gunner would have to shoot while the tank was moving, having ensured that both elevation and traverse readings were correct. They even had a practice session in the park before Friesen was completely satisfied that all was ready.

THE TANK

As we have already described the Panther, let us look at its opponent, the IS-III. Known as *The Pike* by the Soviet tanks troops because of its pointed nose, this was the last and most streamlined version of the Josef Stalin heavy tank, which came into service in early 1945. It weighed nearly 49 tons, had armour 24–120 mm thick and mounted a formidable D-25 L/43 122 mm gun, in a low, flat ballistically shaped turret, which gave maximum protection through shot deflection. Powered by a 519 hp diesel engine, the four-man IS-III had a top speed of 23–5 m.p.h. and a range of just under 100 miles. A formidable opponent for the Panther.

A comparison of the two weapon systems is worth looking at:

Gun	Type of ammo	Penetration in mm of armour at 30°			
		500	1,000	1,500	2,000yd
75 mm KwK 43	APCBC	141	121	104	89
122 mm		140	130	120	110

However, as the ranges were short, there was little in it.

If the Panther was to knock out this tank, then surprise would be crucial, so the infantry fired their automatic weapons to keep the enemy's heads down and to mask the noise of the Panther moving into its firing position. Ehegotz fired and the round struck the IS-III just below the turret ring, penetrating the armour and exploding the ammunition and fuel. It was a total 'kill'. Friesen moved his tank back into its hull-down position. It was 14.15 hrs. A few minutes later, three more

These are Josef Stalin IIIs, like the one which SS Obersturmführer Arnold Friesen managed to knock out at the Vienna bridgehead. They are seen here on the Allied Victory Parade in Berlin. (Tank Museum)

T-34s appeared at the end of the street, supported by Soviet infantry. They were engaged by the Panther and knocked out, while the German infantry eliminated the Russian infantry.

While Friesen had been dealing with the T-34s, a Russian anti-tank gun had managed to get into a firing position and hit the Panther on its glacis plate, just in front of the radio operator's position.

'"Anti-tank gun!" yelled Friesen. An anti-tank round was currently in the breech of the 75

mm, but it was faster to fire it off than to unload it. Ehegotz squeezed the trigger and emptied the breech. "High explosive!" ordered Friesen. The loader obliged by loading an anti-personnel round. "Fire!" Friesen screamed, and round after round sought out the anti-tank gun and its crew. Smoke again filled the turret and Friesen vomited once more, but there was nothing left in his stomach. The anti-tank gun was utterly demolished.'[13]

Friesen and his crew then backed the tank into a hide position and took a well-earned

A Panther crew in relaxed mood. (Author's collection)

break. The hatches were opened, the tank aired out, coffee was brewed and they all relaxed slightly – but not for long. About 17.00 hrs four more T-34s appeared at the curve and roared down the river road towards the bridge, much as they had done that morning. And once again Ehegotz hit them in their flanks, destroying three out of the four. Another assault on the bridge had been stopped – there would be no more tank attacks before last light. It was just as well because the Panther's turret was now well and truly jammed. Friesen informed the infantry that he would have to move his tank into the underground garage of a building near the bridge as soon as it was dark, so that they could attempt repairs.

At dusk the crew reversed their Panther all the way back to the bridge, then they moved forward, across the street and into the safety

of the underground garage. Rau and Friesen stood guard with Panzerfausts, while the rest of the crew worked to free the obstruction in the turret ring. While this was going on, the infantry moved back in small groups across the bridge, fortunately without any Russian reaction. Then, about 20.30 hrs, Russian tanks began to approach the bridge once again, passing close by the building where the Panther was hidden and taking up a 360° perimeter on the plaza. No enemy infantry had accompanied them, so, realizing how vulnerable the enemy tanks were, Friesen decided to do some tank hunting, but first of all he called the infantry command post and reminded them not to blow the bridge whatever happened, until the Panther was safely across.

Friesen and Rau, taking three Panzerfausts, made their way quietly to the plaza, where they found the Soviet crews buttoned up inside their tanks, talking nervously at being out on a limb. They tried to creep closer so as to use their Panzerfausts, but suddenly the Russians started their engines and began to move back towards their own lines. Friesen let two of the tanks pass, then knocked out the other two with the Panzerfausts – their thirteenth and fourteenth enemy tanks killed that day. Returning to the Panther, Friesen found that fortunately the fault had been rectified and the tank was once again fully battleworthy.

The infantry command post then co-located with the Panther, covering the withdrawal over the bridge of the various infantry elements, the tank being placed behind a wall of sandbags which the infantry had erected for them. The night was fairly quiet, and at 22.30 hrs the PzKpfw IV moved back across the bridge, followed at 23.00 hrs by the infantry command post.

‘ "See you in Stammersdorf," said Friesen to Schmidt.

‘ "You sound to be pretty confident about that," Schmidt replied.

‘ "I've been confident all day long," smiled the Panther commander.

'Schmidt laughed. "I'll tell you what, I'll wait on the other side of the bridge."

‘ "And you know what *not* to do before we get there?" queried Friesen.

‘ "Yeah, I know," replied Schmidt. "Don't blow the bridge!" '

At 23.15 hrs on 13 April 1945 the Panther crossed into safety.

A TANK ACE

When Friesen returned to his Regimental Command Post, Enseling greeted him with a bear-hug and said, 'You earned the Knight's Cross today, and if they don't give it to you, I'll give you mine'. He then called Sepp Dietrich at Army headquarters who promised to submit an immediate recommendation for the award. However, war finished before final confirmation was ever received – Hitler had to personally approve all recommendations for the Knight's Cross and there was, to put it mildly, some confusion in the 'Hitler Bunker' at that time.

Enseling toasted the gallant Friesen in champagne at the command post, his heroism had clearly earned him the rating as a tank ace.

Strangely enough, another very well-known tank ace was in the HQ that day and participated in the celebration, but without meeting Friesen face to face. That was Ernst Barkmann, some of whose exploits in Normandy and the Ardennes are covered in the next section. On this occasion Barkmann had been wounded on 12 April in Vienna, when his tank platoon was trying to get back to the bridgehead. His Panther was hit by a Panzerfaust, fired by a German soldier who mistook the tank platoon for enemy. Barkmann was wounded in the stomach and arms, his gunner was blinded and his radio operator also wounded. After leaving his two wounded crewmen with some medics, Barkmann continued on his way, only to have his Panther slide into a large bomb crater. Recovery proved impossible and the tank had to be destroyed. However, Barkmann survived, and was taken into British captivity. He is still alive today.

NOTES TO RUSSIA AND THE EASTERN FRONT

1. *Small Unit Actions During the German Campaign in Russia*, published by the US Dept. of the Army in July 1953.
2. Ibid.
3. Ibid.
4. *The Opposition*, Daniel S. Ibragimov, trs. by Stephen L. Sewell.
5. *Weapons of Glory*, G.T.M. Gorbachev and others, trs. by Stephen L. Sewell.

6. 'Maria's Tank', Maj Y. Miletsky, in *The Tank*, August 1944.

7. *The Opposition*, Ibragimov.

8. I am very grateful to Maj Peter R. Mansoor, US Army, Assistant Professor of the Dept. of History at the US Military Academy, West Point, for supplying the information for this account. It was published in *Armor*, January–February 1986. I have brought the quote up to date, acting on new information which has also been kindly supplied by Maj Mansoor.

9. Although this figure may not be quite accurate (it was his personal count), he did have the Tank Battle Badge in Gold, which signified that he had taken part in 75 to 100 tank battles, so his tally of 'kills' must have been considerable.

10. The Hummel (Bumble-Bee) was a self-propelled 15 cm tracked heavy howitzer, based on the PzKpfw III/IV chassis.

11. Initially Friesen thought this tank was commanded by another famous tank ace, Ernst Barkmann, but this was not the case. (See section on the Battle of the Bulge for more on Barkmann.)

12. Quoted from Maj Mansoor's article.

13. Ibid.

THE NANCY BRIDGEHEAD: THE GERMAN COUNTER-ATTACK ON ARRACOURT

19–22 SEPTEMBER 1944

MOVE AND SHOOT

The advance through France by Patton's Third Army had been spectacularly successful; seven weeks was all that it had taken it from breaking out of the Normandy bridgehead west of St Lô on 25 July, to reaching and crossing the Moselle River in early September. In XII Corps, 4 (US) Armd Div, under Maj Gen 'Tiger Jack' Wood, had played a major part in this lightning advance, bypassing strong points and finding its way around obstacles. Its outstanding characteristics were described by one contemporary commentator as: '. . . its ability to move and shoot, but above all to move. Movement became its middle name, constant momentum its trademark.'[1]

CCA 4 (US) Armd Div, under Col Bruce C. Clarke – later to become famous as the hero of St Vith in the Battle of the Bulge – performed a classic manoeuvre around Nancy as part of the capture of the town, which has been likened to Jeb Stuart's 'ride around Richmond' in the Civil War. All seemed set to tackle the next hurdle, the capture of Metz. Then, without warning, they came under a series of fierce armoured attacks from Gen Hasso von Manteuffel's Fifth Panzer Army,

which resulted in some of the largest tank battles to be fought by the Americans in the Second World War. Centred around Arracourt (see map, p. 194) in September–October 1944, it was a supreme test for 4 (US) Armd Div. Could this fast-driving, fast-shooting division fight and defend as well as it could raid and pursue?

There is not room here to deal with all the battles which took place, so I have chosen two examples, the first one featuring tank destroyers, the second, Sherman medium tanks. In both cases their enemy was the Panther – 'No contest!' one is liable to conclude. Surely the low-velocity 75 mm gun of the Sherman or even the 76 mm of the lightly armoured tank destroyer were no match for such an opponent? However, as the 4 (US) Armd Div history comments:

'When you stand by a wide-tracked Panther it looks as big as a house and the barrel of its high-velocity gun seems to go on for miles. That was the German Mk V tank. It was a *good* tank. The 4 Armd Div killed them and the smaller Mk IVs by the score in one of the biggest armored battles in France.'

The M18 Hellcat had a low silhouette, good cross-country performance and was well liked by its crews. It had a top speed of nearly 55 m.p.h. (Tank Museum)

THE TANKS

This time we shall look at the American tanks – the M18 Hellcat tank destroyer, which was the standard equipment of the 704th Tank Destroyer Battalion (704 TD Bn) of 4 (US) Armd Div, and the Sherman M4A1, with which the 37th Tank Battalion (37 Tank Bn) was equipped.

The Hellcat, as it was popularly called, had been designed as a tank destroyer (TD) from the outset and not merely adapted from an existing tank chassis, as had the M10. It was armed with a 76 mm gun, for which forty-five rounds were carried. The 76 mm was a good gun, but even with the improved M93 HVAP hyper-velocity ammunition, it was unable to penetrate the front glacis of the Panther at battle ranges. However, as we shall see, the TDs managed to beat their opponents by manoeuvre, so that they could get in close

or attack from the flank. Because of its comparatively light weight (just under 18 tons), the M18 was extremely fast (top speed 50–55 m.p.h.), had a good radius of action (150 miles) and an excellent cross-country performance. The crew of five (commander, driver and three gun crew) invariably adored their TDs, epecially the electric turret, radial engines and automatic transmission – 'real quiet and very fast' was how one TD crewman described the Hellcat to me.

The M4A1 was very similar to the M4 and the first model to be produced in quantity at the Lima Locomotive Works, where an assembly line had been established to fill British orders. Like the M4, it was powered by the nine-cylinder Continental petrol engine giving a top speed of some 25 m.p.h. and a radius of action of 120 miles. Its main armament was a 75 mm gun, although later

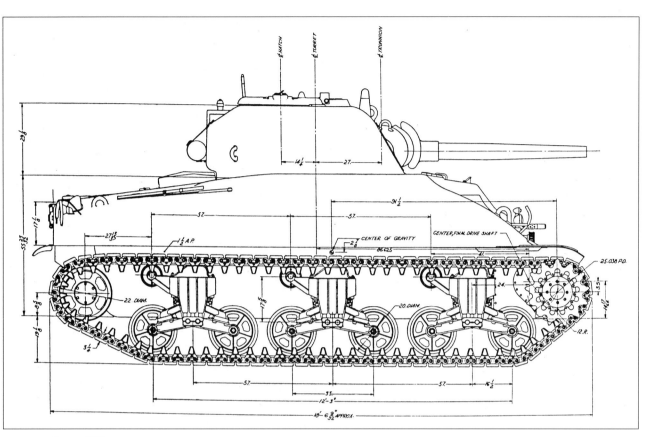

Sherman M4A1.

models were fitted with the 76 mm M1A1 gun. It had a crew of five and weighed some 31 tons. In total, a staggering 49,234 Shermans of all models were produced – that is over half the *total* US tank production for the entire war. Reliable, easy to maintain, rugged, with a good cross-country performance, its virtues made up to some degree for its main faults, which were undergunning and its penchant for 'brewing up' when hit. Part of the reason for this was that the US tank designers would stow ammunition above the turret ring.

Arguably, one reason why Sherman had an 'edge' might have been its electric power-traverse, which enabled it to engage targets faster than tanks with manual traverse. However, both PzKpfw IV and Panther had

power-traverse, although not as good as that on Sherman. The former was electrically powered, the current being generated by a small two-stroke petrol engine, while Panther, like Tiger, had hydraulically operated traverse. This meant that the engine had to be running, although this was rarely a hardship during a tank battle. Far more significant, in my opinion, was the superior cross-country mobility of the Sherman and Hellcat over their German opponents.

THE SETTING

By the night of 18/19 September, CCA 4 (US) Armd Div was located in the area of Arracourt. It was thinly spread because Col Clarke had only a relatively small force at hand (two companies of medium tanks and

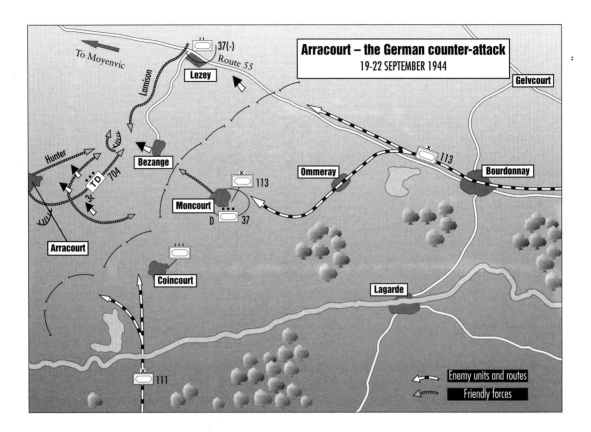

one of lights, a battalion of armoured infantry, a battalion of engineers, a company of TDs and three battalions of artillery). The armoured infantry and a company of medium tanks were deployed on the northern flank, between Chambrey and Arracourt. CCA HQ, the field artillery and a platoon of TDs were grouped in and around the town of Arracourt, while most of the engineers held the south flank. Company C of 37 Tank Bn, formed a combat outpost around the crossroads village of Lezey, 4–5 miles north-east of Arracourt.

Just before midnight the CCA outposts near Lezey called for artillery fire onto suspected enemy movement to their front and the movement ceased. About 07.30 hrs on the 19th, a liaison officer was driving down the road near Bezange-la-Petite when he encountered the rear of a column of Panthers,

but he managed to escape undetected in the thick morning mist. He radioed the information to his Battalion Commander (Bn Comd), Col Abrams, who was at Lezey. About the same time a light tank platoon at Moncourt reported a brush with some German tanks.

In fact what had happened was that 113th Panzer Brigade (113 Pz Bde) (forty-two Panther tanks) had moved up from Bourdonnay, to the south-east of Moncourt, and was now pushing through the heavy fog towards Bezange. First to encounter it was a section of Shermans in an outpost position south of Lezey. A Panther suddenly loomed out of the fog some 75 yd away from the two M4s. Fortunately the US tankers were on the ball and the Panther, plus two more, were destroyed at point-blank range. The German column checked, turned back and hurried off southwards.

Sherman M4A1s like these were to be found in most of the tank battalions of 4 Armd Div. Certainly James Turner tells me that this was the case in his company: 'My tank and most of all those in the battalions were M4A1, with a 75 mm gun and the nine-cylinder aircraft engine.' (Tank Museum)

C Company of 704 TD Bn, who were the TD company in CCA, had two platoons manning the outpost line, while the third was in reserve with CCA HQ. When Col Clarke heard about the enemy attack he ordered the third platoon, under Lt Edwin Leiper, to establish an outpost line between CCA HQ and the direction of the enemy. Leiper raced off into the fog with his TDs. Approaching Rechicourt-la-Petite on the way to Moncourt, where he was to establish his line, he suddenly saw a German tank gun muzzle 'appearing out of the fog 30 ft away'. He gave the signal to disperse and his well-trained platoon quickly deployed and opened fire. Five minutes later, five enemy tanks had been knocked out for the loss of only one M18. They remained in position for the rest of that day and destroyed a further ten enemy tanks, although they lost another two TDs.

One of the platoon's Hellcats, commanded by Sgt Henry R. Hartman, knocked out six of these and lived to fight another day.

THE SHERMANS IN ACTION
The 113 Pz Bde attack developed into a series of consecutive jabs, by tanks and infantry at about company strength, as it probed to find a weak spot in CCA's defences. At least one of these jabs was aimed at Arracourt. B Company, 37 Tank Bn was recalled from Chambrey to help meet this threat and reached the area about 11.00 hrs, taking up a defensive position in defilade some 800 yd east of Arracourt. A Company was released from Luneville about 13.00 hrs and sped back to aid B Company, who was by then being heavily attacked. An eyewitness was James Turner, then a 1st Lieutenant in A Company, who told me:

1st Lt James Turner stands beside the C Company, 37 Tank Bn crest in Germany soon after the war in Europe ended, 20 July 1945. (James Turner)

'My platoon (3rd) was posted to protect the CP of CCA. Shortly after reaching the vicinity of the CP, my tank became inoperable and I took over my platoon sergeant's tank. We sat in defilade and observed the German tanks. They fired some shots into our area from 2,000 yd, but would come no closer. One of the B Company tanks was hit, taking the turret cupola ring off complete with the .50 cal gun and hatch covers. The Germans withdrew at about 15.00 hrs. Maj Hunter, the Task Force commander, advanced the task force ahead about 2 miles, to relieve C Company and 704 TD, and also to survey the area.

'One German tank was on a hilltop 1,500 yd away with its crew on the ground. I had my gunner sight on it and fired an HE shell at it – I knew that AP would not do any damage at that range. The tank answered by firing one AP shell. At 16.00 hrs Maj Hunter decided to sweep forward with A and B Companies (fifteen tanks total). A Company was on the left and B Company on the right. I was on the extreme left and as we proceeded, I saw a Mk V on a hilltop 700–800 yd away with the crew working on the engine. I had my gunner sight on it and fired one round of AP, hitting the engine compartment. The Germans fled on foot. I then came upon some German infantry and chased them down a valley. This led to a German bivouac area with five Panther tanks. I immediately opened fire and we hit these tanks, one round in each engine compartment and one round in the turret. As we engaged I attempted to call my CO (Capt Spencer) to appraise him of the situation and to get some help. I couldn't reach him – his tank had been hit and set on fire.

'Lt De Craene's crewman (2nd Platoon) tried to call the CO to tell him their tank had been hit and De Craene knocked unconscious. I ordered them out of the attack. My platoon had knocked out four of the five tanks, one slowly moving away even though we had hit him twice. I started to move closer to finish it, when three Mk Vs backed into my line of fire. We opened fire and knocked out all of them. I started to move again and three more Mk Vs came into view, one at a time. We hit each of them with two rounds of AP except the last one, which we had hit in the engine compartment, stopping him. We had a delay in reloading; possibly we had expended all the AP in the turret racks or the loose casings on the floor (approx. twenty-one expended) interfered. Anyway, the German rotated his turret and put two rounds through our turret, killing the loader, wounding the gunner (both legs broken), the driver (shrapnel wound in shoulder), the bow gunner (burns and shrapnel wounds) and myself (thirteen wounds) left foot, left side and chest, plus a partially severed achilles right tendon. The first shot knocked me to my knees on the turret seat and the second ejected me from the turret and I rolled to the ground. I looked up and saw Maj Hunter's tank approaching the fire zone of the German tank, so I rolled towards him and stood up to stop his tank. I managed somehow to climb onto his tank and told him of the danger. Darkness was falling and he recalled the units to an assembly area. We started to approach my knocked-out tank to pick up the other wounded, but there was another tank helping.

'After Spencer's tank was hit, B Company (Capt Leach) took his tanks to the right, formed them in line and attacked over the hill, moving through the bivouac area but was too late to assist me. . . . We had

Capt (later Col) James H. Leach, DSC, Commander of B Company, 37 Tank Bn, standing behind his 'Peep' (Jeep). (Col James Leach)

definitely knocked out five enemy Mk Vs and hit three others, disabling them. The wounded crew and I were treated at a forward hospital and evacuated to England. I returned to the 37th after a long recuperation period.'

In the four days 19–22 September the 37th destroyed fifty-five Panthers, many of them being 'factory-new', while losing fourteen of its own tanks. Not long afterwards, the Corps Commander, Gen Eddy, sent a message to Gen Wood in which he said: 'The Germans are frightened by your superior equipment, frightened by your more skilful tactics, and above all frightened of your magnificent courage and will to win.'[2]

THE BATTLE OF THE BULGE: A CLOSE-RANGE ENGAGEMENT NEAR MANHAY

WACHT AM RHEIN

The German offensive in the Ardennes, which began on 16 December 1944, came as a complete surprise to the Allies. It caused panic, especially among some of the green, understrength American troops of V and VII Corps, when eight Panzer divisions, supported by seventeen Volksgrenadier divisions, a Panzergrenadier division and two parachute divisions, burst upon them. At first the Panzers made excellent progress, but eventually the line was stabilized and, although the Battle of the Bulge – as it is now called – delayed the Allied advance for some six weeks, the 120,000 German casualties and the destruction of many AFVs and other precious weapons and equipment, undoubtedly hastened the final defeat of Germany.

THE SITUATION

Just before Christmas 1944 and some eight days after the attack had begun, Field Marshal Montgomery decided that the only way to stabilize the situation was for the US First Army to secure the northern flank, by shortening the line it was holding, prior to a counter-attack by VII Corps. This involved moving troops on Christmas Eve to the line Trois Points–Manhay. 7 (US) Armd Div would merely have an outpost at the Manhay crossroads, while 3 (US) Armd Div would continue to defend the line Trois Points–Manhay–Hotton.

Unfortunately, the Germans had also chosen to move armoured troops that night in the same area – 2nd SS Panzer Division (2 SS Pz Div) was continuing with its assault, while Kampfgruppe Peiper was withdrawing from La Gleize. The two sides were bound to meet and it would be the American armour which would come off worst. One of the key factors was the worry on the part of the Americans over firing at friendly forces, because they knew that the tanks of 3 Armd Div were going to be moving in the area that night. This element of doubt would prove to be their undoing.

The leading German Panzers and Panzergrenadiers of 2 SS Pz Div were moving along a small road from Odeigne towards Manhay and Highway N15, while a US force composed of company of the 40th Tank Battalion (40 Tank Bn) (with seven tanks only) and the 48th Armored Infantry Battalion (48 Armd Inf Bn) was sitting astride

Leutnant Ludwig Bauer won his Knight's Cross during the Ardennes offensive. He served with Pz Regt 33 in 9 Pz Div from 1941 until the spring of 1944, survived the war and rejoined the reformed German Army after the war as a reserve officer. He also held the Iron Cross First and Second Class, Tank Battle Badges 1 and 2 and was wounded seven times. (Ludwig Bauer)

Four were destroyed immediately and the other two badly damaged – small wonder that the Sherman was known to the GIs as the 'Ronson Lighter' as it was guaranteed to 'light' every time. The Panthers and PzKpfw IVs swept on through the shattered Americans who broke in disorder. In the chaos that followed one Panther got itself separated from the rest and continued alone onto Highway N15. This Panther was No. 401, commanded by SS Oberscharführer Ernst Barkmann.

A TANK ACE

Barkmann was already a tank ace, having begun his career as an infantryman in the assault on Poland, where he was wounded and awarded the Iron Cross Second Class. He then volunteered to serve in a Panzer unit and

SS Oberscharführer Ernst Barkmann, one of Germany's great Panzer aces. (Gordon Williamson)

this road. All were alert and ready for the enemy. However, as the unidentified (German) column approached, it was clear to the GIs that the leading vehicle was undoubtedly a Sherman tank – no one could mistake its tall silhouette and the easily recognizable sound of its engine. The GIs manning the position called on their radios to try to confirm that it was a friendly column, but to no avail. Too late they realized that the rest of the vehicles behind the Sherman were German, by which time all but one of the seven tanks had been hit by Panzerfausts.

went on to win his Iron Cross First Class at Kharkov, while commanding a PzKpfw III. Shortly afterwards he was re-equipped with the new medium heavy tank, the Panther, and in early 1944 his unit, SS Panzer Regiment 2 (Pz Regt 2), *Das Reich*, moved to France. Here it would find very different conditions to the broad Russian steppes – the 'bocage' fighting in Normandy was a much closer affair, in which individual tanks often had to fight their battles unsupported and at close range. This was to prove good training for his Christmas Eve battle in the Ardennes. Barkmann knocked out many American tanks during the period June–July 1944 and was subsequently awarded his Knight's Cross. In one particular single-handed engagement

near the village of Le Lorey he destroyed a complete American column of tanks, half-tracks, lorries, jeeps and petrol tankers, including no fewer than nine Shermans.

THE BATTLE

The Panthers of 4 Kompanie, Pz Regt 2 were in the vanguard of the divisional attack, with Barkmann's Panther in the leading section. When they bumped the enemy position they were fired upon and two Panthers received direct hits. Confused fighting followed and the section commander, SS Hauptscharführer Frauscher, radioed that he was pulling away in order to reach the Manhay road, so Barkmann decided to press on as well and managed to reach the main road unscathed.

These were the type of conditions under which the Battle of the Bulge was fought. Here a Panther Ausf A passes a column of German half-tracks. (Tank Museum)

He did not realize that he was now on his own, but thought that Frauscher and the others had gone on ahead and that he must catch up with them, so he motored on. Shortly, in the darkness, he saw another tank. As he recounted later: 'Fifty metres away, on the right, there was a tank . . . with its commander standing in the turret, and which was apparently waiting for me – Frauscher!'[3]

Barkmann moved his Panther up to the other tank, on its left-hand side, stopping as they came level. Ordering his driver to switch off the engine, he then took off his headsets so that he could hear the reply when he shouted across to the other tank commander. However, as he did so, the other commander ducked down into his turret and closed the cupola lid with a clang. A few seconds later the driver's hatch opened and Barkmann noticed that the driver's instrument panel light was wine-red in colour, rather than the normal green of the German Panther. He realized in a flash that it was a Sherman!

Hastily replacing his headsets, he shouted over the tank intercom: 'Gunner! The tank alongside us is enemy. Fire at it!' However, when the gunner tried to traverse onto the target, the long barrel of the 75 mm struck the turret of the enemy tank. They were too near to get a shot at the Sherman. 'Can't fire – turret traverse stuck!' shouted the gunner. Fortunately the driver had been listening out on the intercom and, without waiting for any orders, started the engine and moved back a few yards, until the gun was completely clear. The gunner then immediately fired into the rear of the Sherman, setting it on fire. Barkmann heard the reverberations of the explosion as he ducked down into the safety of his turret.

They moved on past the burning Sherman and saw two more Shermans emerging from the forest on the right of the road. Barkmann knocked out both these tanks, then pressed on, expecting to meet up with Frauscher around every bend. Then, as they negotiated a particularly large S-bend and found that they were entering an open grassy area, he saw a frightening sight – nine enemy tanks, partially dug in and, as he recalled, 'all had the muzzles of their guns pointing threateningly at our tank'. What should he do? To stop or turn back would be suicidal. 'Keep driving,' Barkmann ordered his driver and they pushed on defiantly, past the Americans who all traversed their turrets, tracking the lone Panther, but who still did not fire. Barkmann also did not engage them, as he reckoned that if he did start a battle it would alert the whole front before he could reach Manhay. By now he had also decided that the rest of the company must be behind him, so they could deal with these 'Amis' he was leaving behind.[4]

Barkmann was still in deep trouble because, as the forest closed in on both sides of the narrow road, he overtook numerous straggling columns of American infantry. They cursed as they were forced to jump into the roadside slush to avoid the tank, but did not realize it was German – just the normal infantryman's anger at those who permanently ride into battle. Barkmann stood upright in the cupola, looking down at them, as dawn broke and houses started to appear instead of trees. They had reached Manhay.

Unfortunately, that was not the end of the traumatic drive for Barkmann. Reaching the crossroads in the village where he should have turned left to Grandmenil and Erezee (the company objective), he found three Sherman tanks coming straight towards him from that direction, so, instead, he drove over the crossroads in the direction of Liège. His intention was to turn around at some suitable place and try again to rejoin the rest of his company, but as he moved on north-westwards he encountered more groups of enemy tanks, static at the side of the road,

The 'opposition' were mainly Shermans, such as these two, of which the more interesting is the assault Sherman M4A3E2 on the right. *Jumbo*, as the 37½ ton tank was called, was built in small numbers (254 only) at the Fisher Tank Arsenal in May–June 1944, rushed over to ETO in the autumn and employed throughout the remainder of the fighting. (Tank Museum)

their crews dismounted and 'brewing up', smoking and chatting. Obviously the Panther had to keep moving on, but it was inevitable that someone would eventually recognize them. Fortunately this did not happen until they were past the main American column. Tank crews then began to mount up, start engines and traverse turrets, but as luck would have it, because the Shermans were parked one behind the other, each blocked the others' field of fire, so no one could fire at Barkmann. Nevertheless, as an emergency could occur at any moment, he issued hand grenades to all the crew just in case they had to abandon the tank, and lit a smoke generator, letting it roll over the rear decks and onto the road to help hide their progress.[5]

The next emergency was not long in coming. 'There's a car driving straight at us from in front,' said the driver suddenly. Barkmann put his head out and saw it was true. One of its occupants was waving a traffic control disc at them, clearly trying to get them to stop. 'Run the vehicle over!' ordered Barkmann. At the last moment the jeep driver realized what was happening, put his vehicle into reverse and desperately tried to escape, but to no avail. Crushing the jeep caused the Panther to slew off the road and into a Sherman parked at the roadside, the driving spocket of the Panther becoming entangled in the other's tracks. To make matters worse the engine stalled and they came under infantry small-arms fire.

Shermans like these were easy victims for Barkmann's Panther, as their 75 mm guns could not penetrate the heavy tank's armour except at close range. (Tank Museum)

Fortunately for Barkmann none of his crew panicked. The driver managed to restart the engine and then backed slowly and carefully until the two running gears were disentangled. On went the lone Panther, past more and more American vehicles and equipment, but by now there were American tanks in hot pursuit. Barkmann engaged and destroyed the leading Sherman and some other vehicles, effectively blocking the road. He repeated this process a little further on, leaving a trail of burning vehicles, so that eventually, the road was well and truly blocked and they were able to escape. Reaching a convenient side turning into the forest, Barkmann pulled off the main road and, having made sure that the 'hot pursuit' had now cooled, allowed his crew to dismount. As they stood around, breathing in the cool morning air and grinning with

pleasure and relief, they heard the unmistakable 'crack' of Panther guns firing from the direction of Manhay. Clearly the rest of the company had caught them up and were attacking.

The capture of both Manhay and Grandmenil followed, opening the way to Liège. Barkmann returned slowly past the litter of knocked-out and abandoned American vehicles to Manhay, where he counted twenty American tanks which had surrendered.

As already explained in the last section, Barkmann and his Panther went on to fight again on the Eastern front, then in Austria, surviving the last, hectic days of the war and finishing up as a British prisoner. He is still alive.

KOHIMA AND THE
TENNIS COURT BATTLE

THE SIEGE OF KOHIMA

The siege of Kohima marked the furthest advance the Japanese made into India at any time during the war. Had they been able to capture the whole town and to control its vital road junction, then they would have been unstoppable. Even when the three-week siege was lifted and the first reinforcements were able to reach the tiny garrison, the Japanese still hung on tenaciously and had to be winkled out of the positions which they had managed to capture. One such position was in the area of what was left of the District Commissioner's (DC) bungalow, which the Japanese had been holding since early April and had turned into a virtually unassailable stronghold in which they were prepared to fight to the death. In the epic battle which followed, 2nd Dorsets were materially assisted by a lone tank, commanded by Sgt J. Waterhouse of the 149th RAC Regiment (149 (RAC) Regt.).

THE TANK

The American M3 medium tank was swiftly developed from the M2A1, in order to meet the desperate need for tanks with bigger guns and thicker armour. Its design and subsequent production took place at breakneck speed, as did the building of the factories where it

would be manufactured.[6] More than 6,000 M3s were built, but it was always considered only as a stopgap AFV, being superseded by the M4 Sherman. The 'General Lee' was the standard American version, while the 'General Grant' was the British version of the tank. The Lee was some 500 lb lighter (because of the smaller turret) and 4 in taller (due to the cupola). Within the US Armored Force, the M3 was used on training in 1941–2, and first saw action with 1 (US) Armd Div in Operation 'Torch' in North Africa.

Despite the fact that the Grant was designed specifically for the British, standard M3 Lees were also supplied to them and saw British Army service in both the Middle and Far East. 149 (RAC) Regt was equipped with Lees.

THE BATTLE

For some two weeks 2nd Dorsets had been trying unsuccessfully to winkle out the Japanese from their positions in and around the DC's bungalow on Garrison Hill. Heavy night fighting had resulted in A and C Companies managing to establish themselves at both ends of the feature (see map), but what was necessary for complete success was to effect a link-up and clear the rest of the

M3 mediums operating in burma. (Tank Museum)

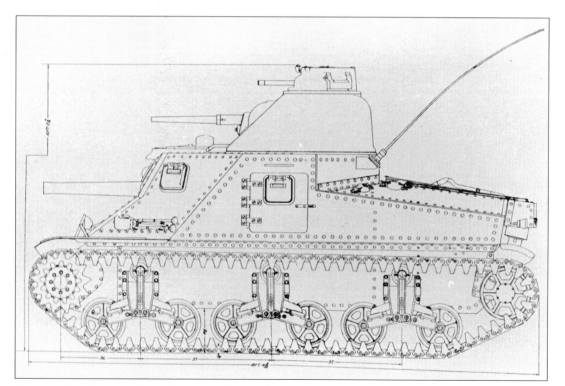

Side elevation of an M3 medium tank, known by the British as the Lee 1. The Lee 2 was the M3A1, which had a cast hull instead of a riveted one. (Tank Museum)

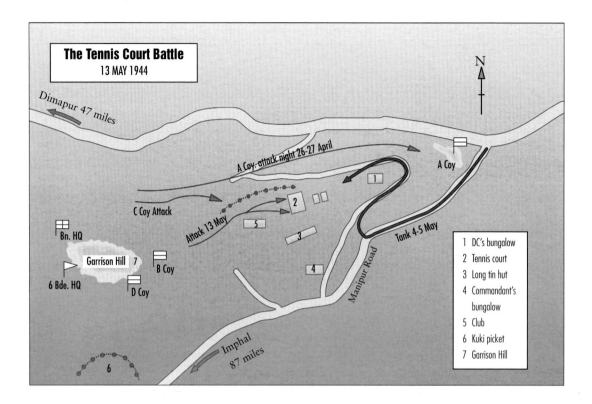

The Tennis Court Battle
13 MAY 1944

N

Dimapur 47 miles

A Coy. attack night 26-27 April

A Coy

C Coy Attack

Attack 13 May

Bn. HQ

Garrison Hill   7

B Coy

6 Bde. HQ

D Coy

1

2

5

3

4

Manipur Road

Tank 4-5 May

Imphal
87 miles

6

1 DC's bungalow
2 Tennis court
3 Long tin hut
4 Commandant's
   bungalow
5 Club
6 Kuki picket
7 Garrison Hill

hill. The only way this would ever be possible, without horrendous casualties, was to get direct, heavy fire-power up to the area of the tennis court, with which to support the infantry attack. Artillery was useless due to the intermingling of both sides, so a tank was the obvious solution. As Col O.G.W. White DSO, then CO 2nd Dorsets, put it in their history: '. . . if we could only get a medium tank on to the tennis court, serving some pretty fast balls from the north end, the Nip would not stay to finish the set.'[7]

The Commander Royal Engineers (CRE) agreed, and on the morning of 28 April a sapper bulldozer, covered by two tanks, one in front and one behind, moved up the road around the Japanese positions on the spur and then began to bulldoze out a rough track straight up the steep gradient. This completed, the driver hitched up one of the tanks and tried to drag it up the slope. No

luck, and when the driver dismounted to make some adjustments the weight of the tank took over and dragged the dozer on top of it. Both then crashed down the rest of the slope, with little chance of recovery.

They tried again on 4 May and this time successfully got a tank into the DC's compound. As it reached the bungalow, B Company advanced and together they attacked the Japanese, killing many of them, before heavy fire forced them to call off the attack. They repeated the attack the following day, only to find that the enemy had dug an anti-tank ditch across the only route. Fortunately, they had been unable to complete it, and, by skilful driving, the tank got around the obstacle and reached the place where it had been hoped that it could climb the steep bank on to the tennis court. This, however, proved impossible and from its current position it could not engage the enemy medium machine-gun post which was

The tennis court. This was the actual area fought over and the bunker in the top left corner was one which gave the Dorsets a great deal of trouble. (Author's collection)

causing all the casualties. So once again they had to withdraw.[8]

More days of stalemate followed and then on 12 May the sappers decided to bulldoze another path, this time straight up Garrison Hill spur and into the perimeter from the rear. Despite all the problems, such as the slope, the state of the ground and the continual heavy rain, they managed the impossible and by that evening all was ready for the tank to do its job. As Sgt Waterhouse wrote in his subsequent report, which is now held in the Tank Museum Library:

'The plan was to attack and capture the tennis court and surrounding area on the high ground south-west of the DC's bungalow. Infantry reports suggested that the tennis court was fairly well defended and covered so well by enfilade and defilade fire that all previous attempts to take this position had failed with extensive casualties.

'My orders were to get down to the tennis court from the top of Garrison Hill and if I could not do so, owing to the ground, I was to approach as near as possible to the objective and dominate it by fire while the infantry went in.

'The attack was set for 09.00 hrs on the 13th and as the forward platoon commander could give me no idea of the ground in front of his positions, I suggested we recce same just before last light on the 12th. This we did and were successful in finding a route to a position from which we could at least dominate.

'The attack went in next day as planned, except that zero hour was delayed one hour. The signal for the infantry to go in was the first round of my 75 mm fire. I would like to mention here that the infantry gave me every assistance possible and even put an officer in my tank who knew one or two enemy positions.

Kohima battle area with one of 149 (RAC) Regt's 'General Lee' medium tanks in the foreground. It is possibly Sgt Waterhouse's tank. (Author's collection)

'We started out well along the route previously arranged and the next thing I remember was my driver shouting " 'old on!" We seemed to slither to one side sharply and our nose went down and "BUMP!", there we were smack in the centre of the tennis court itself. We pulled to the right and found ourselves in front of a steel water tank very heavily sandbagged and small arms fire met us. My 75 mm gunner dealt with this position so effectively that the Nips started to leave in a hell of a hurry without even arms and equipment. They were met by infantry fire from both flanks and very few got away. We next paid our attention to a series of crawl trenches and MG posts all around the court, and had a hell of a party for the next 20 minutes or so. Finally, the infantry commander got me on the IC and told me all the positions had been captured in this area and quite a few Nips liquidated.

'We next went on to the edge of the court which overlooks the DC's bungalow and gave it quite a pasting. After that everything in sight was well and truly plastered. The infantry again went in and took over without a casualty. I learned afterwards that as we came over the top into the tennis court we crashed right on top of one of their main positions and buried a few of the enemy without ever having the privilege of killing them first.

'The whole action lasted about 40 minutes and the infantry suffered only one casualty and even he walked out. We stayed forward to give covering fire until all the positions and the bungalow itself were consolidated, then we came out.

'The infantry officer estimated that we ourselves had knocked out possibly forty of the enemy. I am not prepared to say that this was the full figure, but when we went down afterwards at the invitation of the infantry CO to view the shambles, as he called it, well he was just about right.

'Altogether, quite a useful shoot.'

A TANK ACE

A first-class tank commander with a well-trained crew, it could be argued that Sgt Waterhouse was no tank ace. Yet by his action he undoubtedly played a key role in this operation, which was the major factor in breaking the Japanese stranglehold on Kohima and thus led directly to the Fourteenth Army's subsequent successes in Burma – not bad going for one lone tank!

M3s of the 25th Dragoons bunker-busting in the Arakan.

THE BATTLE OF PELELIU AIRFIELD, SOUTH PACIFIC

'Beginning with its first amphibious assault, the 1st Marine Division (1 Mar Div) had built up a tradition of extraordinary good luck in making its initial landings against the enemy. At Guadalcanal low cloud had covered the approach of the convoy, tactical surprise was complete, and landing conditions perfect. At Cape Gloucester, again tactical surprise was achieved in the selection of the beaches, and D-Day provided the only clear, calm morning which occurred during the entire monsoon season. The sea was placid at Peleliu too, and the temperature the least debilitating that would be encountered in weeks to come. But beyond this point, any resemblance to the "landing luck" of Guadalcanal and Cape Gloucester was purely coincidental.'[9]

The assault was planned for 15 September and the beaches on the south-west corner of the island chosen, because they were negotiable and flat, thus allowing for the employment of both tanks and artillery. However, there was a coral reef some 500 yd off shore, so landing craft would be unable to get in close. Instead, most of the assault force would have to 'swim' in on an Amtrac – the tracked, armoured landing vehicle, which was now organic to US Marine Corps (USMC) units. However, just to complicate matters, because the Amtracs could not be launched far enough from shore to keep the ocean-going transports out of enemy artillery range, there had to be a 'double shuffle' from the transports into landing ship tanks (LSTs) and thence into Amtracs. To make matters still more complicated, the assault force had to embark from a number of widely separated points thus making the co-ordination of the landing even more difficult than usual.

TANK SUPPORT

The assaulting brigades would be supported by a number of Sherman medium tanks, the initial distribution being fifteen to the left-hand brigade, nine to the centre and six to the right. The remaining sixteen of the division's forty-six tanks had to be left behind due to lack of shipping space. Thus, although this would be the very first time that the Marines would have armoured support for a landing, it would not be at full strength.

Peleliu's garrison numbered nearly 11,000 élite, veteran troops, with armoured support, although this turned out to be only light tankettes. They had built an incredibly complex system of bunkers and trenches from which it would be very difficult to winkle them out. They had also dug a deep, almost continuous anti-tank ditch on the beach, so movement inland would be difficult until routes around it could be found.

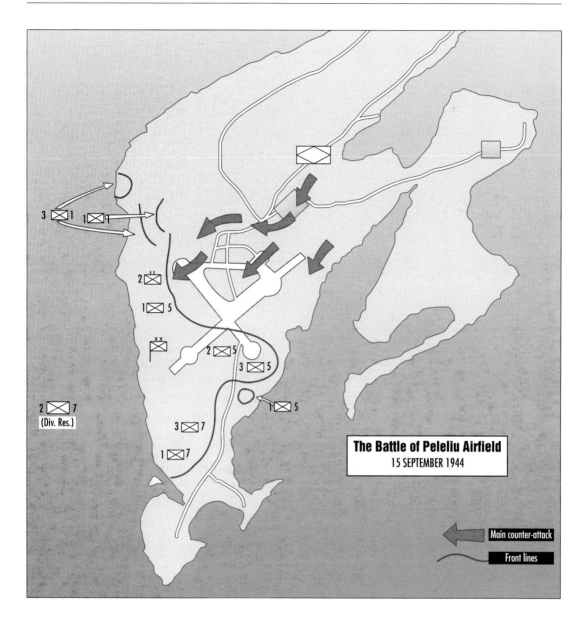

The Battle of Peleliu Airfield
15 SEPTEMBER 1944

Main counter-attack

Front lines

'HIT THE BEACH!'

The Marines 'hit the beach' with their customary *élan* in the early morning, but lost a great number of their LVTs, also DUKWs (amphibious utility vehicles), on the way in, which delayed the landing of artillery and other vital support equipment. The thirty waterproofed tanks waded ashore with the fourth wave, in six columns of five tanks, each led by an Amtrac. Seventeen of them were hit up to four times each by enemy artillery or mortar fire on the run in. However, all but three reached the beach safely, then made their way slowly forward under intense fire, their progress materially hampered by the anti-tank ditch.

By afternoon it was clear that the assault was getting bogged down, so the divisional reserve was ordered in. Then, about 17.15 hrs, the Japanese counter-attacked.

A good comparison between the USMC Sherman M4A2 and a captured example of the little Japanese Type 94 tankette. (Author's collection).

THE TANKS

We have already dealt with the American Sherman (although these were the diesel-engined M4A2) which was to prove to be the battle-winner in this bloody encounter, so it is relevant to look at the Japanese AFVs that were also involved. These were the Type 94 tankette, a 3½ ton two-man vehicle, armed with a 7.7 mm machine-gun and very similar in design to the Vickers Carden-Loyd light tank of the same period. From 1936 onwards a modified version with a better running gear was produced and later a diesel prototype was built. The Type 94 was superseded by the Type 97, which was larger and heavier (4.7 tons), and armed with a 37 mm gun.

THE BATTLE

An increase in mortar and artillery fire had been the first indication that an enemy counter-attack was brewing. Then a company-strength formation of Japanese infantry was seen advancing across the airfield.

'This was no tightly bunched knot of screaming, sword-waving fanatics. These men moved with the cool determination of the veterans they were: keeping well dispersed, taking advantage of the scanty cover of shell holes and ground folds, opening fire as they came within effective range.'[10]

To make matters worse, an air observer reported that he could see a group of enemy tanks forming up to the east of the ridges just north of the airfield, with more infantry hanging on to them wherever they could get a handhold. This group caught up with the dismounted infantry on the airfield when they

USMC Shermans on Peleliu. The original caption for this photograph quotes Kipling: 'Sometimes we goes where the roads are, but mostly we goes where they ain't'. His comment aptly applied to tanks on Peleliu. (USMC)

were about 400 yd away from the Marine positions, combining to form what looked like an unstoppable assault wave.

Fortunately, this was only an impression. The tanks foolishly then speeded up, far too fast for the assaulting infantry and the attack became more like an old-fashioned cavalry charge, as it headed for the 1st Battalion, 5th Marines (1/5) positions (see map). The presence of tanks did not really come as any surprise to the waiting Marines as everyone knew about them and had been expecting them to make an appearance. Most accounts agree that there were between thirteen and nineteen enemy tanks involved in this action, although, as the official history comments: 'There are nearly as many versions of what happened next as there were witnesses!' The official account explains that the Japanese

tanks, having tried to gain as much cover for as long as they could from the jungle to the north of the airfield, then took a south-westerly diagonal path directly in front of the 2nd Battalion, 1st Marines (2/1) positions, who poured devastating fire into their flank. Two[11] of the tanks veered into the lines of this battalion, hurtled over a coral embankment and crashed into a swamp just behind the infantry foxholes.

Meanwhile the men of 1/5 had opened up with everything they possessed – 37 mm guns, bazookas, anti-tank grenades, together with the 75 mm guns of the Shermans – even a US Navy dive-bomber, which happened to be in the area, came in low and dropped a large bomb. The three Sherman tanks that were attached to 1 Bn had been located in partial defilade to the infantry positions, from

213

where they could place pin-point accurate, direct fire, close in front of the infantry. The tank-riding enemy infantry were the first to suffer and were just blown away by all this fire-power. Then the tankettes themselves began to explode. As one marine recalled:

'A tank rushed for the machine-gun on my right. "Stoney" stands up in his foxhole (he's a lad with guts) and lets go a burst of automatic fire. The tank was not ten foot away when it burst into flame, leaving a trailing fire as it still rolled forward.'[12]

The three defilade tanks were not the only ones involved in the battle, although as luck would have it, all but one of the Shermans supporting other battalions had returned to the beach to replenish. However, 2/5 was operating in the woods across the southern end of the airfield, and seeing the enemy

advance, it immediately despatched its supporting tanks to assist, as the executive officer of 5 Mar, who was sitting in a vantage point on the right of 1/5 later explained:

'At the time when the enemy tanks were approximately half-way across the airfield, four Sherman tanks came onto the field in the 2/5 zone of action on the south end of the airfield and opened fire immediately on the enemy tanks. These four played an important role in stopping the enemy tanks and also the supporting infantry, the majority of which started beating a hasty retreat when these Shermans came charging down from the south. They fought a running battle and ended up in the middle of the enemy tanks.'

Unfortunately, other accounts conflict, at least two observers contending that at no time did any Shermans engage in a 'running battle',

Peleliu airfield after the Japanese counter-attack had been defeated on the afternoon of D-Day. (USMC)

while others claimed that even the tanks that were in the re-arming area were able to engage the Japanese by moving just a few yards, as the enemy were only some 50 yd away.

WHO DID WHAT?

Exactly who knocked out which enemy tanks, when and where from, appears to be shrouded in some mystery, which shows just how difficult it is to be certain about claims made in a battle as confused as this one. Obviously to those taking part at the time, all that counted was that the enemy threat was beaten back and all their tanks were either destroyed or withdrew. However, it is perhaps interesting to rationalize all the reports and claims made, and this was done by someone with a flair for figures who calculated that if every claim of knocking out a Japanese tank in that battle were taken at face value, then there would have been 179½ enemy tanks involved, instead of the thirteen (or possibly nineteen) actually taking part. Obviously each of the tankettes was hit many times and by many different weapons, so it would be difficult to say which hit actually destroyed it. Remember the point made earlier by 'Stimo' Stimpson of 5 RTR as to how difficult it is for anyone to claim a 'kill' unless he and the enemy tank were definitely the only two involved. After the battle Marine tankers reported an unexpected problem with the Japanese tanks: they were so thinly armoured that the AP rounds from the Sherman's 75 mm went straight through – in one side and out the other, merely 'ventilating' the tank instead of knocking it out. The USMC tank crews had to change to using HE, which exploded on first impact and devastated the little Japanese light tankettes.

The battle continued the following day, and the next and the next, in fact for over two months. Peleliu was not finally completely captured until 25 November,[13] 1 Mar Div being awarded the Presidential Unit Citation for its capture.

NOTES TO NORTH-WEST EUROPE AND THE FAR EAST

1. Quoted from an article in *Armor* magazine, July–August 1987, by Brig-Gen Albin F. Irzyk (Retd). Gen Irzyk served on the staff of 4 (US) Armd Div as G-3 and commanded 8th Tank Battalion.

2. 4 (US) Armd Div's history, *From the Beach to Bavaria*.

3. *Battle of the Bulge, Then and Now*, Jean Paul Pallud.

4. Barkmann was quite correct and Frauscher's battle report stated that he had subsequently knocked out all nine.

5. At one stage the loader had spoken quietly to Barkmann, pulled him down into the turret and turned his camouflaged jacket collar up so as to hide the Knight's Cross, which was around his neck and shining in the moonlight.

6. In early September 1940 work began on building the new Chrysler tank factory, just outside Detroit, where the M3 would be built. It produced its first tank in mid-April 1941 and was in quantity production three months later.

7. *Straight on for Tokyo*, Lt Col O.G.W. White DSO.

8. This was also Sgt Waterhouse.

9. Chapter III of *The Assault on Peleliu*, Maj Frank O. Hough, USMCR.

10. Ibid.

11. This figure is variously reported as being up to six. However, all confirm that some enemy tanks did get through the lines, but were all disposed of and their crews killed.

12. *US 1st Marine Division 1941–45*, Philip Katcher. The machine-gunners had to jump for safety as the flaming tankette crashed over their MG nest, crushing the weapon to pieces.

13. Actually a party of twenty-six Japanese soldiers and sailors did not surrender until after the war was over – on 21 April 1947!

PART THREE

POSTWAR CONFLICTS

THE PUSAN PERIMETER

AUGUST—SEPTEMBER 1950

OBONG-NI RIDGE: 17 AUGUST 1950

On 25 June 1950 the North Koreans invaded South Korea, their invasion forces spearheaded by blitzkrieg-like armoured units, composed of T-34/85 tanks. For a number of weeks they enjoyed spectacular successes as they pushed the South Koreans and their hard-pressed American allies further and further south, until by early August all that remained to the United Nations was a small perimeter around the vital port of Pusan, through which all supplies passed. As with the case of the Nazi Panzers' lightning advances in Poland and France, a myth arose that the North Korean armour was invincible. This was reinforced especially because the South Koreans possessed no armour of their own, while the Americans could only muster some light M24 Chaffees, which were no match for the more heavily armoured and better armed T-34/85s. However, as the summer progressed, the Americans were able to build up their armour

North Korean T-34/85s driving past 'welcoming' crowds in South Korea, shortly after the North Korean People's Army had invaded. There was little opposition against the army and its blitzkrieg assault. (Simon Dunstan)

Marines advance past a knocked-out North Korean T-34/85 Soviet-built tank. (US Marine Corps)

in the Pusan bridgehead, bringing in both M26 Pershings and M4 Shermans (the M4A3 version) and including at least one battalion of the even more modern M46 Pattons, until there were over 600 tanks in the UN Pusan perimeter.

However, even before this build-up was completed, there were opportunities for positive action against enemy tanks. One such operation concerned USMC tanks in support of 2 Bn, 5 Mar (2/5), who fought an action on Obong-Ni Ridge and succeeded in inflicting heavy casualties on the enemy.

THE TANKS
The USMC tanks involved were M26 Pershings. As these are described in the next

battle report, let us deal here with the North Korean armour, namely the T-34. Those in service in the North Korean People's Army (NKPA) were T-34/85s, the final Second World War version of the battle-winning Soviet T-34, which had been made even more effective towards the end of 1943 by fitting the new 85 mm gun in an enlarged turret. The new gun could penetrate the frontal armour of both Tiger and Panther at 1,000 m, or so the Russians claimed. The improved tank now weighed 31½ tons, had armour 18–75 mm thick, a top speed of over 30 m.p.h. and an excellent cross-country performance. This would be the first occasion when T-34/85s were in combat with Pershings.

Pershings push on past two knocked-out T-34/85s, November 1950. The Pershings' 90 mm gun had no trouble penetrating the armour of the T-34. (Simon Dunstan)

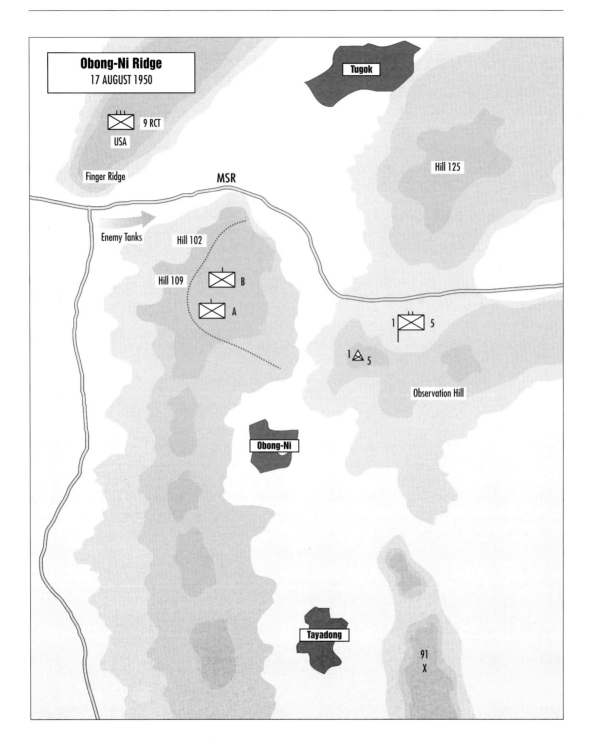

Obong-Ni Ridge
17 AUGUST 1950

9 RCT

USA

Tugok

Finger Ridge

Hill 125

MSR

Enemy Tanks

Hill 102

Hill 109

B

A

1 5

1 5

Observation Hill

Obong-Ni

Tayadong

91
X

THE BATTLE

Shortly after the Marines began their advance on 17 August, the Pershings of 3 Platoon A Company were called upon to give fire support with both main armament and MG fire. The Marine armour, led by 2nd Lt Granville G. Sweet, concentrated heavy fire along 2/5's first objective, knocking out at least twelve enemy anti-tank guns and several automatic weapons. In the return fire, one M26 withstood three direct hits from enemy mortars, while the tanks of Sweet's platoon were struck by a total of twenty-three anti-tank projectiles. This fire did not bother the tanks or the tank crews much, and only one man was slightly wounded. After 1 Bn had passed through 2/5, the tanks moved forward and blasted several more North Korean positions in Tugok. Then, when the Marines had taken their objective, Sweet led his platoon back to a rallying point, about 1,000 yd east of Observation Hill (see map).

At about 20.00 hrs the tanks were refuelling and replenishing with ammunition. As they were doing so they were informed by B Company, who was now consolidating on Hills 102 and 109, that four enemy T-34s and supporting infantry were approaching the brigade position along the main supply route (MSR). They immediately set off, but some 300 yd down the MSR had to stop to move some stationary trucks which were blocking the road. At that time Sweet ordered his leading section to load with AP, 'just in case'. US Navy Corsairs, who were providing close air support, came in immediately, knocking out one tank and dispersing the enemy infantry. The other three tanks came on alone. To quote from the USMC history:

'Preparing a reception for the T-34s were the 1st 75 mm Recoilless Gun Platoon on Observation Hill and the rocket section of 1/5's anti-tank assault platoon on Hill 125. As the first enemy tank reached the bend, it took a hit in the right track from a 3.5 in rocket. Shooting wildly, the black hulk continued until its left track and front armor were blasted by 2nd Lt Paul R. Field's 75s. The enemy vehicle burst into flames as it wobbled around the curve and came face to face with TSgt Cecil R. Fullerton's M26.

'Still aimlessly firing its 85 mm rifle and machine-gun, the T-34 took two quick hits from the Marine tank's 90 mm and exploded. One North Korean got out of the burning vehicle but was cut down instantly by rifle fire. He crawled beneath the burning wreckage and died. The second T-34 charged toward the bend, taking a 3.5 rocket hit from Company A's assault squad. Weaving crazily around the curve with its right track damaged, the cripple was struck in the gas tank by a rocket from 1/5's assault section before meeting the fury of Field's recoilless rifles. It lurched to a stop off the road behind the first tank, and its 85 mm gun fired across the valley into the blue yonder.

'By this time a second M26 had squeezed next to that of Fullerton on the narrow firing line and the two Marine tanks blasted the T-34 with six 90 mm shells. Miraculously, the Communist vehicle kept on shooting, although its fire was quite indiscriminate. Marine armor poured in seven more rounds which ripped through the turret and exploded the hull. Before the kill, one Red tank man opened the turret hatch in an effort to escape. A 2.36 in white phosphorus round, fired by a 1 Bn rocket man, struck the open lid and ricocheted into the turret. The enemy soldier was knocked back into the tank as the interior turned into a furnace.

'The third T-34 raced around the bend to stop behind the blazing hulks of the first two. Marine tanks, recoilless rifles, and rockets ripped into it with a thundering salvo. The enemy tank shuddered, then erupted in a violent explosion and died. Thus the Brigade shattered the myth of the T-34 in five flaming minutes. Not only Corsairs and M26s, but every anti-tank weapon organic to Marine infantry had scored an assist in defeating the Communist armor.'

THE NAKTONG RIVER FRONT BATTLE, NEAR AGOK: 31 AUGUST–1 SEPTEMBER 1950

DEFENDING THE PERIMETER
Throughout August and early September the North Koreans mounted a series of attacks to try to drive the UN forces into the sea. There were many acts of individual heroism during this difficult period, none more worthy of recounting than the action which resulted in the Congressional Medal of Honor being awarded to Sgt First Class (SFC; later Master Sergeant (MSG)) Ernest R. Kouma of A Company, 72nd Tank Battalion (72 Tank

Bn). On 31 August his unit was engaged in supporting infantry elements on the Naktong River front. There was a thick blanket of fog that evening, completely obscuring the river and cutting visibility down to about 40 yd. Light mortar fire began about 20.00 hrs, then, just before midnight, the fog lifted.

THE TANK
SFC Kouma was commanding three M26 Pershing tanks, the heaviest American tank to see service during the Second World War, the 43.4 ton tank being more than a match for the Tiger. Despite its ability, however, only 310 (out of a total wartime production of 1,436) ever reached operational service before the end of the war and of these, only 200 were issued to units and just 20 saw any kind of action. The M26 had therefore had to wait for the Korean War to really prove itself

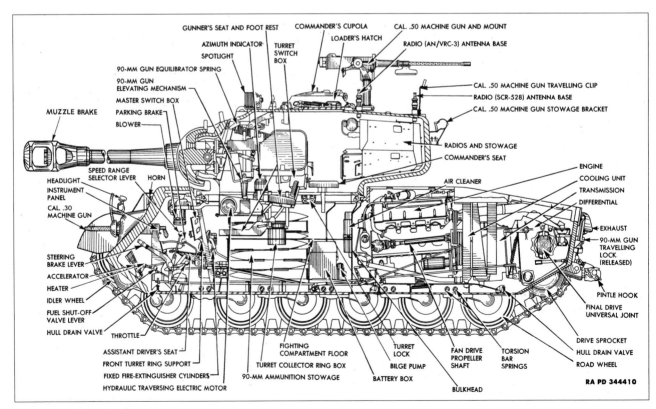

Pershing M26 tank.

A Pershing M26 heavy tank, of the type used by Sgt Kouma, fighting its way through Seoul, 27 September 1950. (Simon Dunstan)

in battle. The Pershing had a crew of five and was armed with a 90 mm M3 gun, for which seventy rounds were carried, plus two .30 cal MGs (one in the bow) and an AA mounted .50 cal on top of the turret. With armour 13–114 mm thick, a top speed of 30 m.p.h., a radius of action of 100 miles and a more powerful gun, it was far superior to the North Korean tanks (T-34/85) in every respect.

THE BATTLE
As the mist started to clear, Kouma was alarmed to see that, under cover of the fog,

the enemy had been building a pontoon bridge across the river and that it was now nearly two-thirds completed. He immediately ordered his gunner to engage with the 90 mm, while he fired the AA mounted .50 cal MG. Then his other two tanks joined in, together with some nearby AA vehicles, firing their dual 40 mm and quad .50 cal MGs. The bridge collapsed under the weight of this fire and the enemy soldiers were thrown into the water, with many casualties. Unfortunately, the enemy had already crossed in another area and soon the infantry positions which Kouma was supporting came under close attack by some 500 enemy. Near midnight the enemy pressure became too strong and the infantry decided to pull back. Kouma's tank platoon was given the task of covering this withdrawal.

The enemy assault came in and one of the other two tanks was immediately knocked out, leaving just two Pershings – Kouma's and one commanded by SFC Oscar V. Berry. Kouma soon discovered that he and Berry were the only obstacles in the path of the enemy, so he decided to stay put for as long as possible, fighting off continual enemy attacks. During one such attack, Kouma's tank was surrounded by a group of Koreans, all wearing US uniforms with 2nd Infantry Division (2 Inf Div) patches on their sleeves.[1] At the time, Kouma was out of the turret, putting a new belt of ammunition into the .50. 'The North Koreans have broken through, A Company has gone,' shouted one of the group to him. Before he could reply, all seven men in the group suddenly tossed hand grenades at him, while a machine-gun opened up from close range. Kouma immediately returned the fire, despite being wounded in the foot by an exploding grenade. He delivered point-blank, withering fire onto the North Korean soldiers who had tried to trick him, killing them all. Then he got back into his turret and continued to engage the enemy.

Making radio contact with Berry, they evolved a plan of action and soon moved forward into open ground where they were able to fire at will on the advancing hordes of North Korean infantry.

After about an hour of heavy fighting, Berry's tank was hit in the engine by a North Korean anti-tank rifle projectile and forced to withdraw. It started to limp back to friendly lines, but after a mile or so of slow going, the engine caught fire and the gallant Berry and his crew had to dismount and make their way back to safety on foot.

Kouma, however, stayed on in his exposed forward position, beating off repeated enemy attacks, for another 7 hours. He constantly got out of his turret to fire the .50 and when that ran out of ammunition, threw grenades and even fired his pistol in order to keep the enemy at bay. Finally, at about 07.00 hrs, running short of ammunition, he withdrew, safely negotiating the 8 miles of now hostile territory and continuing to engage the enemy. SFC Kouma destroyed at least three hostile machine-gun positions en route, with accurate fire from his 90 mm. When he did eventually reach his company command post area, Kouma went straight to replenish his tank and then had to be ordered to report for medical treatment, as all he wanted to do was to rejoin his company, despite his wounds. Thanks entirely to his brave action, the infantry were given the time they needed to be able to re-establish a secure defensive position and the enemy advance was beaten back.

A TANK ACE

After the Naktong 'Bulge' was retaken, over 250 enemy bodies were counted in the area where Kouma had made his heroic stand.

He later rejoined his unit and was offered a battlefield commission, which he refused, subsequently becoming a tank gunnery and tactics instructor at Camp Irwin, California, before joining the army recruiting staff. He volunteered to serve in Vietnam, but was turned down on the grounds that if he had been captured, it might have been used for propaganda purposes. MSG Kouma eventually retired from the Army in 1971, after thirty-one years of service, and sadly died in December 1993. Earlier that year the MSG Kouma Tank Platoon Gunnery Excellence Competition had been inaugurated at the Armor Center at Fort Knox, to be competed for annually within the US Armored Force. As Kouma's citation reads:

Advancing out of the Pusan bridgehead, the UN Forces had to deal with T-34/85s like this one (photographed from the rear). The 'soft shoulders' on the dirt roads made it extremely hazardous to move off the crown of the road. (Author's collection)

'MSG Kouma's superb leadership, heroism and intense devotion to duty, reflect the highest credit upon himself and uphold the esteemed traditions of the US Army.'

A PRESIDENTIAL UNIT CITATION
Following on from MSG Kouma's gallant action, 2 Inf Div went onto the offensive. This action prevented the enemy from obtaining his goal, which was a flanking penetration of the Allied perimeter between Taegu and Pusan; if this had been successful, the enemy could have rolled up the entire Allied defence line. The enemy lost some 1,800 casualties and much equipment and MSG Kouma's unit, 72 Tank Bn, received a Presidential Unit Citation, which closed with the words:

'The 72d Tank Battalion displayed such gallantry, determination and *esprit de corps* in accomplishing its mission under extremely difficult and hazardous conditions as to set it apart and above other units participating in the action, and reflects great credit on its members and the military service of the United States.'[2]

The Last Phase of the Battle of the Imjin River

THE CHINESE ATTACK

One of the most dramatic changes of events during the Korean War took place in late November 1950, when some 180,000 Chinese troops launched a massive offensive in support of the NKPA. From then onwards the hoped-for 'Home before Christmas' promise, made by MacArthur to his UN troops, became an impossible dream. The front was eventually stabilized on the 38th Parallel in the last week of December. There were further Chinese onslaughts in early 1951, however, and the battle see-sawed first one way then the other. By 8 April the latest Chinese offensive had been pushed back and the 38th Parallel line re-established. Then on the night of 22 April 1951 the Chinese attacked once again. By the end of the month they had been contained once more, but at massive cost to both sides – the Chinese alone lost over 70,000 men. There were many feats of courage, one of which was the famous stand of the Gloucesters (Glosters) at the Imjin River, which took place on 22–5 April 1951. However, the Glosters did not fight alone, and as the history of the 8th King's Royal Irish Hussars (8th Hussars) says: 'The Battle of the Imjin has now been woven into the great tapestry of the Regiment's past. It has confirmed the standards by which British soldiers in battle have been recognized

through the ringing centuries.' This is the story of part of the 8th Hussars involvement in the later phases of that famous battle.

THE TANK

8th Hussars were equipped with the Centurion Mk III. Although this British medium gun tank was operating in terrain for which it had never been built, it quickly proved itself to be the best tank of any to fight in Korea, and was probably without parallel throughout the world at that time. Developed towards the end of the Second World War, the Centurion Mk I, with its 17-pounder gun, was on troop trials before war ended, but never saw operational service. By the time of the Korean War, the Mk III was in British Army service. It mounted the 20-pounder gun OQF Mk I gun, for which sixty-five rounds were carried (APDS, HE, Canister and Smoke), plus a coaxially mounted 7.92 mm Besa MG (3,600 rounds carried). Weighing over 49 tons combat loaded, with a four-man crew, Centurion was powered by a 650 b.h.p. Rolls-Royce Meteor petrol engine which gave it a top speed of nearly 22 m.p.h. and an excellent cross-country performance.

Centurion was later upgunned with the highly successful ROF 105 mm gun which itself was a world-beater. Centurion is still in service (or just coming out of service) all over

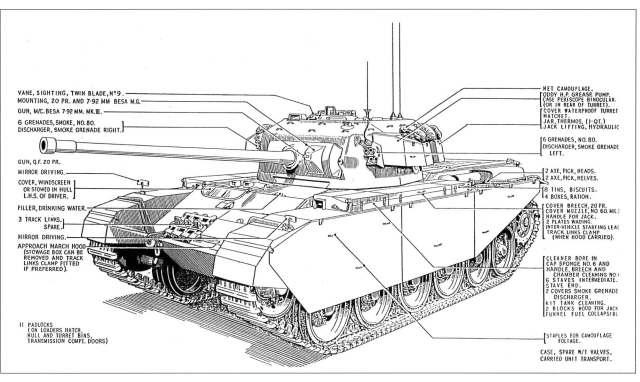

VANE, SIGHTING, TWIN BLADE, Nº 9.
MOUNTING, 20 PR. AND 7·92 MM BESA M.G.
GUN, M/C. BESA 7·92 MM. MK.III.
6 GRENADES, SMOKE, NO. 80.
DISCHARGER, SMOKE GRENADE RIGHT.

GUN, Q.F. 20 PR.
MIRROR DRIVING.
COVER, WINDSCREEN
OR STOWED IN HULL
L.H.S. OF DRIVER.
FILLER, DRINKING WATER.
3 TRACK LINKS,
SPARE.
MIRROR DRIVING.
APPROACH MARCH HOOD
(STOWAGE BOX CAN BE
REMOVED AND TRACK
LINKS CLAMP FITTED
IF PREFERRED).

11 PADLOCKS
(ON LOADERS HATCH,
HULL AND TURRET BINS,
TRANSMISSION COMPT. DOORS)

NET CAMOUFLAGE.
ODDY H.P. GREASE PUMP.
CASE PERISCOPE BINOCULAR.
(OR IN REAR OF TURRET).
COVER WATERPROOF TURRET
MATCHET.
JAR, THERMOS, (1-QT.)
JACK LIFTING, HYDRAULIC

6 GRENADES, NO. 80.
DISCHARGER, SMOKE GRENADE
LEFT.

2 AXE, PICK, HEADS.
2 AXE, PICK, HELVES.
8 TINS, BISCUITS.
4 BOXES, RATION.
COVER BREECH, 20 PR.
COVER MUZZLE, NO. 60. MK.
HANDLE FOR JACK.
2 PLATES WADING.
INTER-VEHICLE STARTING LEAD
TRACK LINKS CLAMP
(WHEN HOOD CARRIED).
CLEANER BORE IN
CAP SPONGE NO. 6 AND
HANDLE, BREECH AND
CHAMBER CLEANING NO. 1
6 STAVES INTERMEDIATE.
STAVE END.
2 COVERS SMOKE GRENADE
DISCHARGER.
KIT TANK CLEANING.
2 BLOCKS WOOD FOR JACK
FUNNEL FUEL COLLAPSIBL
STAPLES FOR CAMOUFLAGE
FOLIAGE.
CASE, SPARE W/T VALVES,
CARRIED UNIT TRANSPORT.

Centurion Mk III.

the world. Probably the most successful British tank ever built, 4,423 Centurions were manufactured between 1945 and 1962 when production ceased. At least 2,500 were exported to a dozen different countries worldwide.

THE SETTING

In mid-April 1951 the British 29th Independent Brigade Group (29 Bde), had been moved up from I Corps reserve, to take over positions along the line of the Imjin River on a 9 mile front. The brigade comprised four infantry battalions: the Northumberlands, the Glosters, the Ulster Rifles and an attached Belgian battalion. 8th Hussars was in support and C Squadron, which is the sub-unit whose actions we will be describing, was in the Yongdungpo area, having just moved up to replace B Squadron.

At about 21.00 hrs on the night of 22 April 2IC B Sqn, Capt Peter Ormrod, was talking on the field telephone to the Glosters Adjutant about an armoured patrol that it was planned would cross the Imjin River the next day. Distant firing was then heard from the direction of 'Gloster Crossing' and the line went dead.

There followed the epic Imjin River defensive battle in which each of the infantry battalions was cut off and had to fight virtually alone, the most often described action being the heroic stand of the Glosters. The 8th Hussar tanks tried on numerous occasions during 23 and 24 April to open routes up to the beleaguered infantry battalions and later helped extricate three of them. However, it was not until 25 April that this final phase of the battle was effected and, with the tanks' assistance, the surviving

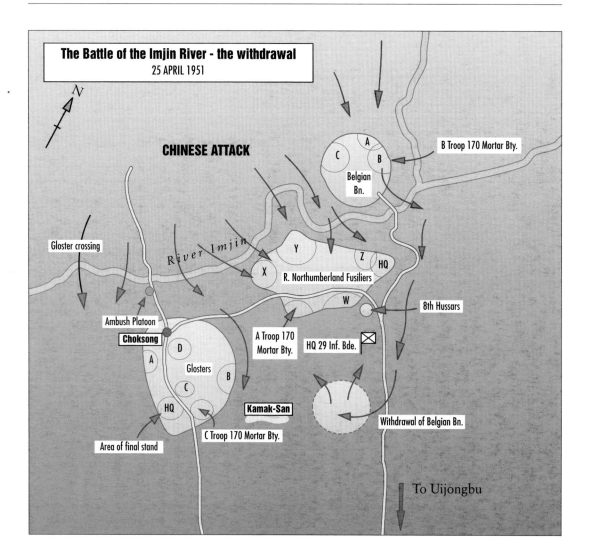

The Battle of the Imjin River - the withdrawal
25 APRIL 1951

N

CHINESE ATTACK

B Troop 170 Mortar Bty.

C   A
B

Belgian
Bn.

Gloster crossing

River Imjin

Y

X   Z   HQ
R. Northumberland Fusiliers

W

8th Hussars

Ambush Platoon

Choksong

D

A   A Troop 170   HQ 29 Inf. Bde. ⊠
Mortar Bty.

Glosters   B

C

HQ   **Kamak-San**

Withdrawal of Belgian Bn.

Area of final stand

C Troop 170 Mortar Bty.

To Uijongbu

infantry could be withdrawn through what has been aptly described as 'one long bloody ambush'.

There is space here to recount only the last phase of the action, described in the 8th Hussars' history as being the '. . . most distinguished single action of the day', and involving Maj Henry Huth, OC C Sqn, and Lt John Lidsey. This is by no means to decry the extremely gallant actions fought by other members of the squadron, such as Capt Peter Ormrod, who had been commanding half the squadron and without whose skilful

management and courage both the Northumberlands and Ulsters might well have been overrun. They had had to force their way down the valley through milling masses of Chinese, the tanks crushing them under their tracks as they 'ploughed them into the paddy fields'. There was a 'continuous iron rain' on the outside of the tanks and few of the infantry riding on them survived the journey unwounded.

Despite all the difficulties, the retreating column finally reached the location of the previous night's tank leaguer, where Maj

'O' Group on the third day of the Imjin battle. Maj Henry Huth is on the left, in the commander's cupola of his Centurion Mk III. Next to him are, left to right, the CO, 2IC of the Belgian Bn, and Capt P. Hartwright (8H LO at Bde HQ). OC's operator, in the other hatch, makes up the party. (Simon Dunstan)

Huth and one other SHQ tank (Lidsey's) were waiting to cover the last lap of the withdrawal. This final phase, however, began with disaster.

The two tanks which had been covering the Belgian battalion's withdrawal were the last ones into the leaguer area because one of them was stuck in low reverse and could only crawl along. They halted and an effort was made to tow the 'lame duck', to try and speed up the withdrawal. While this was being attempted, the enemy began to fire through the surrounding trees from close range. A stray bullet set off a phosphorus grenade in one of the smoke dischargers on the turret of the tank attempting the tow.[3] Unfortunately, as the turret was traversed over the engine decks, the burning phosphorus dripped down into the engine and set the tank on fire. The CO of the Belgian battalion, who was standing close by, was badly burned and had to be evacuated. Maj Huth then ordered the blazing tank and the lame one to be abandoned, after putting an AP shell into the turret of each of them from 50 yd range.

'He then traversed his turret left and engaged the Chinese at a distance of only 70 yd . . . aware that the last Belgian soldiers were still making their way through the trees behind him. . . . For three deliberate minutes he did not budge, but swinging his turret this way and that, firing long bursts of Besa, while bullets smacked against his armour, he held down the advance.'[4]

Only when Maj Huth was sure the Belgians were clear did he order his driver to take the tank out of the leaguer, meeting John Lidsey's tank outside the grove. Together they continued delaying the Chinese as they advanced towards them out of the trees.

Half a mile later came another crisis. The Ulsters, who had cut across the hills, were now coming down their reverse side and were destined to meet the same dirt road along which the Belgians and C Sqn's tanks were now withdrawing. Some were helping wounded friends and all had reached a complete state of exhaustion. They reached the road by a small group of shacks where, to make matters even worse, there were already many Americans crowded together waiting to be evacuated. Maj Henry Huth immediately ordered all his tanks, including his own and Lidsey's, to take on board as many wounded as possible, then to fill up any space remaining with the unwounded. They would endeavour to take them all down to the main supply route.

While they were loading up, a spotter plane flew in low and dropped a message, which said that a force of some 2,000 enemy were approaching from the west and could be expected to overtake the tired troops in under

10 minutes. Huth and Lidsey, being the only two tanks now available to fight, moved back to meet them. For a while they managed to hold the enemy back, but every minute saw the Chinese thickening and widening their advance, the paddy fields providing plenty of cover. As one observer, Capt the Hon. R.D.G. Winn, who was riding on the back of Huth's turret at the time, later wrote:

'The attack developed rapidly, on a wide arc, and was sustained with great ferocity. With no protective infantry, the tanks fought back in short bounds in constant danger of being enveloped from either flank. The enemy came forward at a remarkable pace, taking up fire positions behind the banks, ignoring losses inflicted at every bound. . . . Maj Huth so accurately measured his own fire-power against the fire and speed of advance of the enemy that he imposed the minimum rate of advance upon them, enabling the tired infantry to reach the road at a point behind him and make their way slowly towards the MSR. He was hampered by the presence of personnel on the outside of his own tank, but during the whole of the action none of these were seriously wounded and so far as I am aware not a single casualty was caused among the infantry on the stretch of road to his rear.

'American infantry joined the column en route and came under the protection of his two tanks. Two other tanks also joined us from the East at this point and strengthened the escort. Before the withdrawing infantry had reached safety, the powered traverse of Maj Huth's tank failed and it became impossible to bring fire to bear speedily when required from the coaxial machine-gun. Fire was continued by Brens and other automatic weapons from his tank, and the enemy was still kept at a distance without the speed of retirement being increased. In many instances it was necessary to engage at

Excellent shot of an 8th Hussar's Centurion Mk III negotiating the scrub, paddy fields and steep hills of Korea. (Simon Dunstan)

right angles to the axis of withdrawal. Not until the last infantryman was seen to have reached the MSR, where more powerful friendly fire-power was available, did Maj Huth give orders to draw out of enemy reach.

'Lt Lidsey, whose tank was closer to the enemy throughout, showed an admirable coolness and bravery vital to the operation in carrying out Maj Huth's instructions, but it was Maj Huth's own example of skill and determination which made all those present in the action proud to obey his orders to the best of their ability.'[5]

As the Regimental history explains: 'the last shot fired by Maj Huth ended the Battle of the Imjin.' Maj Huth's squadron had suffered severely, losing a total of six Centurions, one Cromwell, two Bren Carriers, one scout car and one half-track, but had been responsible for saving the major proportion of 29 Bde Maj P.F. Huth, MC was rightly awarded the Distinguished Service Order for his gallantry.

TANK-VERSUS-TANK AT BEN HET, VIETNAM

Despite the effective use of armour on many occasions during the Vietnam conflict, there was only one battle[6] in which American tanks fought directly against North Vietnamese tanks. This battle took place at a special forces camp near Ben Het in the Central Highlands of South Vietnam. The camp was important as it overlooked the Ho Chi Minh trail entrances from the Laos–Cambodia–Vietnam border area.

On the night of 3 March 1969 North Vietnamese tanks and other forces attacked the joint US and Vietnamese troops, who were dug into the barren hills of the camp. The camp had been subjected to intense indirect fire attacks during February, which were thought to be designed to mask North Vietnamese troop movements. To counter this apparent enemy build-up, elements of the 1st Battalion, 69th Armor were sent into the area. Capt John P. Stovall's B Company occupied strong points and bridge security positions along the 10 km road link between Ben Het and Dak To. One platoon of M48A3 tanks was stationed in the camp to support three Vietnamese infantry companies, an American 175 mm artillery battery and two M42A1 'Dusters' (twin 40 mm guns on the M41 light tank chassis). Capt Stovall had also established a temporary command post near to the tank platoon positions, because

the platoon leader had been evacuated to Dak To with multiple fragmentation wounds.

On 2 March, at about 22.00 hrs, SFC Hugh Havermale, the tank platoon sergeant, reported to Capt Stovall that his men could hear the sound of tracked vehicles through the noise of the artillery and the two men went forward together with a night vision device. Although they could hear unidentified vehicles running their engines for some 20 minutes, then shutting them down as though they were carrying out daily maintenance, they were unable to establish even a general location of the reported noises.

The following night the artillery and mortar fire increased sharply, while the track and engine noises were repeated. The platoon loaded with HEAT ammunition[7] just in case and Havermale scanned the area with the help of his Xenon infra-red searchlight. He saw nothing. Another tank commander, Sgt Jerry W. Jones did manage to locate the area of the engine and track noise more accurately, but unfortunately had no searchlight. Everyone stood to and waited. Suddenly, an anti-tank mine exploded some 1,100 m to the south-west. The battle was about to begin.

THE TANKS
The M48A3 Patton was the most powerful American tank to see service in Vietnam. The

An M48A3, belonging to C Company, 1 Tank Bn, 1 Mar Div, prepares to move off some 15 miles south-east of Danang, 12 February 1970. (Simon Dunstan)

48½ ton General Patton mounted a 90 mm M41 gun and had armour 12–120 mm thick. Deliveries began in 1953 to replace the 'stopgap' M47. Widely exported, it saw active service in Pakistan, Israel and Vietnam. The four-man tank was powered by a 750 b.h.p. V-12 diesel engine, had a top speed of 30 m.p.h. and a range of 290 miles.

Its opposition at Ben Hat was the Russian-built PT-76 reconnaissance tank. Weighing only 14 tons, with armour 11–14 mm thick, it was well armed with a D-56T 76.2 mm gun and coaxial MG in a well-sloped, two-man turret. Not only did it have a good cross-country performance (top speed 27½ m.p.h. and range 162 miles), but the three-man tank was amphibious without any preparation and carried a snorkel tube for deep wading. Propulsion was by water jets in the back of the hull.

THE BATTLE
The mine had immobilized the enemy tank, but had not knocked it out and the next

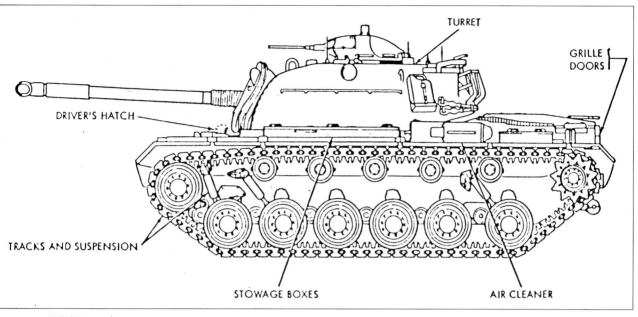

M48A3 Patton tank.

second it fired at the camp, but the round fell short. The rest of the attacking force also opened up and the defenders were able to count some seven gun flashes. Specialist 4 Frank Hembree was the first tank gunner to fire at the enemy and later recalled: 'I only had his muzzle flashes to sight on, but I couldn't wait for a better target because his shells were landing real close to us.'[8] This proved to be all that Hembree needed, his second round turning the enemy tank into a fireball. By the light of the burning PT-76 they were able to locate three more tanks and a tracked open-topped carrier (BTR 50), which were all engaged. Shortly after this action, Stovall received reports of another enemy tank approaching the left flank, near the camp airstrip. He called for illumination via the camp mortar squad, while the tankers continued to fire at the enemy, hitting at least two more tanks and the carrier.

While this firing was taking place, Capt Stovall had been climbing up on to the back decks of Havermale's tank. As he did so an

enemy tank fired at them, the night illumination proving a two-edged sword as the enemy could now see them just as well as they could see him. The enemy projectile struck the M48, blowing Stovall and the tank commander off the vehicle and inflicting severe shrapnel wounds to them both. The explosion also killed the loader and driver, who were manning an externally mounted machine-gun. Nevertheless, actual damage to the M48 was slight and it was soon back in action, manned by spare crewmen.

Sgt Jones then took charge and, dismounting, ran over to another tank which was unable to engage the enemy from its current location. He moved it, under fire, to a new position and then took on another PT-76, close by the burnt-out one, scoring a direct hit. Gradually the enemy fire slackened and it became clear that they were having second thoughts about continuing with the attack. This was just as well because the M48s had by then used up all their readily available HEAT ammunition and were

PT-76s demonstrating very clearly their amphibious capabilities. (Simon Dunstan)

reduced to firing HE with concrete-piercing fuses. Fortunately, they were able to use the lull to replenish. The battle then just petered out, especially after reinforcements in the shape of the tank company's second platoon arrived and the platoon commander, Lt Ed Nickels, took charge.

Next morning the enemy had vanished. An investigation of the battlefield revealed two burnt-out PT-76s and one burnt-out BTR 50, which had all belonged to 16 Company, 4th Battalion, 202nd Armoured Regiment of the NKPA. Total casualties within B Company were two killed and two wounded. Sgt Havermale's tank, which had received the direct hit, had no damage other than a broken machine-gun charging handle. So ended the first tank-versus-tank engagement of the war. The next clash of armour would not happen until two years later, in March 1971, when South Vietnamese M41, Walker Bulldogs, clashed with North Vietnamese tanks in Laos.[9]

AMBUSH AT SUOI CAT

THE 'BLACKHORSE'

Among the many American units that fought in Vietnam, the 11th Armored Cavalry, the 'Blackhorse' Regiment (11 ACR), earned for itself a special reputation for gallantry, discipline and fighting spirit. It was involved in many actions, using a mixture of tanks: M48A3 for heavy fire-power, ACAV (M113 personnel carriers converted into Armored Cavalry Assault Vehicles), heavy 4.2 in mortars and 155 mm SP howitzers, plus Huey scout and Cobra attack helicopters. When it arrived in Vietnam in 1966 the regimental strength was 3,762 troopers.

Convoy protection was one of 11 ACR's main roles and the unit was involved in many ambushes, one of the earliest being near Suoi Cat on 2 December 1966. The action fought by 1st Squadron (1 Sqn) 11 ACR became a classic example and was quoted in the 'SOP' (Standard Operating Procedures) for the Regiment.

THE BUILD-UP

Recent intelligence reports had indicated that there was an enemy battalion operating in the vicinity of Suoi Cat, so 1 Sqn 11 ACR carried out a limited zone reconnaissance of the area, but found no signs of enemy. On 2 December 1 Sqn was going about its routine duties at the base camp, west of Suoi Cat: A Troop on base camp security, B Troop protecting an engineer rock quarrying site some 25 km north near Gia Rev, the rest of

the squadron on vehicle maintenance. Earlier that morning B Troop had sent a resupply convoy (2 tanks, 3 ACAV and 2 trucks) down from Gia Rev to base without incident and now, at about 16.00 hrs, the convoy was getting ready for the return trip. The squadron commander, Lt Col Martin D. Howell, was holding a command and staff meeting at his CP at about 16.30 hrs when suddenly, as one witness put it later, '. . . all hell broke loose!'

THE AFV

Having dealt with the M48 tank in the last battle report, we will look at the ACAV. When agreement was reached on the organization of 11 ACR for Vietnam, it was decided that M113s would replace tanks in the cavalry platoons. These therefore were modified for use as fighting vehicles by adding an armoured shield for the .50 cal machine-gun, plus pedestals and shields for two side-mounted M60 machine-guns.[10] The concept and design had been adopted some years previously by South Vietnamese armoured forces and was recommended to American units by their armoured advisers to the Vietnamese Armor Command.

The basic M113 is probably one of the most widely used AFVs in the world. Development began in 1956 when a requirement was raised for a lightweight armoured personnel carrier for use by armour and infantry, which was both amphibious

Members of M Troop, 3 Sqn, 11 Armd Cav Regt keeping watch for enemy from their ACAVs during Operation 'Cedar Falls', 10 km south-west of Ben Het, 11 January 1967. (Simon Dunstan)

and air portable. Built by the FMC Corporation, the basic M113 weighed about 11 tons combat ready (M113A1). However, the extra weaponry and, in some cases, extra armour increased the basic weight considerably. Nevertheless, it still had a good cross-country performance, a top speed of about 42 m.p.h. and a range of 300 miles. By early 1980 some 70,000 members of the M113 family had been produced.

THE BATTLE

The convoy commander, Lt Will Radnosevich, had arranged his vehicles in the following order: his own tank leading, followed by two ACAVs, then the two trucks, the third ACAV and finally, the last tank. He had full radio contact with his armoured vehicles, with base and also with a forward air controller. They set out and passed through Suoi Cat without incident, although

240

An ACAV on patrol. Note the .50 heavy Browning machine-gun in the leading turret and the raised fording/wading plate at the front. (Simon Dunstan)

everyone noticed that the village was strangely quiet, with no children about. While traversing his commander's hatch to observe both sides of the road, Radnosevich accidentally traversed the complete turret, which evidently alarmed the enemy, who set off a command-detonated mine some 10 m in front of the tank. 'Ambush! Ambush! Claymore Corner,'[11] shouted Radnosevich over his radio as he led his convoy through the ambush site at top speed, blasting both sides of the road and meeting a hail of enemy fire.

His call galvanized the squadron. Under Capt John Landry, B Troop, who was nearest to the ambush, 'saddled up and moved out' within 5 minutes of receiving the message. Meanwhile at the squadron base, C Troop, the howitzer battery, and a resident tank company (D Company) also got ready to move, followed by A Troop as soon as it was released from its perimeter security details.

The tank company, under Maj Bill Peasle, was rolling through the camp gate just 7 minutes after the ambush had been sprung, so action was immediate and help was on its way. In addition, the gunship 'on station' fired at the enemy and also called for additional assistance via the forward air controller. By this time the convoy had driven through the ambush position, under intense fire, with the loss of one ACAV, which caught fire after being hit at least four times.

B Troop (Capt John Landry) was the first relief force to arrive and moved into the ambush position from the east, engaging the Viet Cong strongly. It was estimated that the enemy was in at least reinforced battalion strength (600 plus), with 75 mm recoilless rifles, mortars and other support weapons, including several heavy MGs. Its well-prepared positions, many with overhead cover, varied in location from those close beside the road (grenade throwers who tried to lob hand grenades into the passing American vehicles) to those 1000 m away (support weapons). All were able to bring concentrated, effective fire on to the road. On reaching the western end, Landry turned round and made a second pass through the ambush area, closely followed by the tank company and C Troop, who were all raking both sides of the road with fire. The tanks were firing canister,[12] which mowed down the charging enemy infantry and knocked out at least one 57 mm recoilless rifle.

The squadron commander, Lt Col Howell, had arrived overhead in a scout helicopter some 10 minutes after the first rounds were fired. He had quickly taken hold of the situation, co-ordinating the activities on the ground himself, designating a suitable fire co-ordination line and directing both artillery and tactical aircraft to strike the enemy. A Troop, who was late on the scene due to its perimeter task, now appeared, killing fifteen of a party of Viet Cong apparently scavenging the area. Howell now had his entire squadron, plus the tank company, and was able to subject the Viet Cong to deadly cross-fire as all units converged. As darkness approached the American troops prepared night defensive positions, while the artillery shifted its fire to the south to prevent the enemy from using its escape routes.

The morning revealed over 100 enemy dead including, it was later discovered, three VC battalion commanders and four company commanders, plus numerous weapons and equipment.

Undoubtedly the speedy reaction and overwhelming fire-power had played a vital part in the success of the operation. It is difficult to select a tank ace from this engagement; clearly all tank and ACAV commanders did a first-class job.

AMBUSH NEAR QUAN LOI

Convoys and ambushes continued to take place throughout the war, and during one on Highway 13 in the Binh Long Province in 1969 Lt Harold A. Fritz, then serving with A Troop, displayed such gallantry above and beyond the call of duty that he was awarded the Congressional Medal of Honor.

On 11 January Lt Fritz was leading a seven-vehicle armoured column along Highway 13 to meet and escort a truck convoy. Suddenly his column came under intense cross-fire from a reinforced enemy company, who was deployed in ambush positions. Fritz's ACAV was hit and he was badly wounded. Realizing that his platoon was completely surrounded, vastly outnumbered and in danger of being overrun, Fritz leapt on top of his burning vehicle and directed the positioning of his remaining vehicles and men. Then, with utter disregard

'Find the Bastards. Then pile on'. This evocative painting by James Dietz was commissioned by the Black Horse Association to honour Lt Harold A. Fritz's heroic counter-attack on Highway 13, Quan Loi, for which he was awarded the Congressional Medal of Honor. The painting now hangs in the Patton Museum. (Patton Museum)

for his wounds and safety, he ran from vehicle to vehicle in complete view of the enemy gunners in order to reposition his troops, assist the wounded, distribute ammunition, direct fire and generally provide encouragement to his men.

When a strong enemy force assaulted the position and attempted to overrun the platoon, Fritz manned a machine-gun and through his exemplary action inspired his men to deliver intense and deadly fire, which broke the assault and routed the attackers. Moments later, a second enemy force advanced to within 2 m of the position and threatened to overwhelm the defenders. Armed only with a pistol and a bayonet, he led a small group of his men in a daring charge, which routed the attackers and inflicted heavy casualties.

When a relief force arrived Fritz realized that it was not deploying effectively enough against the enemy positions, so he ran through heavy enemy fire to personally direct its deployment, and did so to such effect that they forced the enemy to abandon the ambush site and withdraw. Despite his wounds he then returned to his men, refusing medical attention until all his wounded comrades had been treated and evacuated.

Fritz's heroism was the subject of an evocative painting and reflected the greatest credit upon himself, his unit and the American forces.[13]

NOTES TO KOREA AND VIETNAM

1. 2 Inf Div wore a distinctive 'Indian Head' patch, with a be-feathered Indian chief's head superimposed on a white five-pointed star on a large black shield.

2. *The Second United States Infantry Division in Korea 1950–51*, Lt Clark C. Munroe.

3. The multi-barrel smoke dischargers are fitted in banks on either side of most modern tank turrets. They are fired electrically by the tank commander when it is necessary for the tank to be obscured from view by a local smoke screen. The grenades must therefore burst instantaneously, so a white phosphorus (WP) filling is normally used. This gives an instant thick cloud of white smoke when it bursts, rather than a slow build-up.

4. *Men of Valour*, Olivia Fitzroy.

5. Taken from a letter written to CO 8th Hussars by Capt the Hon. R.D.G. Winn and held in the Tank Museum Library.

6. North Vietnamese armour had made its appearance before this action, although not against American tanks. This was in the assault on Lang Vei Special Forces camp, during the Tet offensive in 1968, when thirteen PT-76s had spearheaded the assault.

7. HEAT = High Explosive Anti Tank.

8. *Armored Combat in Vietnam*, Gen Donn A. Starry.

9. Sgt Nguyen Xuan Mai, a tank commander in 1 Sqn, 11 ACR, destroyed a North Vietnamese T-54 at Landing Zone 31, where, by the end of the battle, the South Vietnamese M41s had knocked out six T-54 and sixteen PT-76 without loss. (Source: p. 193, *Armored Combat in Vietnam*).

10. Sometimes one of the side or front MGs was replaced by a 57 mm recoilless rifle, while an 81 mm mortar was also carried in support platoons.

11. *Armored Combat in Vietnam*. 'Claymore Corner' was a unit nickname for a well-known point on the road, so everyone immediately knew where the action was taking place.

12. This sophisticated form of canister contained either 1,280 pellets or up to 10,000 lethal little darts called flêchettes.

13. Taken from Capt Harold A. Fritz's citation.

CONTINUAL CONFLICT

From its independence in 1948, through the past half-century of its existence right up until the more hopeful days of 1994, the state of Israel has been almost continually at war with one or other of its Arab neighbours. Now at long last, there seems to be a real chance of peace. However, the Israeli Defence Forces (IDF) will no doubt have to remain ready to meet any emergency, certainly until a lasting peace has been achieved. One of the most important components of the IDF has always been its armour, whose determination, expertise and courage has enabled the Israelis to overcome far larger and better equipped forces time and time again. Their technical expertise, for example, is abundantly clear to anyone who has had any dealings with them. However, it is not often that the commander of any of the world's armoured corps is called upon to show his personal technical expertise in such a practical way as occurred in the first of our accounts in this section.

Maj Gen Israel Tal, known as 'Talik' throughout the IDF, took over command of the Armoured Corps on 1 November 1964. To quote from its history: 'The immediate impact he made upon discipline and training and his insistence upon the achievement of the highest professional standards by all tank crewmen and officers,

Maj Gen Israel Tal seen here on the gunnery range watching his gunners training through high-power binoculars. (Israeli Defence Force)

quickly established the Corps as a most formidable fighting force.'[1]

Talik's gunnery prowess is legendary, as the following account shows.

THE WAR OF THE WATERS

A STRANGE BATTLE

Thirty years ago the Israeli Armoured Corps fought one of its strangest battles. Over a period of months specially selected tank crews fought a 'precision war' against Syrian attempts to divert natural water resources on the Golan Heights. If such attempts had succeeded the very existence of Israel would have been threatened as her survival depended, and still does depend, upon these waters.

On the same day as Maj Gen Tal took over the Armoured Corps in 1964, Maj Gen David Elazar took over command of Northern HQ. It was a period of high tension on the Syrian front, during which Syrian forces, in dominating positions on the high ground above, fired repeatedly on Israeli patrols moving in the valley. Only a few months earlier Israel had started the flow of water through its 'National Carrier', a conduit which carries water from the Sea of Galilee down to the barren Negev Desert in the south. The Arabs were in uproar, Syria demanding war, but Egypt showing reluctance, still cautious after the embarrassments of the recent conflict over Suez (Operation 'Musketeer'[2]). An emergency joint Arab conference resulted in a plan to divert the sources of the River Jordan, in particular the Banias springs on the Golan, thus nullifying the Israeli project. At the same time Syria began building a carrier of its own, aimed at diverting the waters into Jordan,

protecting this work with a series of fortifications along the Golan Ridge, which dominates the entire region.

Gen Elazar, watching the Syrian progress from a vantage point near Tel Dan in the northern sector, contended that tank guns should be able to hit point targets on the Syrian water carrier and to deal with enemy fire coming from dug-in tanks. Some senior Israeli commanders expressed doubts, but Lt Gen Yitzhak Rabin, then Army Chief of Staff, gave his consent and a company of Centurions from the 7th Armoured Brigade (7 Armd Bde), commanded by Capt Shamai Kaplan,[3] was sent to Tel Dan to deal with the situation. 2nd Lt Avigdor Kahalany, who was commanding a Centurion troop in this company, was the first into action. They watched as an Israeli mobile patrol moved along a dirt road in full view of the Syrians. Suddenly, at a range of about 800 m, it was engaged by Syrian machine-gun fire from two vintage Second World War ex-German PzKpfw IV tanks, which had been dug-in, with just their turrets visible. Lt Col David Eshel, a well-known writer on the IDF, told me:

'Within 5 minutes Kahalany's Centurions were in position, well dispersed at 50 m intervals ready to fire. Kahalany's tank was first to fire, aiming for some Syrian recoilless guns placed in the shadow of one of the houses above. The air filled with flying shrapnel, screaming tank shells and clouds of smoke. Syrian mortars pounded the area, while the Panzers joined in. The Centurions fired nonstop for almost an hour before a cease fire was arranged by UN observers.'

Unfortunately, what became known as the 'first Nukheila incident' ended in complete failure. Having fired nearly 100 rounds the Centurions' 105 mm guns had hit very little and no Syrian tanks had been knocked out. Gen Tal, who came to investigate, was naturally furious. Gen Rabin started to have second thoughts about the whole idea, but Tal was adamant that he could deliver the goods. He immediately called a meeting of all Armoured Corps officers above the rank of major and did not mince his words when he addressed them. A new gunnery training

camp would be set up in the Negev, where all tanks crews, in particular gunners, would be subjected to gruelling schedules, firing hundreds of rounds until they could guarantee to hit with the first round at any range. Tal spent many days and nights with his men on the ranges, monitoring their progress. Eshel again: 'Blessed with great technical talent and a stickler for detail, Gen Tal was a hard man to please when it came to tank gunnery. He soon knew every gunner by name.' The results were quickly proven when, only two weeks after the initial failure, Tal was ready to prove his point. Kahalany's Centurions were again put into position, but this time in a secondary role, while a platoon of Israeli-modified Shermans was selected to do the primary job. These had been upgunned locally with the French CN 75-50

The capbadge of the modern day Israeli Armoured Corps. (Tank Museum)

The Israeli M51 Supersherman, which mounted a modified version of the French 105 mm gun (designated as the D1504 tank gun, its barrel length was 4.5 m instead of the original 6 m). It was the next development after the M50 Supersherman. Later, the tank was fitted with the British 105 mm gun. (Israeli Defence Force)

gun, which was based upon the German 7.5 cm Kwk 42 (L/70) which had been mounted in Panther. The gun was preferred by many Israeli tank crews, who had initially found Centurion, with its original 20-pounder gun, totally ineffective. However, the Centurions had now been locally upgunned with the British L/7 105 mm gun, which at the time was the best tank gun in the world. Tal, who had examined the British gun personally, was delighted with its performance and shook off the doubts of the veteran Sherman crews, who still swore by the French gun. Kahalany was also confident that his Centurion was ready to prove its worth. His gunner, Sgt Shalom Cohen, was the best he could get and had delighted Gen Tal with his performance on the ranges.

Col Eshel writes:

'As noon came, the patrol was passing along the dirt track leading towards the springs and soon the Syrians opened the day with machine-gun fire followed by light mortars. Capt Shimon's Sherman platoon was quickly out of its hiding and opened fire, but misfortune hit one of the tanks which slid into a ditch. Kahalany saw the accident and ordered his own Centurion up into position. At 800 m his gunner Cohen took aim and sent his first high-velocity round towards one of the Syrian Panzers hiding in a dugout, which presented a target only 60 x 120 cm. It was a difficult target to hit even at that range at a time when advanced optics were not available, as they are for tank crews today. But Cohen fired and his rounds hit home, the Syrian tank exploded into searing flame. Encouraged with his success, the gunner fired again, taking extra care that his aim was on the mark and the second Panzer burst into flame.'

Soon a fierce battle was in full swing, with Syrian artillery pounding the nearby settlements and the Israelis calling in fighter bombers to silence them, until the UN arranged a cease-fire.

Tal's tankers had done a good job, but there were still doubts among some senior officers as to the effectiveness of tank fire to silence Syrian point targets. However, the water problem did not diminish and it was clear that something had to be done. Failing a solution, the Israelis would be forced to give in, or would have to escalate the matter to full-scale war. Gen Tal was convinced that high-precision tank gunnery would answer the problem, by destroying the Syrian equipment without having to resort to such drastic measures. He had carefully studied the potential of contemporary tank guns and was convinced that they had far more potential than the technical parameters set by the designers. He contended that the first failure had been the result of insufficient training by tank crews and not lack of quality material. So far, current training standards had allowed tank gunners to fire with limited accuracy at ranges of not over 800–1,000 m, a hit within a 4 m target radius being considered sufficient, assuming that ricochets would also be lethal. Gen Tal was totally opposed to this theory, stressing that only point targets should apply in tank gunnery and that engagement ranges should be extended to 1,500 m. A major retraining was now under way, which included both regular and reserve tank crews. Eshel writes:

'. . . professional skill becoming in high demand and emphasis placed on specialization rather than a wide range of skills which were formerly demanded. Thus a

specialist bore-sighting team was given the task of zeroing all the tanks with high precision equipment and test firing, thus bringing every single tank to a common denominator in combat. One of the men chosen to serve in this coveted unit was Shalom Cohen (later Sgt), who thus fired a huge amount of rounds amassing great experience which would serve him well later.'

Despite the Israeli success in the second engagement, the Syrians had clearly decided not to give up. However, they did move their working sites eastward, until they were some 2,000 m from the nearest Israeli positions in the valley, a range at which their experts assumed they were invulnerable to the Israeli tank guns. Without any of today's high-pressure guns, supersonic high-velocity ammunition and ultra-modern optics, such engagement ranges were considered impossible for tank gunnery. Indeed, to hit a precision target at any range above 1,500 m was thought to be a tanker's dream!

Eshel again:

'Gen Tal was faced with two alternatives: one was to use the indirect or semi-indirect firing method, which was used in the Italian Campaign during the Second World War by Sherman crews firing HE shells from the short 75 mm gun usually uphill and in salvoes. But apart from a few Israeli officers who had been taught this practice in France in the early fifties, no one in the IDF had so far fired in this method. Moreover, indirect firing would not guarantee accurate hits on point targets, which was the prime requirement here.

'Thus a more reliable firing procedure had to be found to destroy point targets at long range by direct firing practice. Direct fire, apart from direct laying – in which the target is visible from the gunner's optics – is used when the target is visible from the position of the gun barrel or the fire base. Thus the projectile travels along a straight path trajectory, the gunner setting his reticule as ordered by the commander. But at Tel Dan in the Northern triangle of the then demilitarized zone, the topographical situation introduced an even more intricate matter into the equation. Studies revealed that from a ballistic standpoint, firing uphill would actually increase hit probability substantially, than firing over a straight line of sight. Moreover, aiming uphill also increased the probability of placing the target within the gunner's optics – than actually firing with direct laying. The same would apply to firing downhill, as long as the depression of the gun allowed this (which was not the case with Soviet-built tanks). The ballistic phenomena was little known throughout the professional world, due to the fact that tank gunnery normally applied to combat ranges and worried little about unusual practices of firing at longer ranges which were thought impractical and were given to other forces to deal with, such as air power with airborne guns and rockets, or artillery barrages. Here, due to political restraints, it was up to Tal's theories to solve a strategic problem with his tank guns, which, if successful, would not only destroy the Syrian diversion project, but would also prevent a dangerous escalation to the brink of full-scale war over the issue. The responsibility that Gen Tal and his experts faced was tremendous. It was the first time in military history that tanks were given a strategic task to perform and if he failed there would be no other option but to go to war or give in.'

Naturally Tal wanted to test his theories as carefully as possible, so he fired a large number of rounds on the Negev ranges over a specially designed model. The results were excellent and he was soon convinced that he could do the job.

Tal had proved beyond doubt that rounds fired at high angles of incidence were more accurate than those fired at the same long ranges over a straight line of sight. Thus, firing uphill at the Syrians on the slopes of Mt Hermon would be ideal. However, Gen Tal had to convince his superiors, who still based their views on the dismal past showing of the first encounter. The chance to prove his theories came on 6 March 1965, four months after the last incident, when a Syrian recoilless gun fired on an Israeli tractor near Almagor, killing the driver. Although it had nothing to do with the water diversion project, Gen Tal seized on the opportunity to convince the doubters once and for all. He personally boarded a camouflaged Sherman, mounting a 75 mm French high-velocity gun, of the type which had already proved itself in the last fire fight. He could clearly see the Syrian gun crew preparing to fire at another Israeli tractor which was starting out along the disputed patrol track, with a volunteer driver.

'This was the cue for which the General had been waiting,' writes David Eshel, 'his first HE round scored a direct hit and the enemy gun exploded into fragments, clearly seen by the senior officers watching the scene from a hill nearby.' Encouraged by this success, Rabin talked to the Prime Minister, who authorized Tal's plan and a few days later Gen Tal, together with some of his officers, flew north to co-ordinate the plan with Gen Elazar. The final show-down would be at the current Syrian water diversion site, on the slopes of Mt Hebron, not far from the Nukheila area, where eight pieces of Syrian engineering equipment had been identified, working in two groups to the left and right of a ravine and clearly visible with high-power binoculars. David Eshel again:

'Tal had brought with him his prime gunner, Sgt Shalom Cohen and he decided to split his two tanks, each taking on four of the Syrian tractors. After several hours of tense waiting with the sun blinding the Syrian gunners below the working site on the slope, these opened fire with a Russian Guryanov machine-gun on a patrol along the track in the valley. Within 2 minutes Tal and Cohen destroyed seven pieces of equipment, the General firing HE shells from an M50 75 mm gun Sherman, while Cohen sent his HESH rounds from his 105 mm L/7 gun mounted on Centurion. One tractor Cohen missed, but the general saw it and sent another round to finish it off and the tractor skidded downhill. Fewer than ten rounds had been fired. All were bull's-eyes on the mark – the incident was over in 4 minutes. Both the Syrians and the Israelis were stunned by the brilliant performance. The Syrians did not respond. With a single precision operation the Israelis had deflated a grand strategy of the Syrians.

Tal had chosen an unexpected option and it had paid off.'

Unfortunately that was not the end of the affair. The Syrians were still determined to continue with their water diversion plans and moved their work site further south, the new area being 6 km away from the nearest Israeli positions in the valley below. This time they were convinced that they could work unhindered from tank guns and that if the Israelis did intervene it would be a clear escalation, using air or artillery. However, they had reckoned without 'Talik'! He remained convinced that both the high-power French 105 mm low-pressure GIAT gun and the British L/7 105 mm were both capable of meeting the challenge. The former had been chosen for the Sherman M51 project and had already proved very effective and Tal himself was 'raring to go', as Eshel explains:

An Israeli Centurion Mk 3/5 upgunned with the L/7 105 mm gun. This was the tank in which Gen Tal had so much faith. (David Eshel)

'Having practised long-range firing on the Negev ranges, Tal was ready. As at such ranges the targets were beyond visual range, high-power binoculars were used, manned by expert observers who would direct fire and correct ranging.'

However, range was not the only problem this time. The Syrians had very cleverly hidden their site with an earth embankment; all that could be seen were the earth-moving scoops, throwing their contents over the wall. Split-second timing was therefore required; aiming and firing had to coincide with the showing of the scoops. In addition, to ensure that the hits would be effective, Tal chose to use a bunker-busting HE round, with a delay fuse which would not detonate the round until it had penetrated the earth wall. It worked perfectly, forty rounds being fired in 10 minutes and two Syrian tractors destroyed, the fire being corrected by outside observers using high-power binoculars. This action took place on 13 May 1965 and intelligence photographs taken later showed that one of the rounds had penetrated the earth wall, gone through the elevated dozer blade, and then exploded in the tractor's engine, with devastating effect.

The last occasion in which Israeli tanks were involved came three months later, once again in the Almagor area. After the last engagement, the Syrians had moved their site 10–11 km from the Israeli positions. Surely now they would be able to work unhindered? However, they were in for another painful surprise. Gen Tal ordered a second model to be built on the Negev ranges, on which his gunners tested super-long engagements using L/7 105 mm APDS rounds – the only ones which were thought to be capable of performing effectively at such long ranges. As Col Eshel explains:

'At such extreme ranges the parameters which worked within the 2,000 m range would no longer apply. Here the natural laws of gravity would certainly decrease trajectory of the constant speed round travelling under stress from other parameters as well. Extra care was given to bore-sighting and the firing tests, examined by the use of a hopping helicopter, were encouraging. Once again, outside observers with their high-power binoculars would observe and correct the firing sequence.'

The fateful day arrived on 11 August, and two tanks, both Centurions, moved into position. Sgt Cohen was in charge of the one tasked to fire at the earth-moving equipment at 11 km range, while Gen Tal, in the second tank, would deal with a Syrian PzKpfw IV, located under cover at 1,500 m range. Their opportunity came when the Syrians opened fire on an Israeli tractor with machine-gun and mortar fire. Cohen's first round (at 11 km) scored a direct hit on one of the Syrian tractors. It took some time for this hit to be confirmed by the observers, but it was definitely a clear shot on the mark. By then the Syrians had reacted as David Eshel explains:

'Gen Tal saw that the Syrian tank was preparing to enter into the fight. He aimed and fired two consecutive rounds and the Syrian Panzer exploded into a searing flame. At this moment, the tank commander, Lt Col Binyamin Oshri, who commanded the Centurion battalion, shouted over the tank intercommunication system that he identified a Syrian T-34 coming downhill at great speed. Tal also saw it and aimed at an estimated 3,000 m range. The first round fell short, but a second followed, the tank running directly in a straight forward line so that the second round slammed home. The tank exploded, still in motion, as parts fell off the burning hulk; a fiery ball of flame rolling downhill – an extraordinary sight.'

At that very moment, Tal's Centurion was hit by a Syrian SU-100,[4] which had been hiding behind a protective earth wall.

Col Oshri was wounded and fell onto the general who was in the gunner's seat. An APHE round had hit the commander's cupola, causing a severe shock wave to pass through the tank, which subsequently affected the entire crew who suffered painful after-effects for some three weeks, although none of them (except for Oshri) were

wounded. Oshri was swiftly evacuated and his life saved, although he was never able to return to active duty. The Syrians again moved their site to a new location east of the Sea of Galilee, some 22 km away from the nearest Israeli positions, where a high ridge prevented any further intervention by tanks. A final attack was therefore launched by the air force which destroyed the site, while the occupation of the Golan Heights in the Six-Day War of 1967 finally put paid to any

Gen Tal's Merkava (this is a Mk II), the revolutionary new main battle tank designed by Tal. (Israeli Defence Force)

further Syrian attempts to divert the vital water sources. The Israeli Armoured Corps had undoubtedly revolutionized long-range tank gunnery and had shown that their tanks could be used in a strategic role. Also it was clear that Israeli tank gunners were capable of precision gunnery of the very highest order, despite many of them being young, short-term national servicemen or reservists. And, as David Eshel goes on to explain:

'The experiences over the War of the Waters paved the way to further demonstrations in excellence, when Gen Tal led his regular armoured division in its epic fight on Rafa junction, during the Six-Day War. Once again his top gunners showed their worth, destroying large numbers of Egyptian tanks at long ranges, scoring with high precision, now standard in the Israeli Armoured Corps. Gen Tal's legacy although now thirty years old, still lives on with his Merkava crews who, with far better equipment, still rate among the best in their trade.'

A TRIO OF TANK ACES

As I explained at the beginning, not many senior officers are called upon to display their practical prowess in the way in which Gen Tal did in the 'War of the Waters'. This account can be added to the wealth of other reports of his prowess in so many different facets of armoured warfare, both technical and tactical, which together make 'Talik' a living legend. Two others who took part also went on to become tank aces in their own right: 2nd Lt Avigdor Kahalany became the most decorated officer in the Israeli Armoured Corps and later we shall cover one of his most famous battles in the 'Valley of Tears', while Sgt Shalom Cohen holds the record for the most enemy tanks destroyed by any Israeli gunner. All three are products of the Israeli Armoured Corps, which has proved itself in battle time and time again.

THE SIX-DAY WAR:
TANK BATTLES IN SAMARIA

WAR WITH JORDAN

The 'Lightning' Six-Day War (5–10 June 1967) took place on three distinct fronts, one of which was the war against Jordan.

It had been hoped that King Hussein would keep his country out of the war. When this proved impossible, however, Israel had to fight the formidable Jordanian Army as well as their other Arab foes. The Jordanian Armoured Corps was well trained, highly professional and well equipped, its latest tank being the American-built M48. In a two-pronged advance the crack Jordanian 40th Armoured Brigade (40 Armd Bde) made a dangerous enveloping move in Samaria, with one battalion (4 Bn) pushing towards Kabatiya, through Tubas, while a second (2 Bn) made for Arraba, via Nablus, aiming to encircle and then defeat the Israelis in detail. Col Moshe Bril's 45th Mechanized Brigade (45 Mech Bde) was in a difficult situation. Some of its forces were engaged on the outskirts of Jenin, while the rest were fighting hard in the area of Kabatiya Junction against the Jordanian 4 Bn, who was gaining ground. Further to the west, the brigade supply column had arrived in the area after an 'eventful' night march and was being attacked by enemy tanks coming from the Arraba crossroads and was literally fighting for its life.

Col Bril decided to suspend the attack on Jenin, pull his armour back to the west and occupy a position of all-round defence on nearby hills. This manoeuvre was assisted by two flights of Israeli Air Force *Mystères*, which struck at the Jordanian tanks while the Israelis were rallying. However, as soon as the Jordanian commander realized what was happening he ordered an all-out two-pronged attack on the Israeli positions. One prong would attack from the south-east, while the other would come in from the direction of Arraba, thus cutting the Israelis off from their supply column. It was a good plan, but unfortunately for the Jordanians it was not at all well executed. The south-eastern force destroyed some half-tracks belonging to Bril's engineer company, but was then halted at close range by a number of hastily assembled Shermans, firing at point-blank range, which brought that attack to a standstill. The other attack was halted by heavy artillery fire.

However, there was worse to come for the Jordanians. Using an unchartered goat track, a force of Israeli Centurions and AMX-13s skirted the enemy main positions and then took them in the rear. The tank battle lasted all night and thirty-five Pattons were destroyed.

THE TANKS

We have already covered both M48 and Centurion, so let us look at the third AFV in

An AMX-13, photographed during a lull in the fighting against the Egyptians in 1956. This was exactly the same type of light tank in which Lt Giora Weiss knocked out seven Jordanian Pattons on the outskirts of Nablus during the Six-Day War. (David Eshel)

this night tank battle. This was the French-built AMX-13 light tank, some 150 of which had been obtained by Israel in the 1950s. The AMX-13 Model 51 was armed with a 75 mm gun similar to the one used in the wartime German Panther, mounted in an oscillating turret, with automatic loading (forty rounds carried). The autoloader was situated in the turret bustle and consisted of two revolving cylinders, each holding six rounds, positioned one each side of the recoil path of the breech. They were revolved mechanically by the gun recoil. The 14½ ton, three-man tank had a top speed of over 40 m.p.h. and a range of 300 miles. Designed initially as an airborne tank, it proved most successful in a variety of roles and its chassis has been used for mounting a range of special variants, including an ARV, a

bridgelayer and a driver-training tank. Other versions have mounted 90 mm and 105 mm guns, plus a selection of missiles. The French had deliberately designed the vehicle for small crewmen, placing a height limit of 5 ft 8 in on anyone manning an AMX-13. It is not recorded if the IDF did the same, but it is thought to be highly unlikely.

The Egyptians also used a 'hybrid AMX-13' during the Six-Day War; having bought some AMX-13s in 1955 they had received only the turrets before an arms embargo prevented delivery of the hulls. The turrets were therefore fitted to Shermans.

THE ENGAGEMENT

It is not often that a light tank can get the better of a heavy tank, which makes Lt Giora

Weiss's action all the more remarkable. In the battle, Weiss's 14½ ton AMX was up against 40 ton Pattons, at point-blank range. The citation for valour which he was awarded after the Six-Day War states that:

'Weiss, exposed in his turret, knocked out the first Patton from a ten yard range and then the second and the third, seven in all, acting with supreme coolness, skill and resourcefulness, loading and aiming the gun (the commander had many duties in a light tank) and at times even operating the machine-gun. His total score also included an enemy recoilless gun and an armoured personnel carrier. Weiss was seriously wounded in a later battle and suffered severe burns.'[5]

A TANK ACE

Many Israeli tank men qualify as 'aces', but what makes Weiss special in my opinion is that, although working with a light tank he succeeded in knocking out much heavier opponents by using all his skills as a superlative tank commander.

Yom Kippur and the 'Valley of Tears' ,

7–9 OCTOBER 1973

THE SYRIANS ATTACK

On 10 October 1973 the Yom Kippur War began on two fronts, with a massive Egyptian surprise attack over the Suez Canal and, simultaneously, a Syrian assault on the Golan Heights. The Israelis had always appreciated that, just as in past wars, they would have to fight on more than one front. Nevertheless, they were taken by surprise at the speed and ferocity of both the assaults.

As the situation had deteriorated in September 1973, one battalion of the crack 7th Armoured Brigade (7 Armd Bde) – the 77th under the already legendary Lt Col Avigdor Kahalany, whose Centurion troop featured in our first report in this section, was moved up to the Golan to boost the desperately thin defensive line located there, based upon the 188th Barak Brigade (188 Bar Bde). Then, on 5 October, GOC of the Armoured Corps, Maj Gen 'Bren' Adan, ordered the rest of Col 'Yanosh' Ben-Gal's brigade to join the 77th Battalion (77 Bn) as quickly as possible. This force comprised the 82nd Tank Battalion (82 Tank Bn) under Lt Col Haim Barak and the 75th Mechanized Battalion (75 Mech Bn) commanded by Lt Col Yossi Eldar. They were destined to fight an epic defensive battle in the area which is now known as the 'Valley of Tears', but first 82 Tank Bn was 'exchanged' with the 74th Battalion (74 Bn, CO: Lt Col

Yair Nofshi) in 188 Bar Bde, so as to make the two brigades better balanced.

The main task of 7 Armd Bde was to secure the northern part of the Golan and ensure that the Syrians did not reach the Kuneitra–Mas'ada[6] road (see map, p. 261). Col Ben-Gal told his tank commanders that he was expecting the Syrians to attack that evening, but had sensibly moved his tanks into position early in the afternoon. The enemy attack started at 13.50 hrs with heavy air attacks, followed by wave upon wave of Syrian tanks in mass formation.

A DEFENSIVE BATTLE

The Israeli defensive positions behind the 'Purple Line' (the 1967 Cease-fire Line) comprised an obstacle belt of minefields and anti-tank ditches. These were watched over by tanks on built-up earth ramparts, which gave them excellent fields of view and of fire but left them rather exposed to enemy artillery fire and air attack. The Syrians had equally comprehensive defence lines on their side of the Purple Line, backed up with large armoured forces. In all the Syrians had some 1,400 tanks, including 400 T-62s, while the rest were mainly T-54/55s.

THE TANKS

The Israelis were using twenty-year-old Centurions, now equipped with 105 mm

The Valley of Tears battle. The commander of 77 Tank Bn of 7 Armd Bde, Lt Col Avigdor Kahalany (right), talks with Lt Col Yossi Eldar (comd. 75 Mech Bn). (David Eshel)

The MTU-55 bridgelayer, which played an important part in the opening stages of the Valley of Tears battle. (Tank Museum)

Soviet-built T-62s, like this one knocked-out in the desert, were used by the Syrians to equip their crack Republican Guard. They fought bravely during the Valley of Tears battle, but were eventually the victims of superior Israeli gunnery. (David Eshel).

guns, while the Syrians had mainly more modern Soviet-built equipment, including the T-62 main battle tank and the MTU-55 bridgelayer, developed by Czechoslovakia, the latter being a vital component in order for the Syrians to be able to bridge the anti-tank ditch. It was basically a T-55 chassis onto which was fitted a scissors-type bridge, 18 m long, which was launched hydraulically over the front of the tank, to span a 16 m gap. It had a 50 ton load capacity, weighed 37 tons and had a crew of two men.

The T-62 MBT was developed from the earlier T-54/55 series in the late 1950s, entering production in 1961. It was widely used by both Syria and Egypt during the 1973 war, but suffered from a slow rate of fire (4 rpm) and limited depression of its 115 mm smooth-bore main armament and associated fire control system, which was no match for the 105 mm rifled guns on the Israeli tanks. It had a crew of four, weighed some 40 tons (combat loaded), was powered by a 580 b.h.p. diesel engine, which gave it a top speed of over 31 m.p.h. and a range of 280 miles (over 400 miles with additional fuel tanks). Forty rounds were carried for the main 115 mm U-5TS (2A20) smooth-bore gun. After firing, the main armament automatically elevates to the correct loading angle and the turret cannot traverse while loading is taking place – this was to prove a decided drawback.

THE 'VALLEY OF TEARS'
In typical Soviet tactical 'steamroller' style, the Syrians attacked en masse, in a three-pronged assault by three mechanized divisions, each led by its tank brigade. Once the initial breakthrough had been achieved, the plan was for a joint airborne/armoured operation to be mounted to capture the

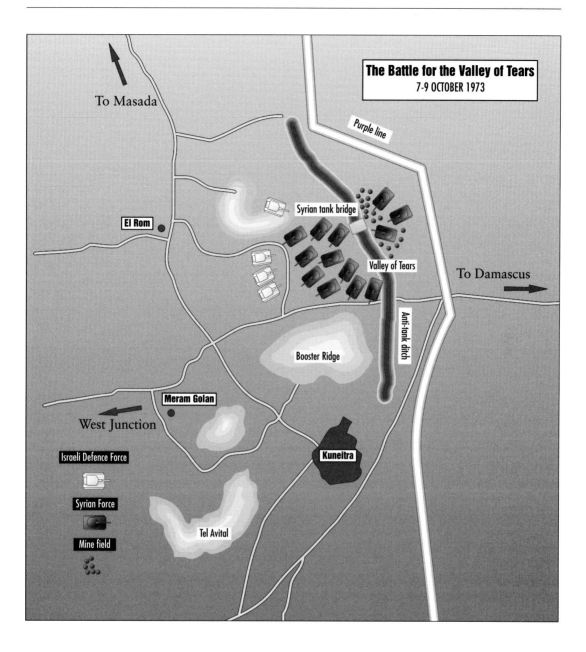

The Battle for the Valley of Tears
7-9 OCTOBER 1973

To Masada

Purple line

Syrian tank bridge

El Rom

Valley of Tears

To Damascus

Anti-tank ditch

Booster Ridge

Meram Golan

West Junction

Israeli Defence Force

Kuneitra

Syrian Force

Mine field

Tel Avital

Jordan bridges, thus cutting off reinforcements from the Golan front. The Israeli tanks began engaging the Syrian 'armoured steamroller' at long range, destroying dozens of vehicles as they struggled through the minefield towards the anti-tank ditch. Col Ben-Gal had given orders that the Syrian bridgelayers were to be priority targets and many were knocked out. Nevertheless, the extremely brave Syrian engineers managed to get two MTU-55 bridges into position over the ditch and their tanks streamed across, then pushed quickly on into the valley. Here, however, they came under direct fire from Nofshi's 74 Bn positioned on Booster Ridge and the rest of 7 Armd Bde's tanks located further north.

In the south 188 Bar Bde was fighting hard

but starting to lose ground, each tank being faced by at least ten of the enemy. Little control was possible as all were engaged in individual battles, the brigade commander, Col Ben Shoham, fighting in his command tank, along with the rest of his brigade: '. . . the Israeli tanks dwindled one by one as they were hit. Crews continued to fight in their turrets until they died, gaining precious minutes.'[7]

On the 7 Bde front the situation was much the same, as the brave Israeli crews and their equally brave Syrian enemies fought a desperate battle to gain ascendancy. Soon dozens of Syrian tanks littered the floor of the valley, but still they kept coming, so that within a few hours there were severe ammunition shortages among the defenders. The Israeli Air Force was called in, their Skyhawks flying so low that they were almost scraping the ground. Initially they did well but,

confronted by an almost impenetrable curtain of gun and missile fire, which took its toll, the ground commanders turned them away.

By now it was starting to get dark and this presented yet more problems to the IDF, as the Syrian night-viewing equipment was much more modern than that of the Israelis, while Syrian commando tank-hunting parties used the darkness to try to infiltrate the Jewish positions.

'Yanush ordered his tanks to fire at anything moving in the darkness. By now the range had closed to 200 yd. . . . Although the silhouettes outlined against blazing Syrian tanks in the valley below provided some visual target acquisition, the Israeli gunners had to improvise with flares, Xenon light projectors, and the seeking out of the tell-tale "cats-eyes" characteristics of vehicles equipped with infra-red.'[8]

Israeli Centurions under fire near Kuneitra. (David Eshel).

Knocked-out Syrian T-55s in the Valley of Tears. (David Eshel)

Daylight brought a brief lull as both sides licked their wounds and prepared for the next onslaught, which was not long in coming. All that day the Syrians tank forces attempted to advance out of the 'Valley of Tears' but were beaten back. Then, at about 22.00 hrs, they attacked again with two brand new divisions, spearheaded by the 81st Tank Brigade (81 Tank Bde), composed entirely of T-62s. By now down to thirty-five tanks, many of them damaged, 7 Armd Bde still managed to hold off the enemy during more bitter night fighting. At one stage the Syrians almost reached the top of Booster Hill, but were beaten back.

Somehow the Israelis held on, then on the 8th the Syrians put in yet another assault, this time led by their crack Republican Guard, also equipped entirely with T-62s. Just south of Kuneitra the 'Tiger Company' of Kahalany's battalion was outflanked by a brigade-sized force. Led by Capt Meir Zamir, the seven Centurions, which was all that 'Tiger Company' could muster, not only held off the enemy, but also destroyed over thirty T-62s. Later that night Zamir's company outflanked another enemy force which had almost succeeded in taking the Booster Hill position, knocking out some twenty T-55s without loss to themselves. By now, however, the Israeli 7 Armd Bde had only 32 tanks operational out of the 105 that had begun the battle just three days previously. Col Ben-Gal formed a reserve force with five of these Centurions and located it half a mile behind his FDLs[9] as a 'last resort' should the Syrians manage to break through.

08.00 hrs 9 October heralded the most ferocious attack the Israelis had yet experienced, with thousands of artillery shells, rockets and air strikes, plus helicopter-borne commandos and of course massed armour and mechanized infantry. The Syrians literally swamped the tank ramps, so that the Centurions found themselves fighting enemy on all sides. Samuel Katz tells of how Avigdor Kahalany found himself surrounded by four T-62s and ordered his gunner to fire 'rapid fire' and '. . . in a space of ninety seconds four T-62s were set ablaze'. The Syrians fought as bravely as the Israelis and had soon infiltrated the entire 7 Armd Bde position, so that hand-to-hand fighting was taking place. Just when all seemed lost, the remnants of Col Ben-Shoham's Bar Bde, just thirteen tanks in all, raced to the rescue, firing at point-blank range and knocking out over twenty-two enemy tanks in its first assault. This was the turning point in the battle and the demoralized Syrians began to withdraw. 'You have saved the people of Israel!' Col Ben-Shoham told his men and those of 7 Armd Bde over the radio.

'Lying silently below in the "Valley of Tears" were the remains of more than 500 Syrian tanks and vehicles. Their presence a testament to the determination and bravery of the Syrian tank soldier, and to the men of the 7th Armoured Brigade who had managed to stop them.'[10]

It had been quite a remarkable battle, in which the skill and bravery of the individual tank commander had triumphed. The Syrians had fought just as bravely, their tanks and associated equipment had been on a par with the Israelis – better in some respects, worse in others. However, what they were unable to match in the end was the sheer professional expertise of the Israeli tank commanders, men like Avigdor Kahalany, whose battalion would subsequently lead the Israeli counter-attack into Syria, threatening Damascus and bringing the war in the Golan to an end.

NOTES TO THE ARAB–ISRAELI WARS
1. *Chariots of the Desert, the Story of the Israeli Armoured Corps*, Col David Eshel.
2. Operation 'Musketeer' was the

British/French assault on Egypt in November 1956, which resulted from Nasser's nationalization of the Suez Canal. Despite the success of the operation, world opinion was very much against Britain and France, who had to withdraw.

3. Capt Shamai Kaplan was later killed in the Sinai during the Six-Day War.

4. The SU-100 was a Soviet-built heavy tank destroyer of Second World War vintage, mounting a 100 mm gun on a T-34 chassis. It was the most effective Soviet tank destroyer of the war.

5. *The Israeli Defence Forces – The Six-Day War*, Col M. Bar-On (ed.).

6. Mas'ada, a Druze village near Lake Birket Ram, to the north of Kuneitra, not to be confused with the ancient, massive cliff top fortress of Masada, south of the Dead Sea.

7. *Chariots of the Desert.*

8. *Israeli Tank Battles. From Yom Kippur to Lebanon*, Samuel M. Katz.

9. FDLs = Forward Defensive Localities, i.e.: the front line.

10. *Israeli Tank Battles.*

TANKS! TANKS! DIRECT FRONT!¹

BRAVO COMPANY WAS UNIQUE

Only one company among the US Marine Corps armoured units that fought in the Gulf War was armed with America's latest main battle tank, the M1A1 Abrams, and that was Bravo Company, 4th Tank Battalion, 4th Marine Division, (4 Tank Bn, 4 Mar Div) commanded by Capt 'Chip' Parkinson, USMC Reserve, from Yakima, Washington. All the rest had the older-generation M60s. Parkinson and his men had trained long and hard for this honour; now the 109 reserve officers and enlisted men, who came from all walks of life in Yakima and the surrounding area, would have a chance to show the world how much they had learned in two years as 'weekend warriors' and how quickly they could master the new AFV. The first people they had to persuade were their active-duty counterparts, who were sceptical that in two short weeks (all the time available) the reservists would be able to reach the same standard as the regulars achieved at the end of their normal eleven-week course. However, at the end of the short period of retraining they were rated as the best tank company ever to be trained at the Marine Corps Base in California.

They arrived in Saudi Arabia on 18 January 1991 and prepared for the dangerous mission which lay ahead, namely supporting the 2nd Marine Division (2 Mar Div) in the land battle. The division's first task was to carry out breaching operations just north of

the point along the Saudi–Kuwaiti border known as the 'Elbow', where it makes a sharp turn to the north. The division was aiming to make a penetration six lanes wide, through the double minefield belts, with Bravo Company protecting the combat engineers breaching the two easternmost lanes, codenamed 'Green 5' and 'Green 6'. Late in the afternoon of 23 February, the fourteen M1A1s of Bravo Company were occupying a position just south of the border, ready for the ground war to begin at 04.00 hrs the next day. They were anticipating the enemy using chemical weapons, so all had on their protective gear and carried their gas masks. It was raining when they held a quiet reveille at 03.00 hrs on the 24th and made their final preparations for the coming battle.

THE TANK

The M1A1 was the logical development of the M1, which had begun its life when the XM1 Program was established in December 1972. The prototype MBT was accepted by the US Army in February 1976 and the first production model appeared in 1980. The original build was to be 3,312 M1s, but this was later increased to 7,467. The first M1A1s were delivered in 1985, while production of the M1A2 began in 1992. Constructed of similar material to the British Chobham armour, the four-man 57 ton tank is armed with the 120 mm Rheinmetall smooth-bore gun and has an integrated NBC system,

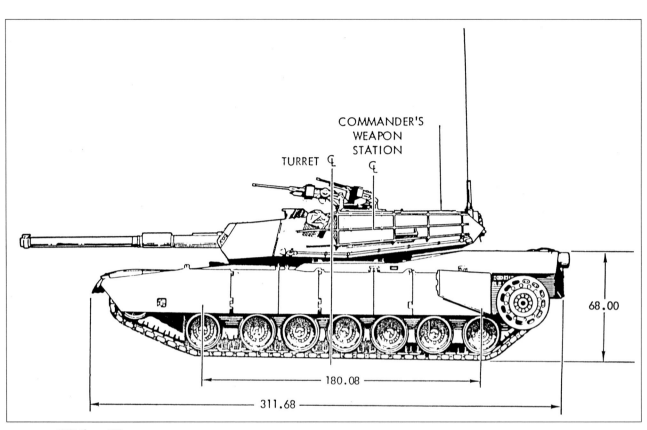

M1A1 Abrams MBT.

providing conditioned air for the crew to breathe. Its 1,500 hp Lycoming Tetxron AGT 1500 gas turbine engine gives the MBT a top speed (roads) of 42 m.p.h., a road range of 290 miles and a good cross-country performance.

Forty rounds are carried for the main armament and there is both a 12.7 mm AAMG for the commander and a 7.62 mm AAMG for the loader, in addition to the coaxial 7.62 mm MG. It performed spectacularly well in the Gulf War, with a 90 per cent reliability rating over the 100 hours of offensive operations. Of the 1,956 M1A1s in the theatre, none were destroyed by enemy fire, although four were disabled and a further four damaged. At least seven were hit by fire from an enemy T-72, none suffering any

serious damage – one even survived a hit at 400 m. The Rheinmetall gun also proved itself in the Gulf. In one engagement, for example, an AP round from an M1A1 hit the turret of a T-72, passed straight through it and penetrated the side armour of a second T-72.

THE BATTLE

Getting through the minefields was not easy and took the Marines 7 hours. The engineers lost three tanks and an Amtrac, while one of the Abrams was blown up on a mine – fortunately there were no human casualties. Once through, the Marines were swamped by hundreds of Iraqi soldiers rushing to surrender. Not all gave up so easily, however, and there was some hostile fire from infantry in foxholes, while enemy tanks could

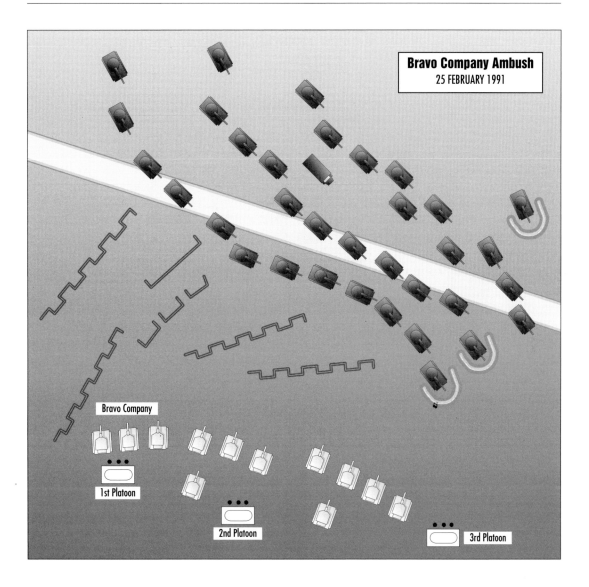

Bravo Company Ambush
25 FEBRUARY 1991

Bravo Company

1st Platoon

2nd Platoon

3rd Platoon

occasionally be seen on the horizon. Bravo Company therefore had to 'jockey around' to engage the unfriendly troops without hitting the hordes of men who were trying to give up. This went on until the early hours of the 25th, when Parkinson was finally able to pull his remaining thirteen tanks into a circular desert-type leaguer, establish a duty watch and take a couple of hours sleep before continuing the attack – reveille being scheduled for 05.45 hrs.

Capt Alan Hart woke up at 05.30 hrs, still about 30 minutes before dawn, and went over to talk to Parkinson, who was sleeping on the back of his tank, *Predator 6*. As they were talking, Cpl 'Brad' Briscoe, who had been scanning with the thermal-imaging sight (TIS) fitted in his tank, ran over to tell Capt Parkinson that he was picking up armoured vehicle movement to the north. 'Probably just our own amtracs running around in front of us again,' Hart said. 'Don't worry about it.' But Briscoe was not convinced and before he returned to his own tank he asked Hart's

An M1A1 shows its speed during Operation 'Desert Sabre', which began at 04.00 hrs on 24 February 1991 and lasted a mere 100 hours. (General Dynamics Land Systems Division)

gunner to turn on his TIS and watch for anything unusual.

As the two officers continued their chat, both heard the faint rumbling of diesel engines and both realized that they were listening to enemy tanks not Amtracs. Hart raced back to his own tank, shouting for everyone to stand-to. Looking through his own TIS, Hart saw at least twelve T-72 tanks moving across his front, from left to right, along the near side of a hard-surfaced road that ran along the top of a small ridge, with low ground on both sides. The only tanks he could see were those on the side of the ridge closest to him; he could not see into the low ground immediately in front of, or behind the road.

Hart quickly took stock of the situation. The Iraqi tank column had all its guns pointed straight ahead, so clearly they had not seen Bravo Company. He surmised that the enemy unit was a counter-attack force, looking to surprise and intercept the advancing US forces. For the time being, Bravo Company had the initiative, especially in the dark, with their TIS and static location. However, at the time when the T-72s were seen, none of the company's thirteen tanks were fully prepared to engage the enemy. It takes about 40 seconds to warm up the system, then a further 2 minutes for the TIS to cool down to its working temperature – as it 'sees' by locating targets as heat sources.

270

They had also to check the danger area around them, to ensure they did not hurt any friendly forces from blast when they started to fire. For example, although Hart was immediately ready to fire, he could not do so, as that might possibly have injured the crews of other Abrams still on the back decks of their tanks and located slightly ahead of him. Therefore, before any firing could take place, all the tanks had to pull abreast of each other. Hart stood up in his turret and shouted to the men who were scrambling into their tanks: 'Tanks! Tanks! Direct front!' He followed this by calling over his radio: 'Predator 6. This is Hawk 1. Enemy tanks to my direct front! Come on line!' None of the company reacted, so he called again: 'This is Hawk 1. Come on line *now*!'

The rest of the company still did not move, so Hart let go with a few expletives, then realized that all were still in their warming up/cooling down process and it would be a few more minutes before they were ready to fight. He therefore had to move his MBT forward to enable his tank to fire safely. As this manoeuvre was in progress, his gunner, Cpl Lee Fowble, said: 'Sir! We've got to shoot! They're traversing!' The nearest T-72s were now only some 1,100 m away, well inside the maximum effective range of their main armament,[2] so it was vital to get in a first-round hit before the enemy could engage them. Hart gave the order and they fired – a direct hit on the leading enemy tank. Without pause, Hart traversed onto another enemy tank and turned it into a second fireball. Then they heard an M1A1 fire off to their right, but its first two rounds were high. Hart ordered his gunner to traverse right and fired at a third target. Another Iraqi tank burst into flames. However, they were in for a shock. They had destroyed three enemy tanks out of the twelve they had originally located yet, looking through his sight again, Hart could

count at least a dozen plus enemy tanks still moving across his front.

Then he realized that there were even more enemy tanks emerging from the other side of the hill – three columns, in total at least thirty to forty tanks, against Bravo Company's thirteen. Hart and his crew continued to acquire targets, load and fire their 120 mm gun just as fast as they could, a fourth fireball acknowledging their fourth 'kill'. Then they began to see the strike of other rounds from Bravo Company's guns, as the Marine tanks came on line and started to engage the enemy. A TOW[3] missile detachment supporting 1st Battalion, 8th Marines also joined in the fire fight and one observer records seeing Hart's tank and the TOW both engage the same target – the missile fired first, but as the 120 mm round travels roughly three times as fast as a TOW missile, both projectiles arrived on target at the same time and the enemy tank literally disintegrated.

As the battle progressed the inherent fault of the T-72's tank gun control system (its automatic reload capability, highlighted in the Valley of Tears battle) was again apparent. Every time the Iraqi tanks fired their main armament, the gun was taken off target and automatically elevated. Although this system had saved a crewman in the turret, it had also seriously affected the crew's ability to fight effectively as there was no 'gun on target hold' during an engagement.[4] As a result, the Abrams were able to get off two rounds during the 12 seconds it took to raise the T-72's main gun and reload it automatically.

Some 90 seconds into the battle and twenty of the Iraqi tanks had been destroyed. Only 5½ minutes later it was all over. Parkinson, who had destroyed three T-72s during the battle, broke the silence by commenting over the radio: 'What a way to wake up in the morning!' Thanks to the

Knocked-out or abandoned Iraqi tanks, such as these T-55s, littered the battlefield after Operation 'Desert Sabre' was over. (Tank Museum)

vigilance of Cpl Brad Briscoe, the amazing TIS, the quick-thinking of Capt Alan Hart and, of course, the shooting ability of all the Bravo Company crews, the Marine tankers had virtually annihilated a crack Iraqi tank battalion in an impromptu ambush. It later transpired that the Iraqi force (a tank battalion of 8th Mechanized Brigade, 3rd Armoured Division, accompanied by two mechanized infantry battalions) had been hoping to catch the Marines by surprise at first light. Just as Bravo Company opened fire they had located a Marine supply convoy and were about to engage it.

In the engagement, Bravo Company knocked out thirty-four of the enemy battalion's thirty-five tanks – all were T-72s except for four T-55s. The battalion had fought well during the Iran–Iraq war and were both competent and courageous, which enhances the performance of the 'Yakima Volunteers'. Two days later, just 100 hours after the ground war began, the cease-fire went into effect. Bravo Company's total 'bag' was 59 tanks, 32 APCs, 26 non-armoured vehicles and 1 artillery gun, all without the loss of a single life.

TANK ACES

Bravo Company, and in particular Capt Alan Hart and his crew, deserve their place in our classification as tank aces. However, just as with Michael Wittmann and his memorable battle at Villers-Bocage versus the advance guard of 7 Armd Div, his MBT was so superior to those of his opponents that it made his task relatively easy. Had Wittmann been in a paper-thin Cromwell, or Hart in a T-72, then perhaps neither contests would have been quite so one-sided. Nevertheless, it shows what a properly trained tank crew can do, especially when the element of surprise is on their side.

THE BATTLE OF 73 EASTING

DRAGON'S ROAR

On the night of 26 February 1st Battalion, 37th Armored Regiment (1 Bn, 37 Armd Regt.) fought a battle against the 29th Brigade (29 Bde) of the Iraqi Tawakalna Division, part of Saddam Hussein's Republican Guard, who was established in a blocking position in an attempt to cover the retreat of Irai forces to the north.

The battalion had arrived in Saudi Arabia in December 1990 and the Battalion Commander, Lt-Col Edward L. Dyer, had made some equipment changes to better fit his scouts and company first sergeants for their missions. The scouts initially had three M113 APCs and three M901 Improved TOW Vehicles (ITV), but they turned in the ITVs and drew in return six HMMWVs[5] from theatre reserve. These six, plus the first sergeants' HMMVs from B, C and D Companies, were given to the scouts and organized into three sections of three HMMWVs. Each vehicle had an M060 machine-gun mount and a crew of three scouts (one with an M16A2 rifle, one with an M203 grenade launcher and one manning the M60). Thus organized they were 'lower profile' and better suited to getting information without confrontation. Each of the first sergeants received an M113 APC in exchange for their HMMV, giving them battlefield armoured protection. In addition, the M577 was considered to be unsuitable as

a Tactical Operations Centre (TOC), and TOC personnel found they could operate more efficiently from a HMMWV with lapboards. They therefore used the CO's vehicle, which had a three-radio net capability.

In early February the battalion was reorganized into an armour heavy battlegroup, exchanging A Company for C/7-6 Infantry, but the CO decided to keep the infantry company concentrated and not to split it between tank companies, in case he was called upon to clear trench systems, a task which would require large numbers of dismounted troops.

THE AFVS

Having dealt with the M1A1 in the last battlefield report, let us look at one of the other AFVs involved, namely the M2 Infantry Fighting Vehicle (IFV)/M3 Cavalry Fighting Vehicle. The tank was more commonly known as the Bradley, after Gen Omar N. Bradley of Second World War fame. Development began in 1972, the contract being awarded to the FMC Corporation, and first production deliveries were made in May 1981. The US Army initially had a total requirement for some 8,000 plus Bradleys, although that figure has since been modified. Saudi Arabia has also bought some Bradleys. With a crew of three + six, the combat-loaded vehicle weighs some 22½ tons and is armed with a 25 mm cannon plus a 7.62 mm MG

The Bradley Infantry Fighting Vehicle in training in the USA prior to the Gulf War. (US Armor School)

mounted coaxially in a small one-man turret. The Bradley has a top speed of 38 m.p.h. and a range of over 250 miles. Its cross-country performance is comparable to that of the Abrams and it is a natural amphibian. It has many advantages over the M113 series it complements and is used for other roles. One version, for example, mounts twin TOW launchers, another a 35 mm cannon and a third the Ground Launched Hellfire Heavy (anti-tank) system.

In March 1991 the US Army issued a report on the Bradley's performance in the Gulf War, which stated:

'Crews reported that the sights were very effective, even during sandstorms. Other crews reported that the 25 mm Bushmaster cannon was more lethal than expected. There were no reports of transmission failures during offensive operations. Of the 2,200 Bradleys in theatre only three were disabled.

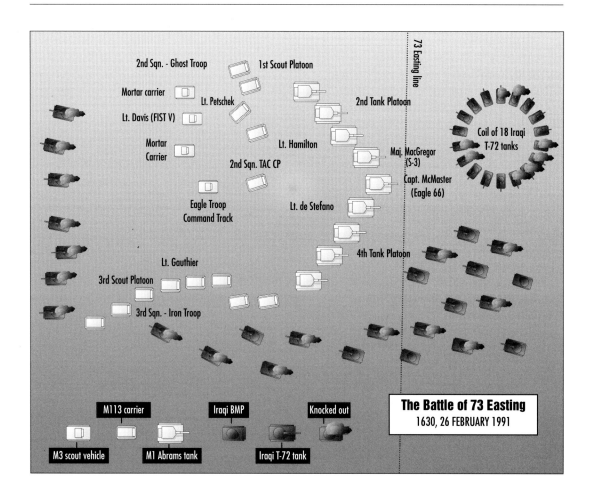

2nd Sqn. - Ghost Troop
1st Scout Platoon
Mortar carrier
Lt. Petschek
Lt. Davis (FIST V)
2nd Tank Platoon
Mortar Carrier
Lt. Hamilton
Maj. MacGregor (S-3)
2nd Sqn. TAC CP
Capt. McMaster (Eagle 66)
Eagle Troop Command Track
Lt. de Stefano
4th Tank Platoon
Lt. Gauthier
3rd Scout Platoon
3rd Sqn. - Iron Troop

73 Easting line

Coil of 18 Iraqi T-72 tanks

The Battle of 73 Easting
1630, 26 FEBRUARY 1991

M113 carrier
Iraqi BMP
Knocked out
M3 scout vehicle
M1 Abrams tank
Iraqi T-72 tank

To date we have no information on the number damaged. Overall, Bradley operational rates remained at 90 per cent or above during combat.'[6]

THE BATTLE

On the afternoon of 26 February TF 1-37 was advancing east as the right flank task force in the 3 Bde 'wedge' and as the flank task force of 1 Armd Div A balanced task force TF 7-6 led the brigade, while TF 3-35 covered the left flank. Their mission was to attack and destroy the Republican Guard Medinah Division on Objective 'Bonn'. At about 16.00 hrs reports were received from the brigade's air scouts that fifty enemy tanks and other vehicles had been spotted in revetments along the axis of advance about 35 km west of the objective. The detection of such a large enemy force in the area was a surprise, especially as, before 'Desert Storm', the Tawakalna Division had been templated some 50 km to the north-east. Now its new location straddled the boundary between 1 and 3 Armd Divs. While USAF A-10s struck the enemy positions and 2 Bde, 3 Armd Div began to attack with artillery and illumination in the south, 3 Bde approached to within about 10 km of the enemy. Visibility had worsened thanks to rain mixed with a sandstorm. However, TIS effectively saw through the haze, although vehicle identification above 1,500 m was virtually impossible.

Direct support artillery (155 mm) began to fire onto the enemy positions, while the brigade manoeuvred into line formation, with TF 1-37 up on line with TF 7-6, and TF 3-35 as brigade reserve. Within the TFs, teams/companies were also all on line, while TF 1-37's scouts moved out to screen the right flank and maintain contact with 3 Armd Div Enemy dismounted troops opened fire with machine-guns, but were generally ineffective. TF 7-6 replied by engaging enemy vehicles at long range with Bradley-mounted TOWs. The advance began and soon D/1-37 saw enemy troops 900 m to its front, advancing in short rushes. These were destroyed with coax MG fire. Both TFs also reported additional troops and vehicles at range of 2,000–4,000 m. These were engaged and destroyed with main tank gun fire, TOW and 25 mm (on the Bradley). Some enemy vehicles were seen fleeing to the east from the enemy positions, but were not engaged because they were over 4 km away.

Direct supporting artillery fire ceased on the objective and MLRS rockets[7] shifted to hit targets in depth, while TF 7-6 fired illumination rounds to improve surveillance on the objective. The commander of 3 Bde, Col Daniel Zanini, ordered TF 1-37 to sweep across the objective and halt 3 km past the far side. TF 7-6 would lift its fire and remain in position to overwatch. The attack began about 20.30 hrs, with the infantry company following a kilometre to the rear of the line of forty-five tanks in order to 'police up' any enemy troops that tanks missed. The advance was at a slow rate (just 5–10 km.p.h.) and by 21.00 hrs at least eight enemy vehicles were on fire.

Control of so many tanks in line at night can be extremely difficult. However, prior to 'Desert Storm', 37 Armd Regt had practised this manoeuvre in theatre training, giving it the codeword 'Dragon's Roar'. This helped enormously, as did the use of company

command-directed radio nets as opposed to platoon nets. Another simple but effective means of command and control was the fitting of coloured filters to tail lights (one colour identified the vehicle's brigade, the other its battalion).

Targets during the attack were mainly T-72s and BMP-1s,[8] with ranges of engagement being 2,200–2,800 m, although some were beyond 3,000 m. One M1A1 on the move hit a BMP with a HEAT round at 3,250 m, while the longest confirmed kill was at 3,750 m. Apache helicopters joined in on the flanks. There was some enemy return fire, but this was mainly small arms and machine-gun, with a few T-72 main armament rounds. As with the USMC ambush, the M1A1s' fire control system dominated the battlefield.

To quote now from a description of the action, written by 2nd Lt Richard M. Bohannon, who was an M1A1 tank platoon leader in 1-37 during the battle:

'We fought a close battle on the objective. As we manoeuvred around burning vehicles and bunkers, we lost four tanks to enemy fire[9]. . . . Secondary explosions of burning Iraqi vehicles threw shrapnel and other debris in all directions as pillars of flame rose to a ceiling of black smoke. Virtually all enemy vehicles in the area were destroyed, but dismounted troops remained hidden in trenches and bunkers. Companies C and D both reported receiving small arms fire from their rear as they swept towards the east. Fortunately, physical clearing of the trenches wasn't necessary. The Iraqis surrendered in force and came forth voluntarily. . . . Speculation continues concerning what shot our four tanks. The three most probable answers are T-72 main gun, dismounted anti-tank missile, or Apache launched Hellfire missile. The fact that Apaches were operating to our rear and witnesses's reports of high round trajectory support the friendly fire theory. However, ballistic reports suggest that 125 mm HEAT rounds produced the damage on some of the tanks. Visual examination of others reveals one obvious sabot hole. Overall, the physical evidence implies that T-72 fire took out our tanks, but the friendly fire possibility cannot be excluded. . . . At 23.00 hrs the infantry reported the area clear, and at 00.50 the next morning, the brigade reformed and continued the attack east.'

Final enemy casualties for TF 1-37's sector of the Battle of 73 Easting included 21 T-72s, 14 BMP 1s, 2 57 mm AA guns, 1 T-62 and 1 MTLB destroyed and over 100 prisoners taken. All this for the loss of just six wounded. After adding two more successful battles to its credit by 28 February, TF 1-37 found itself a few kilometres inside liberated Kuwait.

This was not a battle from which to single out tank aces, but does give a good impression of the superiority of the Abrams over the enemy AFVs. A report, kindly supplied to me by the FMC Corporation, contains these words:

'The Abrams tanks were faster, more mobile and able to outrange the Iraqi tanks. M1A1s had better guns, better ammunition, an exceptional thermal-imaging system, better rangefinder, better fire control system and much better armor than the Iraqi tanks. M1A1s did, in fact, dominate the battlefield.'

EAGLE TROOP BATTLE

Also engaged in the Battle of 73 Easting was Eagle Troop, 2nd Squadron, 2nd Armored Cavalry Regiment (2 Sqn, 2 Armd Cav Regt).

Sand berms like this were no protection against the Abrams gun. In one case, an M1A1 kinetic energy round went through a sand berm surrounding an Iraqi tank, hit and went completely through the vehicle, then went through the berm on the opposite side. (Tank Museum)

278

Eagle Troop commanders. Left to right: Lt Timothy Gauthier (3 Plt, scout), Lt Jeffrey DeStafano (4 Plt, tank), Capt H.R. McMaster (OC), Lt Michael Hamilton (2 Plt, tank) and Lt Michael Petscheck (2 Plt, scout). (Capt H.R. McMaster)

The troop comprised 140 soldiers equipped with 9 M1A1s main battle tanks, 12 M3A2 Bradley fighting vehicles, 2 4.2 in mortar carriers, an artillery fire support vehicle (FIST-V), several armoured personnel carriers (APC), a command post vehicle and a maintenance recovery vehicle. It had arrived in Saudi Arabia on 4 December 1990 and went into action on 23 February, having been reinforced with an engineer platoon and an armoured earth mover (ACE) to break through the two large dirt berms which delineated the border. Here is how Capt H.R. McMaster, the troop commander, described crossing the frontier:

'At 1.30 p.m. the Troop crept to within sight of the 12 ft high earthen mounds as the artillery dropped a thunderous barrage on suspected enemy OPs in Iraq. The first platoon scouts and the engineers bolted forward across the flat and rocky ground to effect the breach. The engineers quickly reduced the obstacle and the tanks sped forward in a large column. My tank went through first and, once through the gap, the others emerged through the dust to take up positions in a large wedge formation. We were elated. We were finally in enemy territory. The flank scouts came through next. Finally, the scouts who had gone forward to secure the obstacle poured through and raced to resume the lead in the Troop's formation. My tank and others used our machine-guns to fire into anything that looked like an enemy position.

'The air cavalry OH-58 scout and Cobra gunship helicopters flew low overhead and cleared the path to the first day's objective. The Troop halted 20 km into Iraq and established defensive positions. . . . The weather had been unpredictable and heavy rains made rest difficuLt'

Now that the border area was secure, the remainder of VII (US) Corps could move forward and, shortly after dawn on the 24th, Eagle Troop moved north another 20 km. The first contact came just after the sun had set, when the leading scouts detected an enemy defensive position, with three distinct squad trenches and bunkers. Enemy troops were visible through the tank and IFV TI sights from a range of 2 km and it was clear that they had no idea that they were being observed. McMaster ordered the scout platoon around the left flank of the enemy position, covered by the guns of his tank and the Bradleys belonging to the 1st Platoon (1 Plt) commanded by Lt Mike Petschek:

'At a range outside that of the enemy's rocket propelled grenades (RPG) SSgts Lawrence and Magee's Bradleys opened up with HE rounds from their 25 mm chain guns. The

muzzle flashes from their gun barrels and the streak of their tracers arcing towards the enemy were followed by innumerable explosions along the enemy positions. My tank then fired a 120 mm HEAT round into an enemy bunker. The fireball from the tank's gun illuminated the area between our combat vehicles and the enemy position. Almost immediately, a violent explosion erupted at the center of the enemy position. The scouts reported ten enemy soldiers running to the north.'

As the troop moved on the following day, it was faced for the first time with the gruesome sight of enemy dead, plus countless groups of enemy soldiers who had thrown away their weapons and were walking south in small groups. Many greeted the troop with 'thumbs up' signs, others actually cheered. All were quickly searched for concealed weapons, given food and water, then left to their own devices as the troop moved swiftly on, turning the main direction of advance eastward.

More engagements followed, and when enemy armoured vehicles were reported, McMaster decided to switch the formation to tanks in the lead:

'It was 4.18 p.m. The sandstorm had not let up. I was issuing my final instructions to the Troop when my tank crested a rise. As we came over the top SSgt Koch yelled: "Tank direct front". I then saw more of the enemy position at which Moody was firing. In an instant I counted eight tanks in dug-in fighting positions. Large mounds of earth were pushed up in front of the vehicles and they were easily discernible to the naked eye. . . . They were close! Koch hit the button on the laser range finder and the display under the gun sight showed 1,420 m. I yelled: "Fire, fire SABOT." A HEAT round was loaded but Taylor (the loader) would load a high velocity

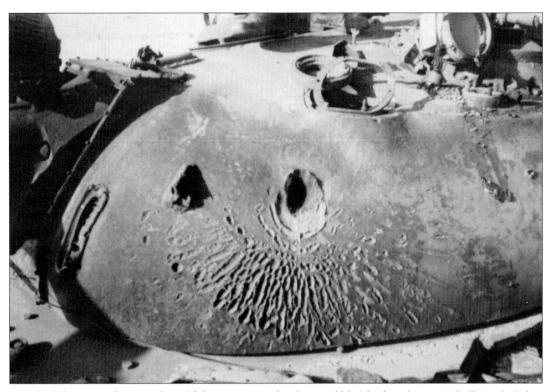

Another knocked-out enemy tank. HEAT rounds were lethal, penetrating Iraqi tanks with ease, as did the Sabot (long-rod penetrator) 'dart-like' rounds. (Tank Museum)

kinetic energy round next; a tank defeating depleted uranium dart which travels at about 1 mile/sec. As Koch depressed the trigger, the gun breech recoiled and the HEAT round flew toward the enemy tank. We were still moving forward but the tank's stabilization system kept the gun right on target. The enemy tank exploded in a huge fireball as Koch swung onto another tank. This tank was much closer and was positioned forward of the main defense. It was swinging its turret toward our tank. Taylor actuated the ammunition door. As the door slid open, he grabbed a SABOT round, slammed it into the breech and screamed: "Up!" Only 3 seconds had elapsed since we destroyed the first tank. I was talking on the radio as Koch let the round go. The enemy tank's turret separated from its hull in a hail of sparks. The tank hull burst into flames as the penetrator[10] ignited the fuel and ammunition compartments.'

McMaster's driver had slowed the Abrams down to about 12½ m.p.h. as he had spotted an enemy minefield and was busily weaving in between the mines while trying to keep the tank's thick frontal armour towards the most dangerous enemy tank. All the tanks in the troop were by now firing, while enemy fire from the T-72s was also coming their way although most of it was wildly inaccurate. The troop cut a 5 km wide swathe of destruction through the enemy's defences, the Bradleys and TOW missiles adding to the death and destruction. By the time it halted at about 4.40 p.m. it was just short of the 74 Easting, slightly south of where the enemy reserve position had been sited.

The battle went on as has already been described, and towards midnight they heard the whine of the tank engines and rattle of tracks, as the AFVs of 1st (US) Infantry Division moved through and took up the lead. Later, on the way back, they passed through the enemy positions which they had assaulted the previous afternoon, McMaster commenting that: 'The enemy tanks and BMPs were devastated. Tank and BMP turrets lay separate from their hulls. Dead enemy soldiers lay next to the unrecognizable hulks of twisted steel.' Of his own soldiers he has this to say:

'In general the Iraqis were unprepared for the United States Army. Our Army was better trained and equipped. The most decisive factor, however, was the American soldier. Our soldiers were aggressive in battle yet demonstrated great discipline and compassion for their enemy. They were exceptionally well led by their NCOs and platoon leaders. Because of strong leadership and confidence, gained through tough, realistic training, the soldiers approached their first combat action without any hesitation or sense of foreboding. I am grateful that I had the opportunity to serve with them in this action.'

A Desert Rat's 'Tail'

The other modern main battle tank in the Allied forces was the British Challenger with which the armoured regiments in 1 (BR) Armd Div were equipped. Their mechanized infantry were equipped with the Warrior MICV, which resembled the Bradley. 1 (Br) Armd Div comprised two brigades (4 Bde and 7 Bde), both famous 'Desert Rats', whose forebears had served in the great 7 Armd Div of the Second World War. The Division was a part of VII (US) Corps in the main assault force, the Challengers and Warriors proving to be every bit as effective as the Abrams and Bradley.

THE TANK

Design work on Challenger 1 as the successor to Chieftain had begun in the late 1960s, but had been superseded in 1970 by the Anglo-German MBT 70 project, which was cancelled seven years later. However, before this, in 1968, the Military Vehicles and Engineering Establishment (MVEE) at Chertsey had produced a prototype of a tank with an externally mounted gun,[11] which was followed in 1971 by another AFV, based on Chieftain and incorporating Chobham armour. It was known as FV 4211. In 1971 the MOD defined the basic requirements for the new tank thus:

'The new tank must be in service by the late 80s, when Chieftain, despite improvements, would be coming to the end of its useful life. The successor to Chieftain will be required to match anticipated Warsaw Pact armoured and anti-armour capabilities well beyond the turn of the century and will be designed to the highest practicable standards of firepower, protection and mobility. Project Definition will be based on a tank of conventional turret design carrying a four-man crew, protected by Chobham armour and mounting a British rifled bore 120 mm gun.'

In 1979 it was announced that the tank would be powered by the Rolls Royce CV 12 diesel engine.

Work continued at MVEE, then at the Royal Ordnance Factory, Barnbow, Leeds. By December 1982 Challenger, as the new MBT was called, had been accepted by the General Staff and seven prototypes were produced. The first British Army order was signed for 243 Challengers (enough to equip four regiments) and the first of these was handed over in March 1983. In layout, the tank is very similar to Chieftain, but incorporating Chobham armour on the turret and hull. Before 'Desert Storm' tanks were uparmoured to provide added protection. A fuel tank that could be jettisoned was also added.

The 120 mm rifled gun proved to be the most accurate tank gun at long range, even outperforming the Abrams. The longest confirmed kill by a tank gun in the Gulf War was at a range of 5,100 m (over 3 miles) by the Challenger's remarkable main armament.

Challenger 1 performed much better in the Gulf War than its critics ever anticipated. There were three Challenger-equipped armoured regiments within 1 Armd Div: the Royal Scots Dragoon Guards and Queen's Royal Irish Hussars in 7 Armd Bde

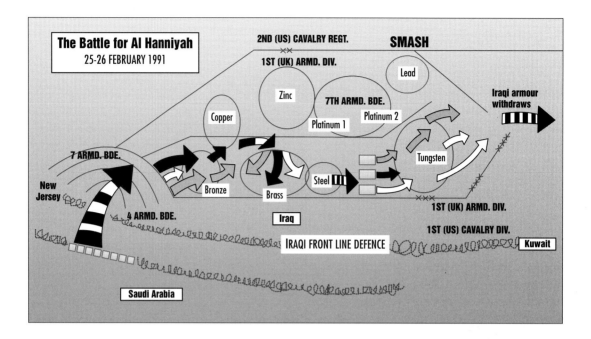

The Battle for Al Hanniyah
25-26 FEBRUARY 1991

2ND (US) CAVALRY REGT.

SMASH

1ST (UK) ARMD. DIV.

Lead

Zinc

7TH ARMD. BDE.

Iraqi armour withdraws

Copper

Platinum 2

Platinum 1

7 ARMD. BDE.

Tungsten

New Jersey

Bronze

Brass

Steel

4 ARMD. BDE.

1ST (UK) ARMD. DIV.

1ST (US) CAVALRY DIV.

Iraq

IRAQI FRONT LINE DEFENCE

Kuwait

Saudi Arabia

(Commander: Brig Patrick Cordingley), and the 14th/20th King's Hussars in 4 Armd Bde (Commander: Brig Christopher Hammerbeck). Three Warrior-borne mechanized infantry battalions made up the balance – 1 Staffords in the armour-heavy 7 Armd Bde and 1 Royal Scots and 3 RRF in the infantry-heavy 4 Armd Bde Divisional troops included an armoured reconnaissance regiment (16/5 Lancers).

THE BATTLE FOR AL HANNIYAH
One of the major battles they fought in the short 'Desert Sabre' conflict was known initially as the battle of 'Copper South', but was later named Al Hanniyah. Brig Hammerbeck later recalled his memories of the battle thus:

'A modern tank battle at night is a curious affair since it is fought entirely on thermal sights and therefore is green and white or black; much of the drama is removed. Crews cannot see the enemy firing at their own tank, but are aware that it is happening as the effect of the supersonic bang is heard as a

round passes close by. A hit on the enemy is simply a black or white spot on the target, followed by a wisp of thermal smoke. In reality it hides a catastrophic explosion within the tank, with the consequent loss of its crew. For my own crew the battle was a confused jumble of target acquisition followed by the engagement sequences. Small groups of enemy who had baled out, terrified witless, were sheltering in the blackness, which must have been broken by the flash of our gun as we engaged targets some 2 km away. Inside the tank there was pandemonium as targets were spotted and engaged. Pervading all was a mix of smells, ranging from the smoke from the main armament to that curiously acrid smell that humans give off when they are charged with adrenalin and, to be frank, are scared. This nasty little battle was best described by Cpl Slade of 14/20 Hussars, who said: "The effect on the tanks was devastating. There was nothing left – absolutely horrendous. I don't think that anyone could have lived through that. You think you are safe encased by steel

Challenger 1s advance. Note the additional 'add-on' Chobham armour, used to strengthen the already impressive front glacis. (Tank Museum)

but you are not. It turns the interiors white hot. That's not a very nice situation to be in."'

14/20 Hussars (14/20H) fought their way through the enemy position which was held in some depth by a strong enemy battlegroup and contained the HQ of the Iraqi 52nd Armoured Brigade. Here are some of the reminiscences of B Sqn, 14/20H, taken from their 1991 Journal:

'At 22.27 hrs, first contact was made by Lt Gimlette in callsign 40, when he reported infantry and APCs on the right flank at a distance of 1,200 m. Initially it was thought that the contact might have been an artillery recce party from our own divisional artillery group and we were ordered to hold firm while the situation was clarified. Meanwhile, the Squadron Leader ordered 4th Troop forward to investigate. As they did so they were illuminated by an IR searchlight, suggesting that a T-55 was observing them. At the same time we received confirmation that no friendly forces were in the area of our contact and that we should open fire. The Squadron Leader ordered 2nd Troop to open fire and allow 4th Troop to withdraw into squadron line and engage the enemy. The first tank to open fire was the troop leader's tank, callsign 20 with a HESH engagement against infantry in the open. Meanwhile, 1st and 3rd Troops were ordered to swing right and take up positions on the left of the squadron firing line. We were now in a squadron firing line at 90 degrees to the axis of advance (which was

Getting ready for the off. Challenger crews making final preparations before H-Hour. (Tank Museum)

Good shot of a Challenger 1 advancing at speed. Note the additional fuel tanks on the rear. (Tank Museum)

east) engaging an enemy position to our south. As the troops came into line and identified targets, tanks engaged enemy to our front with a mixture of APFSDS (because most tanks had that loaded already),[12] HESH and machine-gun. The engagement continued for about an hour during which approximately eight transport targets were destroyed on the left. On the right, several trench systems were engaged and at least one section of infantry destroyed with a well-placed HESH round. In addition a BTR 60PA and two MTLBs were destroyed.[13] The enemy returned fire, principally with machine-guns. However, Lt Dingley's tank was engaged by two rounds of anti-tank fire

(later discovered to be D30s (122 mm howitzers) in the direct fire role) and Capt Thomas's tank was illuminated by IR searchlights, although no T-55s were subsequently discovered on the position. . . .

'At about 02.45 hrs B Squadron moved back to the Battlegroup axis, linked up with A Squadron and prepared to continue the advance east. The mission remained unchanged: to destroy all enemy armour and mobility assets within boundaries. . . . At 04.15 hrs contact was made by Cpl Adesile on the right. He reported a large articulated lorry to his front. This was rapidly engaged and destroyed with one round of APFSDS. From the dramatic fireball that followed, we

Allied armour concentrates after the end of the war, close to knocked-out enemy tanks. (Tank Museum)

assumed this was carrying ammunition. Soon afterwards, we had multiple contacts of tank turrets dug in to our front. Maj Sherreff ordered squadron line to be formed and all tanks were quickly into action. We had contacted the bulk of a tank company to our front and soon there were several T-55s burning. The ammunition on board them continued to explode as the fires took hold inside. Several enemy tanks returned fire but fortunately no Challengers were hit. Meanwhile, B Squadron took on the bulk of the tank company on the right, A Squadron and the Queen's Company cleared the position on our left which also included a number of T-55s.

'At first light, we had a clearer view of our night's work; burning tank hulks and debris of battle littered the desert. Disconsolate groups of Iraqis wandered about in a daze looking for someone to accept their surrender. At about 07.00 hrs the commander of the Iraqi 52 Armd Bde surrendered to Capt Joynson, together with a large number of other Iraqis, presumably his brigade staff. After the war, the Squadron Leader returned to the battlefield with a regimental expedition. A total of five T-55s destroyed by B Squadron using both APFSDS and HESH were found. All were dug in facing south and most had died with their guns traversed right as they faced the sudden and deadly threat posed to their right flank.'

For a last word on Operation 'Desert Sabre' back to Brig Hammerbeck:

'We had come 350 km in 97 hours, of which 54 had been in contact with the enemy. We had knocked out some 66 tanks, 90 armoured personnel carriers and 37 artillery pieces. Three divisional commanders, four

Commander 4 Armd Bde, Brig Christopher Hammerbeck, in the turret of his Challenger. (Tank Museum)

brigade commanders and their staffs, together with 5,000 officers and men had surrendered to us. Of the much-vaunted chemical capability there had been no sign, nor had the enemy manoeuvred against us in any numbers.

'But above all the officers and men of the Brigade had proved that they were courageous and fair in battle. They had kept faith with the high standards which had been set by our predecessors in the Second World War. We felt that we had done everything that had been expected of us and were overcome by a sense of relief at having survived. As we looked at the ruins of a once-proud Iraqi Army we felt that enough was enough and that it was time to go home.'

NOTES TO THE GULF WAR

1. Extracted from an article by Lt Col J.G. Zumwalt USMC Reserve, which appeared in *Proceedings* Magazine, published by the US Naval Institute.

2. The maximum effective range of the T-72 main armament is some 2,000 m, while that of the M1A1 is well beyond 3,000 m, giving the Americans a significant advantage. Their other two gunnery advantages were their ability to fire accurately on the move and the TIS.

3. TOW = Tube-launched, Optically tracked, Wire-guided missile. TOW is a two-stage solid projectile weighing 40 lb, with a range of 3,280 yd.

4. In addition, of course, an automatic loader makes a lousy cup of tea and does not stand guard well, or help with the chores. Such systems may save space, so that the AFV can be smaller and require fewer men to crew it, but, in my opinion, reduce a main battle tank's all-round performance to an unacceptable degree.

5. HMMWV = High Mobility Multi Weapons Vehicle. With a top speed in excess of 65 m.p.h. and a range of 310 miles, the 3.8 ton 'Humvee', as the GIs call it, first came into service in the mid-eighties. Now there are over 80,000 in service in a wide variety of roles.

6. *Janes Armour & Artillery*.

7. MLRS = Multi Launch Rocket System.

8. BMP-1 = Soviet-built APC.

9. Within days, all four disabled tanks were recovered and put back into full running order, so none were a complete loss. More importantly, of the sixteen crew members, ten emerged almost unscathed, while the other six had non-life-threatening injuries, which says much for the high degree of protection which the Abrams provided.

10. The long-rod penetrator is another name for the fin-stabilized depleted uranium dart, which forms the tank-killing part of the modern SABOT round. Its power can be gauged by the fact that one hit the turret of a T-72, passed completely through it and hit – and destroyed – a second T-72.

11. Known aptly as 'Contentious', the AFV can now be seen at the Tank Museum, Bovington.

12. APFSDS = Armour-Piercing Fin-Stabilized Discarding Sabot (see also note 10). It would be normal to have this loaded in case of meeting enemy armour.

13. BTR 60PA = eight-wheeled APC, MTLB = tracked APC.

SELECT BIBLIOGRAPHY

I have deliberately tried to include as many books as possible on this fascinating subject.

Baily, Charles M. *Faint Praise, American Tanks and Tank Destroyers During World War II*, Archon Books, Hamden, Connecticut, 1983.

Bar-On, Col Mordechai (ed.). *The Israeli Defence Forces – the Six-Day War*, Israeli MOD, Tel Aviv, 1968.

Bender, R.J. and Law, R.D. *Uniforms, Organization and History of the Afrika Korps*, R. James Bender Publishing, San Jose CA, 1973.

Bradley, Gen Omar. *A Soldier's Story*, Henry Holt and Co. Inc, New York, 1951.

Brisset, Jean. *The Charge of the Bull*, Bates Books, Berkeley CA,1989.

Cole, H.M. *The Lorraine Campaign*, Historical Division of the US Army, Washington DC, 1950.

Connell, John. *Wavell, scholar and soldier*, Wm Collins, 1964.

Eshel, Col David. *Chariots of the Desert, the Story of the Israeli Armoured Corps*, Brassey's Defence Publishers Ltd, 1989.

Fitzroy, Olivia. *Men of Valour (3rd Vol in the history of VIII KRIH)*, published by the Regiment, 1961.

Forty, George. *Tank Commanders*, Firebird Books, Poole, 1993.

——. *United States Tanks of WWII*, Blandford Press, Poole, 1983.

——. *Patton's Third Army at War*, Ian Allan, Weybridge, 1978.

——. *XIVth Army at War*, Ian Allan, Weybridge, 1982.

Graham, Andrew. *Sharpshooters at War*, The Sharpshooters Regimental Association, 1964.

Guderian, Maj Gen Heinz (trs. Christopher Duffy). *Achtung – Panzer!*, Arms and Armour Press, 1992.

Hingston, Lt Col *The Tiger Strikes*, New Delhi, 1942.

Hough, Maj Frank O., USMCR. *The Assault on Peleliu*, US Marine Corps, USA, 1950.

Hoyt, Edwin P. *The Pusan Perimeter*, Military Heritage Press, USA, 1984.

Icks, Col Robert J. *Famous Tank Battles*, Profile Publications, 1972.

Katcher, Philip. *US 1st Marine Division 1941–45*, Osprey Publishing Ltd, 1979.

Katz, Samuel M. *Israeli Tank Battles. From Yom Kippur to Lebanon*, Arms and Armour Press, 1988.

Koyen, Capt Kenneth. *The Fourth Armored Division from Beach to Bavaria*, PRO 4th Armd Div, USA, 1946.

Kurowiski, Franz. *Panzer Aces*, J.J. Fedorowicz Publishing Inc, Winnipeg, 1992.

Lefevre, Eric. *Panzers in Normandy, Then and Now*, After the Battle, 1983.

Liddell Hart, Capt Sir Basil. *The Tanks*, Cassell, 1959.

Moore, William. *Panzer Bait*, Leo Cooper Ltd, 1991.

Munroe, Lt Clark C. *The Second United States Infantry Division in Korea 1950–51*, Toppan Printing Co. Ltd, USA, 1951.

Onslow, The Earl of. *Men and Sand*, St Catherine Press Ltd, 1961.

Pallud, Jean Paul. *Blitzkrieg in the West, Then and Now*, After the Battle, 1991.

——. *Battle of the Bulge, Then and Now*, After the Battle, 1984.

Province, Charles M. *The Unknown Patton*, Hippocrene, New York, 1983.

Ramspacher, Col E.G. *Le General Estienne, 'Pere des Chars'*, Charles Lavauzelle, Paris, 1983.

Ritgen, Oberst aD Helmut. *The 6th Panzer Division 1937–45*, Osprey Vanguard, No. 28, 1982.

Roberts, Maj Gen G.P.B., CB, DSO, MC. *From the Desert to the Baltic*, William Kimber & Co. Ltd, 1987.

Starry, Gen Donn A. *Armored Combat in Vietnam*, Blandford Press, Poole, 1981.

Swinton, Maj Gen Sir Ernest D. *Eyewitness*, Hodder & Stoughton Ltd, 1932.

US Dept. of the Army. *Small Unit Actions During the German Campaign in Russia*, Dept of the Army Pamphlet 20-269, Washington DC, 1953.

——. *Russian Combat Methods in WWII*, Dept of the Army Pamphlet 20-230, Washington DC.

White, Lt Col O.G.W. *Straight on for Tokyo*, Gale & Polden, Aldershot, 1948.

Wilson, Dale E. *Treat 'em Rough!*, Presido, Novato CA, 1989.

Zaloga, Steven J. and Grandsen, James. *The T-34 Tank*, Osprey Vanguard, No. 14, 1980.

INDEX

References for illustrations are given in italic